D. H. LAWRENCE AND THE CHILD

D. H. Lawrence, *A Holy Family.* 1926. Oil 30 × 26 inches. (Collection of Saki Karavas, Taos, NM).

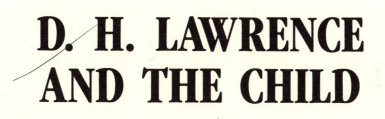

D. H. LAWRENCE
AND THE CHILD

Carol Sklenicka

UNIVERSITY OF MISSOURI PRESS
Columbia and London

Copyright © 1991 by
The Curators of the University of Missouri
University of Missouri Press, Columbia, Missouri 65201
Printed and bound in the United States of America
All rights reserved

5 4 3 2 1   95 94 93 92 91

Library of Congress Cataloging-in-Publication Data

Sklenicka, Carol, 1948–
    D. H. Lawrence and the child / Carol Sklenicka.
        p.   cm.
    Includes bibliographical references (p.   ) and index.
    ISBN 0-8262-0778-2 (alk. paper)
    1. Lawrence, D. H. (David Herbert), 1885–1930—Characters—
Children.   2. Lawrence, D. H. (David Herbert), 1885–1930—
Knowledge—Psychology.   3. Psychoanalysis and literature.
4. Children in literature.   I. Title.
PR6023.A93Z9154   1991
823'.912—dc20   90-29322
                                                          CIP

Designer: Elizabeth K. Fett
Typesetter: Connell-Zeko Type & Graphics
Printer: Thomson-Shore, Inc.
Binder: Thomson-Shore, Inc.
Typeface: Garamond Book

For Rick

Contents

Acknowledgments

I would like to thank Deborah Denenholz Morse and Naomi Lebowitz for their enthusiastic and pertinent encouragement of this project, and my mother, Dorothy Johnston Sklenicka, for her patience and generosity. I am grateful, also, to the late Gene Minard, and to others with whom I learned, one year in St. Louis, that the novel is indeed the "bright book of life." Many others have generously read and commented on the manuscript: Martha Bergland, Leo Hamalian, Keith Cushman, Deborah Robbins, Mark Spilka, Peter Balbert, L. D. Clark, Alice Gillam, William Van Pelt, Linda Weinhouse, Jack Zipes, Dennis Jackson, Wayne Fields, Howard Nemerov, and R. M. Ryan. My thanks to them all.

During the writing of this book my children, Katherine Ryan and Robert Ryan, have contributed vividly to my understanding of my subject, and my husband, R. M. Ryan, has provided for me, body and soul. To these gifts Louise Ryan has added her wit and counsel; the memory of my father, Robert Sklenicka, gave me confidence in myself. My appreciation to all of them.

Material from my article "Lawrence's Vision of the Child: Reimagining Character and Consciousness," was published previously and is reprinted here with the permission of the editor of the *D. H. Lawrence Review*. A version of Chapter 2 was delivered at the International Conference on Narrative Literature at the University of Wisconsin in Madison, on April 8, 1989; an abridgement of Chapter 5 was presented at the International Conference on D. H. Lawrence at Université Paul Valéry, Montpellier, France, on June 25, 1990.

Abbreviations

The following abbreviations are used to cite primary sources and appear parenthetically in the text.

AR	*Aaron's Rod*
CP	*The Complete Poems of D. H. Lawrence*
EC	*The Escaped Cock*
FU	*Fantasia of the Unconscious*
Kangaroo	*Kangaroo*
LCL	*Lady Chatterley's Lover*
Letters	*The Letters of D. H. Lawrence* (Cambridge edition)
LG	*The Lost Girl*
PS	*The Plumed Serpent*
PU	*Psychoanalysis and the Unconscious*
Rainbow	*The Rainbow*
SL	*Sons and Lovers*
TR	*The Trespasser*
WL	*Women in Love*

D. H. LAWRENCE AND THE CHILD

My heart leaps up when I behold
    A rainbow in the sky:
So was it when my life began;
So is it now I am a man;
So be it when I shall grow old,
    Or let me die!
The Child is father of the Man;
And I could wish my days to be
Bound each to each by natural piety.
                    William Wordsworth

Even the rainbow has a body
made of the drizzling rain
and is an architecture of glistening atoms
built up, built up
yet you can't lay your hand on it,
nay, nor even your mind.
                    D. H. Lawrence

Introduction
Reimagining Character and Consciousness

Late in the twentieth century, we are accustomed to encountering children and children's perspectives in literature and popular narratives. That such was not always the case comes as a surprise to many readers. It may be even a greater surprise to hear D. H. Lawrence recommended as a writer on childhood. My study proposes that Lawrence made a significant, pivotal, and unrecognized contribution to literature's notion of what a child means and what it means to be a child.

The subject of the child has long tantalized and challenged the artistic imagination. In mythology, art, and literature, children may personify innocence or the bestial nature beneath humanity's civilized surface; they may be manifestations of supernatural power, or symbols of human weakness. Rarely, though, before the Romantic period, was the child represented as a subject of intrinsic interest, and even then such a portrayal remained problematic. The creation of a literary child in a realistic genre entails peculiar difficulties. *Infans,* the Latin root of our word "infant," means one who cannot speak. Because young children are not articulate, and because adults cannot readily recall their childhoods, the child's point of view is nearly inaccessible to the writer whose work is drawn from observation.

This book studies the development of a modern idea of childhood in the novel. This development occurred in the context of a debate that had persisted through the eighteenth and nineteenth centuries: Is the human child an innocent or a sinful being? The innocent or Romantic position, promoted by Rousseau, was represented by such writers as Wordsworth and Dickens. The medieval Christian view, based on the concept of original sin, was kept alive by Evangelicalism and disseminated by numerous writers of popular books for children and adults, but pilloried by autobiographers such as Edmund Gosse and Samuel Butler. Charles Darwin's work variously influenced the debate: It lent support to the view that human beings are like animals in need of training but, at the same time, challenged biblical sources. It encouraged a naturalistic analysis of childhood and, at the same time, implied that the species might be perfectible.

The complexity of children's experiences and feelings, and the importance of these in shaping the adult psyche, was demonstrated by Sigmund Freud early in the twentieth century. Freud not only changed the ways we think about childhood but also offered many modern novelists a subject they found enticing and—at last—approachable. Among them, D. H. Lawrence is prominent because he portrays parenthood and childhood with variety and extensiveness; because he represents children of unusually young age; because he makes childhood central to his aesthetic opinions and literary achievements; and because he offers a theory of child consciousness that stands in fruitful contrast to both the Romantic attitude and the Freudian model. Lawrence's work offers, in fact, an important, comprehensive, non-Freudian interpretation of childhood.

The significance that Lawrence attaches to the subject of childhood may be gauged from his description of his longest, most ambitious philosophical work, *Fantasia of the Unconscious,* as "an essay on Child Consciousness" (*FU,* 179). Although the book expands into a description of the origin and nature of all consciousness, its constant touchstone is childhood. Lawrence believed that the young child's unconscious exists in a pristine (not innocent) state, as yet undistorted by mental conceptions. In his novels, his detailed, unsentimental, and sustained attention to vivid, carefully individuated child characters separates his creations from both the Romantic notion of the child as a morally free and superior being and the naturalistic, or Freudian, analysis of the child as a victim of social or personal history. Childhood is a significant subject in the major novels of Lawrence's middle period, *Sons and Lovers* (1913), *The Rainbow* (1915), and *Women in Love* (1920), which form the central subject of my study.

Virtually all of Lawrence's novels have something to say about childhood, though, and a brief catalog of them may be illuminating. In *The White Peacock* (1909), children figure in the stories of Lettie Beardsall's and George Saxton's marriages and failures of personal development. Already in this first novel Lawrence sees parenthood as an indication of self. *The Trespasser* (1912), examines the painful effects of a bad marriage and an unsatisfying affair on a husband who, nonetheless, feels great tenderness for his daughters. *The Lost Girl,* a novel Lawrence began in 1913, dropped during the middle period, and completed in 1920, traces the development of Alvina Houghton as the only child of a sickly mother and a neurotic father. It relates Alvina's childhood retrospectively through her experience as a maternity nurse in a lying-in hospital, where she witnesses "the inferno of the human animal" (*LG,* 33), and through her closing episodes as a pregnant war bride in an isolated Italian mountain village. The three novels of Lawrence's extreme masculinist (or "leadership") period, *Aaron's Rod* (1922), *Kangaroo* (1923), and *The Plumed Serpent* (1926), show predictably little affinity for children. Nonetheless, the subject is conspicuously resisted. Aaron Sisson leaves his family in England because, as Lilly puts it, "when a woman has got children, she thinks the world wags only for them and her. . . . I'll be hanged if I can see anything high and holy about children. I should be sorry to, it would be so bad for the children" (*AR,* 99–100). In *Kangaroo* a girl named Gladys appears on the edge of the political world in which only one character, Richard Somers, "seemed actually aware that the child was a little human being" (*Kangaroo,* 68)—an awareness that foreshadows his eventual rejection of the others' machine-like civilization and fascistic politics. Don Ramón, the originator of the "plumed serpent" myth, has two sons; one represents Mexico's history, the other its future. These two aspects of Mexico have already divided Don Ramón and his wife. In *The Boy in the Bush* (1924), the novel Lawrence wrote with Mollie Skinner, the bildungsroman of Jack Grant is structured by his dialectical meditations about his upbringing by an Australian mother and an English father. *Lady Chatterley's Lover,* which I will discuss in my closing chapter, ends with Connie Chatterley pregnant by Oliver Mellors, her former gamekeeper—a sign promising rebirth for them and for England itself. Lawrence's posthumous novel *The Virgin and the Gipsy* (1930) recalls the situation in which Frieda Lawrence's children (by her first husband) grew up under the dominance of their paternal grandmother. The prominence of some aspect of childhood—sometimes exalted, often depreciated—in many of Lawrence's works is not coincidental. It is congruent with his emphasis on cycles of birth, death, and rebirth and with his belief that knowledge of the self in relationships is the crucial human project. More examples of this emphasis appear in Lawrence's short stories, poems, plays, criticism, and essays. My particular concern in this study is the novel, because it is the form that most engages Lawrence's aesthetic commitment.

The novel, Lawrence believes, can reveal a deep structure of life and death, an unchanging being, enigmatically both individual and unindividuated, that resides beneath the ego. This being—Lawrence calls it the soul, but then concedes that that word no longer serves to say what he means—is essential to his conception of the child's nature and consciousness:

> The nature of the infant does not follow from the natures of its parents. The nature of the infant is *not* just a new permutation-and-combination of elements contained in the natures of the parents. . . . There is in the nature of the infant something entirely new, underived, underivable, something which is . . . *causeless.* And this something is the unanalysable, indefinable reality of individuality. (*PU,* 14)

This "reality of individuality" is fundamental both to Lawrence's view of the child and to the difference he wishes to make in the novel. Lawrence's attention to childhood thus dovetails with his revolutionary intentions for fictional characterization—and for the novel itself.

The remarkable realism of child characters in Lawrence's fiction is, paradoxically, an aspect of their symbolic function in the moral code that prevails in his novels and essays. Lawrence insists that art should have a moral bearing, though the terms of his morality are not the conventional ones; the old dichotomy between good and bad becomes, in his work, an opposition between vitality and deadness. Therefore, Lawrence's reimagining of childhood must be seen as part of the change in the representation of consciousness that he brings about in the modern novel. Conversely, his conception of the fictional character as something deeper than ego or personality is rooted in his view of the child. Without claiming that children are morally superior, Lawrence nonetheless privileges them within his iconoclastic value system. In contrast to Freud, Lawrence sees childhood as a source of direct renewal, a realm in which a healthful spiritual balance may be *re*covered, rather than as a locale where repressed complexes may be *un*covered and disentangled. The vitality and pristine quality of the child are ideals for the soul in Lawrence, a state of being to be reclaimed and cherished by adults.

In the first chapter of this study, I distinguish Lawrence's debt to two Romanticists, Rousseau and Wordsworth, and to three nineteenth-century novelists whose child characters have shaped our notions of literary childhood: Charles Dickens, Charlotte Brontë, and George Eliot. I also review and interpret Lawrence's personal experience with children, in preparation for my four principal critical chapters about the evolution of the literary idea of childhood in Lawrence's most productive period, that which extends from *Sons and Lovers* (1913) through *Fantasia of the Unconscious* (1921).

My second chapter focuses on *Sons and Lovers,* the first novel to illustrate a Freudian understanding of childhood. This novel has endowed the literary history of childhood in two particular ways. First, in enacting an oedipal attachment, *Sons and Lovers* popularized Freud's theory for English readers and rapidly began to alter the way the sexuality of children is addressed in twentieth-century literature and criticism. It was the novel that brought English literature into the psychoanalytic age. Second, by writing this novel based upon his own childhood, Lawrence achieved the psychologically complex vision of family life and child growth that later enabled him to make an even larger contribution to the history of the literary child. Already in *Sons and Lovers,* Lawrence has discovered rich veins that yield a different, non-Freudian ore. My reading of *Sons and Lovers* regards these non-Freudian subtexts as the basis for the visionary realism of Lawrence's later work on childhood.

Once Lawrence had written about his own childhood, he went on to create, through visionary realism, other versions of the child's experience. Chapter 3 examines Lawrence's adoption and modification of inherited conventions regarding childhood. Taking the childbirth scenes and the metaphor of birth in the first generation of *The Rainbow* as examples, I show how Lawrence allies realistic and transcendent modes of language and character development. Lawrence creates the novel's patriarch, Tom Brangwen, by beginning with his boyhood and his longing for something he cannot articulate; the maturing of Tom's character follows his quest toward that "beyond" which he seeks but cannot name and culminates in his recognition that this unknown is embodied by his marriage to Lydia Lensky. In Lydia's story, Lawrence invokes the early years as a means of healing the spirit, both recovering the Romantic conception of innocence and advancing it beyond the guilt of the Freudian model of psychic development, toward a more direct connection between childish impulses and their adult expressions.

Anna Brangwen, the most successful and vivid of Lawrence's child creations, is the subject of my fourth chapter. To the portrait of Anna, Lawrence brings both his sense of a visionary component in the child and his realist's awareness of complex family relations. The little girl's adjustment to Tom as a stepfather shows that taking on even a kindly parent may be as difficult as losing parents was for orphans in Victorian novels. The sections of *The Rainbow* that present Anna's childhood are more intricate than previous Lawrence critics have noticed, particularly in Lawrence's manipulation of chronology and in the deft, sensitive witnessing of the growth of the child's unconscious through an objective, largely external narrative perspective. This narrative style conveys Anna's otherness and independence by relying on dramatized scenes and dialogue rather than on either interior monologues or interceding metaphors.

In Chapter 5 I turn to Ursula Brangwen, the main child figure of *The Rainbow*'s second half. Ursula represents a new conception of the child, one in which the relation of the unconscious and the conscious is crucial. The complexity of her identity and the difficulty of balancing conflicting impulses form the subject of both Lawrence's and Ursula's own examination of her being from her earliest years.

Lawrence's darkening vision of the modern world, and of the relations of modern men and women, also infuses Ursula's childhood. Through her relations with her father, terror enters Ursula's consciousness that must eventually be exorcised in *Women in Love,* when she enters the marriage relationship with Rupert Birkin. The primary child in that novel, Winifred Crich, and the German sculptor, Loerke, are then considered as Lawrence's final extrapolations of modern childhood.

Altogether, the stories of the two generations of Brangwen girls and their fathers form a primary text in the neglected study of daughters and fathers in literature, a "virtually unmapped" but not "unmarked" territory about which Lynda Boose and Betty Flowers write, "The terrain that this family relationship occupies has been written all over by tacit injunctions that have forbidden its charting."[1] There are many more girls than boys in Lawrence's fiction. Aside from the autobiographically based Paul Morel and his symbolic counterpart in "The Rocking-Horse Winner," there are only three boys that I know of: Johnny of "Sun," and Cyprian and Pedro in *The Plumed Serpent.* Yet in *The Trespasser* and *Aaron's Rod* the unwilling fathers have three girls each. The Vicar and the Horse-

---

1. Lynda E. Boose and Betty S. Flowers, Introduction to *Daughters and Fathers,* 1–14. This collection of essays begins to establish a theoretical background for analysis of daughter-father relations. My readings, however, in bringing forward the children and analyzing some uses and abuses of paternal power, initiate the mapping of Lawrence's explorations in this area.

Dealer have daughters, as do the families of "The Old Adam" and "England, My England." Gerald Crich and Cyril Beardsall have younger sisters to watch over, and Anna Brangwen has seven daughters and just one son. Alvina Houghton is a daughter, as are Lou Witt of *St. Mawr,* Dollie Urquhart of "The Princess," and Virginia Bodoin of "Mother and Daughter." The most important children in Lawrence's oeuvre, I think, are *The Rainbow*'s Anna Lensky and Ursula Brangwen. In seeking an explanation for this preference of Lawrence's for female protagonists, I have found Carolyn Heilbrun's comment about women writers suggestive.

In *Reinventing Womanhood,* Heilbrun discusses the difficulty women novelists have had in imagining "autonomous" female characters, noting for instance that George Eliot herself triumphed over greater handicaps than those facing any of her heroines. For great autonomous heroines we must look to male writers like Henry James or Ibsen. Heilbrun concludes that (until recently, anyway) when a woman writer imagines autonomy she imagines *maleness.* [2] If one applies the same logic to Lawrence's portrayal of an outstanding number of strong female characters, and especially to his repeated inclusion of girls rather than boys in stories that call for a child, one realizes that it was somehow more compatible to Lawrence's imagination to invent girls. They are like that strongest role model in his early life, his mother. The stories in which he does portray a male child are clearly anchored in personal history and actual events ("Sun" and *Sons and Lovers*). If Daniel Dervin is correct when he says that Lawrence does not completely form a male identity until the leadership period, the fact that Don Ramón's children are sons, one devoted to his mother and the other loyal to his father, would seem to mark a breakthrough for Lawrence in the establishment of his male identity. This interpretation is supported by the fact that, after their mother dies, Don Ramón, the ideal patriarch, frees his sons from his love as Lawrence must have wished to be freed by his parents: "She called thee her own. I do not call thee mine own. Thou art thyself" (*PS,* 357).

After completing *The Rainbow* and *Women in Love,* the novelist who wrote the celebrated oedipal novel sought another explanation of the nature of childhood. Lawrence's theories of childhood, expounded in *Psychoanalysis of the Unconscious* (1920) and *Fantasia of the Unconscious* (1921), show that he was still refining his thoughts about childhood during the years when he was not includ-

2. Carolyn Heilbrun, *Reinventing Womanhood,* chap. 3.

ing children as central figures in his fiction. These two essays were, according to Lawrence, "deduced from the novels and poems, not the reverse. The novels come unwatched out of one's pen. And then the absolute need which one has for some sort of satisfactory mental attitude towards oneself and things in general makes one try to abstract some definite conclusions from one's experiences as a writer and a man" (*FU*, 57). The "definite conclusions" of *Psychoanalysis* and *Fantasia* provide helpful glosses to Lawrence's novels and introduce a vocabulary that is sometimes useful in discussing the fiction, but they really do not decode the novels. Lawrence was a writer whose thought and style altered dramatically from experience to experience and book to book; his nonfiction writings are just as variable as his fiction. Among other things, *Psychoanalysis* and *Fantasia* create a language for the description of biological and psychic periods of childhood, particularly for the months before birth and during infancy, that are *not* represented in the novels. I view these essays as independent texts in Lawrence's treatment of childhood, texts that underscore his conflict with other theorists and show the connection between his thinking about child consciousness and his overall prophetic effort. For these reasons, I have placed my analysis of them where it fits chronologically rather than establishing it in the foreground as a key to the novels. Readers who are not acquainted with Lawrence's theoretical attitudes and vocabulary are, nonetheless, invited to turn to Chapter 6 for some commentary on these matters before reading about the novels in Chapters 3, 4, and 5.

The remainder of my final chapter discusses the reasons for an apparent decline in Lawrence's interest in the child after the writing of *Fantasia of the Unconscious* and *Aaron's Rod* (a novel in which a father leaves his family) in 1921. Finally, I note that in two stories, "England, My England" (1915, revised 1922) and "The Rocking-Horse Winner" (1925), Lawrence revives certain attitudes of Dickens's and James's in order to create symbolic child-victims, while in two of his last works of fiction, *Lady Chatterley's Lover* (1928) and *The Escaped Cock* (1929), he closes his tales by leaving the female protagonist with child, using the traditional image of the child as a symbol of regeneration, within novels that are otherwise iconoclastic.

Lawrence's approach to the subject of childhood displays a courage of vision comparable to that which he recognized in Paul Cézanne's still lifes. Both writer and artist worked against a tide of conventional expectation—expectation of what an apple ought to look like or of what a child ought to mean in a novel.[3] Lawrence's comments on Cézanne provide a close description of his own project: "Cézanne's apples are a real attempt to let the apple exist in its own separate entity, without transfusing it with personal emotion. Cézanne's great effort was, as it were, to shove the apple away from him, and let it live of itself."[4] Just as Cézanne abandons the Fantin-Latour apple that is "no more than enamelled rissoles,"[5] Lawrence challenges the prevailing image of the child as an innocent, a highly spiritual being, sometimes a savior but as often a victim of the sins of the adult world, as well as the Freudian implication that the child is a puppet animated by instincts and guilts. Another writer on Cézanne, Rainer Maria Rilke, praises the painter for his "good conscience" in painting only what he knew and refusing to paint "sentiments" in place of the thing itself.[6] Likewise, to present the child anew, and in good conscience, Lawrence shoves away many conventional sentiments about childhood and lets the child live of itself.

3. John Russell comments on Lawrence's essay "Introduction to These Paintings": "Where the essay has an indestructible relevance both to Lawrence himself and to the predicament of the artist in no matter what medium is in the long section on Cézanne, and on Cézanne's lifelong struggle to re-invent the language of art. When Lawrence says of Cézanne that 'he *never* got over the cliché denominator, the intrusion and interference of ready-made concept, when it came to people, to men and women' [as opposed to apples], he was not making a contribution to art-history. He was making common cause with someone who, like himself, had 'uttered the foreword to the collapse of our whole way of consciousness, and the substitution of another way'" (John Russell, "D. H. Lawrence and Painting," in *D. H. Lawrence: Novelist, Poet, Prophet,* ed. Stephen Spender, 243).
4. D. H. Lawrence, "Introduction to These Paintings," in *Phoenix,* 567.
5. D. H. Lawrence, "Art and Morality," in *Study of Thomas Hardy and Other Essays,* 167.
6. Rainer Maria Rilke, *Letters on Cézanne,* 50–51.

"The Mother Tongue of Our Imagination"
1 Lawrence's Heritage from Literature and Life

The child became a literary figure in the late eighteenth century, and the theme of childhood flows through both the Romantic and the realist streams of nineteenth-century English literature, appearing prominently in Romantic poetry and in the Victorian novel. Lawrence adopted elements from both the Romantic and the realist representations of the child and transformed these into his own visionary realism. Although his emphasis on the child's vitality and individuality—rather than on its spiritual superiority—is original, Lawrence's respect for the child's consciousness may be traced to Jean Jacques Rousseau and William Wordsworth, while his novelistic handling of the psychology of the child descends from Charles Dickens, Charlotte Brontë, and George Eliot.

Besides the inclination to regard the child as an unspoiled representative of human nature, Lawrence shared with his Romantic predecessors the belief that childlike consciousness ought to be maintained in later life as a source of salvation, sanity, and even happiness for the adult. I shall illustrate Lawrence's use of childhood as salvation in my study of Lydia Lensky's in Chapter 3. It is important to recognize the idea's correspondence with experiences Rousseau records in his *Confessions* and with his description of childhood in *Émile*. One of his peculiarities, Rousseau admits, is a propensity to rapid and drastic shifts of interest: "a mere nothing frequently calls me off from what I appear most attached to; I give in to the new idea; it becomes a passion, and immediately every former desire is forgotten." This ability to immerse himself utterly in one thing partakes of a childlike "sleep of reason" that allows Rousseau to give up his adult sense of relativism and perplexity and to enjoy periods of extraordinary, unalloyed happiness, such as this one spent at Charmettes: "I rose with the sun and was happy; I walked, and was happy; I saw Madame de Warrens, and was happy; I quitted her, and still was happy! . . . happiness continually accompanied me; it was fixed on no particular object, it was within me, nor could I depart from it a single moment." The intensity of this state is matched by an unusually strong memory of it: "Nothing that passed during this charming epocha, nothing that I did, said, or thought, has escaped my memory. The time that preceded or followed it, I only recollect by intervals . . . but here I remember all as distinctly as if it existed at this moment."[1] Thus a blossom of periwinkle that Rousseau, short-sighted, scarcely saw when it was pointed out to him by Madame de Warrens impressed so deeply in his memory that thirty years later he is rapturous when he sees another such plant. The image of the periwinkle, like that of Proust's madeleine, recalls and reinstates the old happiness. The sensory connection between the two occasions bypasses mental deliberations about cause and effect that often hobble adult experience. Such transcendence of the conscious mind through the memory of sensation is something like Wordsworth's youthful "spots of time," which "retain / A renovating virtue, whence . . . our minds / Are nourished and invisibly repaired."[2] In a distinction that would be adopted and elaborated on by both Wordsworth and Lawrence, Rousseau usefully separates the child's perception and the adult's reason:

Before the age of reason the child receives images, not ideas; and there is this difference between them: images are merely the pictures of external objects, while ideas are notions about those objects determined by their relations. An image when it is recalled may exist by itself in the mind, but every idea implies other ideas. When we image we merely perceive, when we reason we compare.[3]

Lawrence draws a similar contrast between sensory and mental experience, wherein he emphasizes that a child's perception is pre-rational and thus preferable because it is visionary: "The sheer delight of a child's apperception is based on *wonder;* and deny it as we may, knowledge and wonder counteract one another. So that as knowledge increases wonder decreases."[4]

1. Jean Jacques Rousseau, *The Confessions of Jean Jacques Rousseau with Thirteen Etchings,* 34, 207–8.
2. William Wordsworth, *The Prelude,* 12.208–15, in *Selected Poems and Prefaces,* ed. Jack Stillinger, 345.
3. Jean Jacques Rousseau, *Émile or Education,* 71–72.
4. D. H. Lawrence, "Hymns in a Man's Life," in *Phoenix II,* 598.

As broad similarities exist between Lawrence and Rousseau, so do important temperamental, moral, and historical differences. In an essay written after the Great War, Lawrence accuses Rousseau and other eighteenth-century French "critics of life" of being "stale fish of sentimentality and prurience." Those men, Lawrence thought, promoted a species of reasonable feeling that lacks passion. According to Gregory Ulmer, Lawrence shared with his contemporaries T. E. Hulme, Irving Babbitt, and others a view that Rousseau bears responsibility for the crisis in modern culture. Unlike his contemporaries, Lawrence was not critical of Rousseau's liberating sensibility; rather he objected that "Rousseau's mentality had in turn become a controlling, limiting convention."[5] The *homme de bien* of the Rousseauists, Lawrence charges, has since grown "into a slight deformity, then into a monster, then into a grinning vast idiot. This monster produced our great industrial civilization, and the huge thing, gone idiot, is now grinning at us and showing its teeth." Lawrence's critique of Rousseau is a stringent one. The individual feelings that Rousseau wishes to liberate are, Lawrence says, not really individual: "The feelings of all men in the civilized world today are practically all alike. Men *can* only feel the feelings they know how to feel. The feelings they don't know how to feel, they don't feel. This is true of all men, and all women, and all children."[6]

Lawrence's polemical essay on the French philosophers is written in the energetically bitter rhetoric of his postwar years. One should be cautious in using it as an indicator of his attitude during those earlier years when he produced his most substantial child characters. Nevertheless, it is significant that he considers children's feelings to be as vulnerable to social determination as are those of adults:

> It is true, children do have lots of unrecognized feelings. But an unrecognized feeling, if it forces itself into any recognition, is only recognized as "nervousness" or "irritability." There are certain feelings we recognize, but as we grow up, every single disturbance in the psyche, or in the soul, is transmitted into one of the recognized feeling-patterns, or else left in that margin called "nervousness."
> This is our true bondage. This is the agony of our human existence, that we can only feel things in conventional feeling-patterns.[7]

The Rousseauistic ideal of natural, innocent fellow feeling that was

---

5. Gregory L. Ulmer, "Rousseau and D. H. Lawrence: 'Philosophes' of the 'Gelded' Age," 69.
6. D. H. Lawrence, "The Good Man," in *Phoenix,* 751-52.
7. Ibid., 753.

meant to liberate us has, Lawrence claims, become a new form of bondage, one that joins with an inherent human tendency toward a bondage by ideas. The very children in whom Rousseau had found the ideal exhibited are now bound with a new variety of what Blake called "mind-forg'd manacles" that exaggerates and exploits their innocence. Underlying Lawrence's disagreement with Rousseau, Ulmer proposes, are differing philosophies of time: "Rousseau wants to *escape* from time by returning to 'paradise' prior to the fall into mortality; Lawrence wants to immerse himself in cyclical time by submitting to the rhythms of death and regeneration."[8]

Rousseau's view of time as linear and regressive and Lawrence's view of it as circular and regenerative affect each author's treatment of childhood. For Rousseau the question is how to protect the virtues of childhood from the encroachments of adult life, society, and language; for Lawrence it is how to maintain the virtues of childhood within the adult life. Characteristically, Lawrence rejects conventional patterns in his attempts to create a form and style within his novels for expressing "unrecognized" feeling. His child characters are allowed to act out a range of feeling that eclipses both the Romantic designation of them as innocent and good-natured and the psychoanalytic diagnosis of their nature as potentially neurotic ("'nervousness' or 'irritability'"), which Lawrence finds dismissive of the child's real vitality.

Wordsworth, himself one of Rousseau's heirs, contributed a good deal to Lawrence's thinking about childhood. Of the poems Lawrence listed as having given shape to his life, Wordsworth's "Ode: Intimations of Immortality" addresses the very subject of the child's superior knowledge and affinity with nature.[9] As I will show later, some of Wordsworth's poems exemplify the weaknesses of the Romantic treatment of children; nonetheless, Wordsworth at his best and Lawrence, at his, respect the child and the childish experience as powerful and admirable. They present the child's vision, spontaneity, and individuality as an inexhaustible source of joy and meaning that feeds the adult mind. They disagree, though, on the reason for the child's admirable qualities. Wordsworth attributes them to a spiritual source—"trailing clouds of glory do we come / From God who is our home: / Heaven lies about us in our infancy"[10]—and

8. Ulmer, "Rousseau and D. H. Lawrence," 79.
9. Lawrence, "Hymns in a Man's Life," 597.
10. Wordsworth, "Ode: Intimations of Immortality from Recollections of Early Childhood," 64–66, in *Selected Poems,* 187.

Lawrence to a natural one—"From the solar plexus you know that all the world is yours, and all is goodly. . . . the great centre, where, in the womb, your life first sparkled in individuality" (*FU,* 69). Thus, one might conclude that from Wordsworth, Lawrence took a commission to explore further the growth of child consciousness into adult consciousness. Lawrence turned the spiritual aspect of Wordsworth into his own version of the visionary experience: blood consciousness. Lawrence admires Wordsworth's spiritual vision—"The joy men had when Wordsworth made a slit [in the umbrella of convention] and saw a primrose!" Yet he despairs of him because he chooses weak vessels, child *victims,* to embody his vision:—"Lucy Gray, alas, was the form that Wordsworth saw fit to give to the Great God Pan."[11]

Likewise, Lawrence does not hesitate to make a cynical allusion to the great Immortality ode when he assaults the too distant, too abstract Romantic notion that at birth "our little baby mind begins to stir with all our wonderful psychical beginnings" like a flower bud ready to bloom. If you come down off the mountain and really look at the "Promised Land" of childhood, Lawrence says, ". . . you won't see all that milk and honey . . . All the dear little budding infant with its tender virginal mind and various clouds of glory instead of a napkin" (*FU,* 65). The source of Lawrence's mixed reaction to Wordsworthian childhood lies, I think, in the complexity of both their visions, which coincide at the center but differ radically at the edges, particularly in their views of how the childlike sensibility is to be maintained in adulthood. Wordsworth is more wistful, Lawrence more resilient. While Wordsworth is sad that childhood's "time is past, / And all its aching joys are now no more," Lawrence is confident that this time can recur, and that the adult's consciousness need not be less visionary nor his experience less sensuously joyful than the child's. The Wordsworth of "Tintern Abbey" tries to convince himself that the "joy of elevated thoughts" is "abundant recompense" for the loss of the "aching joys" and "dizzying raptures" of youth.[12] Lawrence continues to be enraptured:

> But all the time I see the gods:
> the man who is mowing the tall white corn,

11. Lawrence, "Preface to *Chariot of the Sun* by Harry Crosby," in *Phoenix,* 256; Lawrence, "Pan in America," in *Phoenix,* 23.
12. Wordsworth, "Lines Composed a Few Miles above Tintern Abbey," 83–85, 85–101, in *Selected Poems,* 110.

suddenly, it curves, as it yields, the white wheat
and sinks down with a swift rustle, and a strange, falling
    flatness,
ah! the gods, the swaying body of god![13]

Though Romanticism finds sustenance in images from childhood, there is a strong inclination, even in Wordsworth, to exaggerate the innocence and unworldliness and freedom of the child. Such exaggeration seemed to Lawrence to be veneration of a false idol. As the spiritual nature of adult, civilized life in the nineteenth century became increasingly puzzling, some writers exalted the child and hoped fervently that the clouds of glory, the child's "unutterable" and presumably more spiritual being, might indeed stay with him into adulthood. Thus Wordsworth addresses six-year-old Hartley Coleridge:

To H. C.

O THOU! whose fancies from afar are brought;
Who of thy words dost make a mock apparel,
And fittest to unutterable thought

. . . .

O blessed vision! happy child!
Thou art so exquisitely wild,
I think of thee with many fears
For what may be thy lot in future years.

Wordsworth consoles himself that if H. C. survives his childhood Nature will, ". . . lengthening out thy season of delight, / Preserve for thee, by individual right, / A Young lamb's heart among the full-grown flocks." Although Wordsworth wonders fearfully what will become of H. C. if he grows up, he reminds himself that this fragile being may not live all that long:

Thou art a dew-drop, which the moon brings forth,
Ill fitted to sustain unkindly shocks,
Or to be trailed along the soiling earth;
A gem that glitters while it lives,
And no forewarning gives;
But, at the touch of wrong, without a strife
Slips in a moment out of life.[14]

13. D. H. Lawrence, "Name the Gods!" in *The Complete Poems of D. H. Lawrence,* ed. Vivian de Sola Pinto and Warren Roberts, 651.
14. William Wordsworth, "To H. C.," in *Selected Poems,* 175.

In the same way that Hartley Coleridge, the child's real name (given him for the rather abstract reason that his father's favorite philosopher at the time of his birth was David Hartley) became H. C., a literary title, the real child, the son of the poet's friend, became a literary child. The very ephemerality of the child is part of his charm, his exquisite wildness. This literary child is idealized, a figuration of the poet's desire to believe that he has preserved his own childlike heart. H. C.'s original did survive childhood, but many others, including two of Wordsworth's own children, did not. Upon the death of his son Thomas in 1812, Wordsworth wrote:

> Six months to six years added he remained
> Upon this sinful earth, by sin unstained:
> O Blessed Lord! whose mercy then removed
> A Child whom every eye that looked on loved;
> Support us, teach us calmly to resign
> What we possessed, and now is wholly thine![15]

Wordsworth's grief for his own son finds expression in conventional sentiments for consolation—the child is untainted, the child has returned to God. The contrast of Wordsworth's styles and attitudes in his response to the hypothetical death of H. C. and to the actual death of Thomas Wordsworth is instructive. The romanticization of the child's spiritual condition that occurs in the literary address to H. C. is severely curbed in the poet's contemplation of his own child. Here the simple form of a prayer and the unelaborate claim that Thomas was "A Child whom every eye that looked on loved" testify to the poet's emotional and physical attachment to earthly life and to *this* child.

Lawrence disliked posturing about childhood or any other topic. Of Crèvecoeur, for example, Lawrence complains that his pastoral view obscures individuality, making of a woman a mere " 'amiable spouse,' just as an oaken cupboard is an oaken cupboard."[16] Like-

15. Wordsworth, Elegiac Piece II (untitled), in *Poetical Works,* ed. Thomas Hutchinson, rev. Ernest de Selincourt, 451.

16. Lawrence uses the phrase "amiable spouse" quite similarly in *Fantasia of the Unconscious:* "But to come at last to a nice place under the trees, with your 'amiable spouse' who has at last learned to hold her tongue and not to bother about rights and wrongs: her own particularly. . . . The best thing I have known is the stillness of accomplished marriage, when one possesses one's own soul in silence, side by side with the amiable spouse, and has left off craving and raving and being only half one's self. But I must say, I know a great deal more about the craving and raving and sore ribs than about the accomplishment" (*FU,* 169). It would seem that the later Lawrence still scorns Crèvecoeur's diction but adopts his attitude.

wise, to Crèvecoeur a little boy is "a healthy offspring, and when this same healthy offspring is seated on his father's plough, the whole picture represents the children of Nature—sweet and pure—toiling in innocence and joy."[17] What Lawrence objects to in Crèvecoeur is a kind of intellectualizing that blinds one to individual circumstances. Therefore he mocks the Frenchman-turned-American-farmer for suppressing the fact that his farm was burned down by Indians and for producing, as an appropriate ending for his letters, a vision of himself living peacefully among the Indians while he was, in fact, "off to France in high-heeled shoes and embroidered waistcoat, to pose as a literary man, and to prosper in the world."[18]

As Philippe Ariès has taught us, childhood is phenomenon shaped by history and culture.[19] Like any of the theories about children (or any disenfranchised group) that have prevailed in history, the Romantic idea of the child takes advantage of the child's inability to describe his own condition in abstract terms. It imposes on him definitions that best suit a particular view of politics, theology, philosophy, or psychology. Such impositions occur as commonly in fiction as elsewhere. Lawrence, who abhorred any turning of a living being into an abstraction, found the idealization of children especially dangerous. His advice to parents in *Fantasia* speaks to this problem, and may be taken as intended for the novelist as well: "Let us beware of having an ideal for our children. So doing, we damn them. All we can have is wisdom. And wisdom is not a theory, it is a state of soul. But nowadays men have even a stunt of pretending that children and idiots alone know best. This is a pretty piece of sophistry, and criminal cowardice, trying to dodge responsibility" (*FU,* 91).

In the history of the novel, the child's assumption of a major role seems delayed. Recognition of childhood as a "period with its own distinctive requirements" occurred in England during the eighteenth century, according to Lawrence Stone,[20] along with the growth of

17. D. H. Lawrence, *The Symbolic Meaning: The Uncollected Versions of Studies in Classic American Literature,* ed. Armin Arnold, 55.

18. D. H. Lawrence, *Studies in Classic American Literature,* 35.

19. The definitive history of childhood has yet to be written. See, though, the seminal work *Centuries of Childhood: A Social History of Family Life* by Philippe Ariès and Lawrence Stone's *The Family, Sex and Marriage in England, 1500–1800* and Jean-Louis Flandrin's *Families in Former Times: Kinship, Household, and Sexuality.* An accessible but poorly documented introduction is provided by Barbara Kaye Greenleaf in *Childhood through the Ages: A History of Childhood,* while a more polished and also finely illustrated one is offered by Anita Schorsch in her *Images of Childhood: An Illustrated Social History.*

20. Stone, *The Family, Sex and Marriage,* 258.

the middle class and the development of the novel itself. Enduring and vital interest in childhood does not enter the novel, however, until the Victorian period, where it accompanies an increasingly anxious fascination with the moral development and protection of the self among threatening, realistic social circumstances.

The challenge of childhood to the novelist is beautifully observed by George Eliot in *Adam Bede*:

> So much of our early gladness vanishes utterly from our memory; we can never recall the joy with which we laid our heads on our mother's bosom or rode our father's back in childhood; doubtless the joy is wrought up in our nature as the sunlight of long-past mornings is wrought up in the soft mellowness of the apricot; but it is gone forever from our imagination, and we can only *believe* in the joy of childhood.[21]

Eliot's lyricism evokes the joy and gladness that she says have vanished. Such joy and gladness, however, are not what convincing childhood narratives are made of. There must be the minutia and conflict of everyday life: When Goethe decided to write his autobiography, he sent off to Frankfurt for a truckful of old household accounts and receipts from his parents' home. Although he knew that "a fact only counts when it means something in our life," he needed the right facts to make his meaning.[22] For many writers since the eighteenth century, those first years, seldom present to the conscious memory, have provided fertile territory for belief, wish fulfillment, and blame, but difficult terrain for applying the conventions of realistic novels.

Yet can a novelist approach the subject of childhood with the kind of empiricism that has characterized the development of the novel as a genre? Young children are not articulate; adults cannot readily recall their childhoods. Moreover, the mind of the very young child is inaccessible. Infantile amnesia, which Freud brought to our attention by connecting it with infantile sexuality, makes even one's own early childhood a period that can be reconstructed only through stories told by others, through psychoanalysis, and through fantasy. Myths and legends often include details of an unusual conception, birth, or childhood, testifying to a strong urge to create narratives that find meaning in childhood: Hecuba, mother of Paris, dreams that she is delivered of a firebrand that sets Troy aflame; Thomas

21. George Eliot, *Adam Bede,* chap. 20, p. 9.
22. Johann Wolfgang von Goethe, *Autobiography* [*Dichtung und Wahrheit*], 1:xxiv.

Hardy is found asleep on a summer afternoon with a large snake, also asleep, on his breast. Early on English novelists adopted and adapted this custom of reciting lineage and beginning pro forma at the beginning of a protagonist's life. Perhaps, as Avrom Fleishman suggests, this recitation of "pseudoautobiography" in eighteenth-century novels influenced the development of true autobiography in the nineteenth century, which in turn influenced the growth of the autobiographical novel. In *Moll Flanders* (1722), Defoe's first-person narrator meets head-on with the problem of how to begin at the beginning: "This is too near the first hours of my life for me to relate anything of my self but by hearsay; 'tis enough to mention that as I was born in such an unhappy place [Newgate Prison], I had no parish to have recourse to for my nourishment in my infancy, nor can I give the least account of how I was kept alive." Henry Fielding in *Joseph Andrews* (1742) and *Jonathan Wild* (1743) and—much later—John Barth in *Lost in the Funhouse* (1968) parody the convention of the lineage. Sterne's *Tristram Shandy* (1760) makes a fantastic tale of the narrator's conception, and Tobias Smollett's *Roderick Random* (1748) begins with a premonitory dream that occurs to Roderick's mother while she is pregnant: "she was delivered of a tennis ball, which the devil (who to her great surprise acted the part of a mid-wife) struck . . . forcibly with a racket"—which is interpreted (accurately, foretelling Smollet's plot) by a Highland seer.[23]

While these eighteenth-century novelists seemed to think that the form demanded that they give some account of their hero's earliest history, they became increasingly arch in their manner of doing so. Rarely did they devote more than a page or two to the actual years of childhood. In the refined realism of Jane Austen, the conventional early history disappears almost entirely.[24] Austen, who surely had ample opportunity to observe children, finds little place for them in her novels except when their rearing becomes an indicator of an adult's character. The weaknesses of Lydia Bennett in *Pride and Prejudice,* Marianne Dashwood in *Sense and Sensibility,* and Maria Bertram in *Mansfield Park* are interpreted by Austen

---

23. Avrom Fleishman, *Figures of Autobiography: The Language of Self-Writing in Victorian and Modern England,* 198; Daniel Defoe, *Moll Flanders,* 10; Tobias Smollett, *Roderick Random,* chap. 1, p. 161.

24. There is an exception in Jane Austen's work, but it occurs in *Northanger Abbey,* Austen's parody of a Gothic novel: "No one who had ever seen Catherine Morland in her infancy, would have supposed her born to be a heroine." Obviously, Austen does not think much of those who predict a character's development from her appearance in infancy (1).

as reflections of their parents' flaws or inattentiveness. Fanny Price, the orphaned heroine of *Mansfield Park,* suffers as a child but proves her worth by responding to her adoptive family's problems with the equanimity of an adult.[25]

Much nineteenth-century fiction that portrays children uses the child as the Romantic poets did, as a symbol for innocence. Eliot's most widely known child character, *Silas Marner*'s Eppie, is a typical symbolic child; despite her very realistic predilection for crawling into the coalhole and dirtying her frock, her true role in the novella is that of Marner's savior: "We see no white-winged angels now. But yet men are led away from threatening destruction: a hand is put in theirs, which leads them forth gently towards a calm and bright land . . . and the hand may be a little child's."[26] Charles Dickens's many angelic child characters also often lack individuality as he employs them, somewhat subversively, to reveal the corruptions of adult society. The girls—Esther Summerson, Agnes Wickfield, Florence Dombey, Little Dorrit—are sexless and hardly seem to be children at all under their burden of care for others. Little Nell dies young, graciously consigned to a better world: "Dear gentle, patient, noble Nell, was dead. . . . . Where were the traces of her early cares, her sufferings, and fatigues? All gone. Sorrow was dead indeed in her, but peace and perfect happiness were born; imaged in her tranquil beauty and profound repose." Paul Dombey's death scene, narrated by himself, also extends hope and comfort as he sees his mother waiting on the bank he approaches: "Mama is like

25. Julian Moynahan in "Lawrence and the Modern Crisis of Character and Conscience" suggests, though, that Lawrence rediscovers a tradition of conscience of which Austen is a primary exemplar, one in which the "force of fate" is positioned "within the character." Moynahan cites Fanny Price as a character who has "intuitive conscience" and is thereby able to save Mansfield Park (32). This "conscience in the blood" is inborn, not acquired from her family. This line of thinking might lead to the conclusion that Austen believes children are born with good character and allowed to lapse by inadequate parents; it seems to me, though, that there are more of Austen's young adults who must be educated into conscientiousness than there are of those who arrive with a reliable innate conscience. In fact, Fanny's education by Edmund is a necessary stage in her development from a well-behaved child to a woman of good character.

26. George Eliot, *Silas Marner,* chap. 14, p. 882; Sandra M. Gilbert's "Life's Empty Pack: Notes toward a Literary Daughteronomy," in Boose and Flowers, eds., *Daughters and Fathers,* 256–77, offers a reading of *Silas Marner,* showing how patriarchal assumptions in that text disenfranchise both the mother and the child.

you, Floy. I know her by the face . . . the light about the head is shining on me as I go!" Dickens closes the story of Paul Dombey's death with a prayer that again emphasizes the child's role as savior: "Look upon us, angels of young children, with regards not quite estranged, when the swift river bears us to the ocean."[27] Other boys in Dickens who are less than angelic—Oliver Twist, Richard Carstone, even David Copperfield—tend not to mature much as they become older. Add to these the sometimes endearing, sometimes annoying childlike grown-ups such as Mr. Dick (in *David Copperfield*) and Harold Skimpole (in *Bleak House*). While Dickens has the sensitivity to portray children and to see in them an indictment of the adult world, he rarely—Pip (in *Great Expectations*) seems an exception— has the visionary will power to see them into convincing adulthood.

Although infant mortality remained high throughout the century (despite progress in particular areas and classes), in literature child mortality is practically epidemic. Many of the children in these novels either die in childhood or remain children mentally or sexually. They are descendants of the disembodied, unrealistic child figures of the Romantic poets, those glorified for their inarticulateness, sensitivity, or purity. The not-so-latent message of the early deaths of children like Little Nell, Paul Dombey, and nunlike Helen Burns in *Jane Eyre* is that a child is better off to die young than to grow into adulthood where she will lose all innocence.[28] Such extreme idealization pervades much of Victorian fiction about children, in which a moral dimension is assigned to the fragility of a child's life. Death saves these unreal children from the worse fate of becoming economic, social, and sexual adults. In the works of J. M. Barrie, Maria Corelli, W. H. Hudson, and others, interest in childhood had become, Peter Coveney argues, "morbid withdrawal toward psychic death."[29]

27. Charles Dickens, *The Old Curiosity Shop*, chap. 71; *Dombey and Son*, chap. 16.

28. Maggie Tulliver is another example, as Raymond Williams's comments in *The English Novel from Dickens to Lawrence* suggest: neither the Dodsons' "unattractive rituals of survival" nor the "rash independence" of Mr. Tulliver offers Maggie a way to any fullness of life. Maggie's trip on the river with Stephen Guest offers only temporary escape. What is "made to happen, because it is all that can happen, is a return to childhood and the river; a return, a releasing feeling, to a transcending death" (83).

29. Peter Coveney, *The Image of Childhood: The Individual and Society: A Study of the Theme in English Literature*, 241.

So, little more than a century after the publication of *Émile*, Rousseau's endowment of the child as a source of salvation for a corrupt society was bankrupt. Published in 1762, *Émile* had been considered so revolutionary that one contemporary reviewer wrote of it, "To know what the received notions are upon any subject, is to know with certainty what those of Rousseau are not." Rousseau faults previous writers because "they are always looking for the man in the child, without considering what he is before he becomes a man."[30] Though Rousseau merely proposed to rectify the oversight, those who adopted his more sympathetic view saw the actual child distorted through lenses of their own. The romanticized image of the child evolved from Rousseau's effort to overturn the older view that children carry the blight of original sin. Ironically, by the end of the century, that image had withered into a popular, escapist fantasy for adults who were appalled by the difficulties of mature life. The future life of the child could then be compromised to preserve the belief that somewhere innocence must still exist.

As we have seen, one major motive for the Victorians' intense preoccupation with childhood was moral nostalgia, the desire to escape the difficulties of adult life. But there was a more admirable motive as well. It was, in Mark Spilka's words, the desire "to come to grips with the terms of childhood conflict so as to renew the ground for value and selfhood." Indeed, Victorian novelists give us—and gave Lawrence—"a number of powerful evocations of the emotional conflicts of childhood, its guilts and fears and psychic damages, for which there is simply no precedent in previous literature."[31] In the novels of Emily and Charlotte Brontë, and sometimes in those of Dickens, Eliot, Samuel Butler, Henry James, and others, the child is an independent human being. These novels represent the child's consciousness in order to criticize the social world from his or her perspective or to obtain better comprehension of the adult characters. In a few outstanding novels, the vivid presentation of children themselves transcends authorial, political, or social agendas about children. Three novels that Lawrence studied carefully as a young man, *Jane Eyre* (1848), *David Copperfield* (1849–1850), and *The Mill on the Floss* (1860), can serve as examples of the emergence of

---

30. The anonymous reviewer is quoted by William Kessen in *The Child,* 72; Rousseau, *Émile,* 1.

31. Mark Spilka, "On the Enrichment of Poor Monkeys by Myth and Dream; or How Dickens Rousseauisticized and Pre-Freudianized Victorian Views of Childhood," 172–73.

a pre-Freudian psychological realism about the consciousness of the child. To appreciate Lawrence on the subject of childhood, it is worth considering the uniqueness of his achievement with these three nineteenth-century counterparts in mind. Like Lawrence, all of them insisted that childhood matters.

The protagonists of two of those novels, Jane Eyre and David Copperfield, are orphans, a circumstance that may be seen as a metasymbol in a psychologically complex world of symbols. The orphan is such a common type in Victorian fiction that the trope leads most often to sentimentality—Little Nell and Oliver Twist being the most enduring examples. Thus the helplessness of the child characters is emphasized by a fiction that strips them of even the amount of stability that their authors enjoyed as children. It would seem that the Victorian novelists' imaginations gravitated to the orphan's condition, regardless of the personal circumstances that informed their fiction. This step toward isolating the child from family relations is, potentially, a radical one, for it forces a deeper study of the self. Yet it seems to me that maternal death is often an abused plot device that allows authors to veer around the heavily mined territory of parent-child, particularly mother-child, relations. Wouldn't we, after all, gain by knowing something of Becky Sharp's, or Little Dorrit's, or Eustacia Vye's relations with their mothers? Nonetheless, in *David Copperfield,* Dickens's somewhat autobiographical bildungsroman, the well-worn trope of the orphan is redeemed by those autobiographical elements that inform the fiction. The depth and authenticity with which David's consciousness is represented in the first fourteen chapters is an important precursor of Lawrence's evocation of the child mind, especially within his extended study of mother-son relations in *Sons and Lovers.*

While the stories of most well-known child characters remain cursory until the child reaches age nine or ten, Dickens, like Lawrence after him, did not hesitate to present the very young consciousness. David Copperfield's first-person narrative is retrospective, but the slightly surreal evocations of the little boy's experience are vivid and seemingly unmediated by a narrator. In the following passage, for instance, David recalls his first thoughts of his father:

> There is something strange to me, even now, in the reflection that he never saw me; and something stranger yet in the shadowy remembrance that I have of my first childish associations with his white gravestone in the churchyard, and of the indefinable compassion I used to feel for it lying out alone there in the dark night, when our little parlour was warm and bright with fire and candle, and the doors of our house

were—almost cruelly, it seemed to me sometimes—bolted and locked against it.[32]

In that passage, comic, morbid, nostalgic, and even oedipal elements are perfectly enfolded and balanced by the sheer ingenuousness of the childish perspective. Dickens and Lawrence share an ability to represent the consciousness of extremely young children that sets them apart from the other novelists I am discussing.

David Copperfield's attachment to his mother expresses oedipal energy similar to that which develops between Paul and Gertrude Morel. David's father has, in fact, already died. David's oedipal conflict is played out against his stepfather, Mr. Murdstone, who forbids David's mother to express affection for her son and brings about her death when David is nine years old. In both cases, a mother draws solace from her son because it is unavailable from her husband. (Mrs. Copperfield is first a widow and then a co-victim of the Murdstones' cruelty; Mrs. Morel is spiritually divorced from Paul's father.) The failure of David's mother to protect him from the Murdstones, followed by her early death, truncates the oedipal story and greatly delays David's achievement of maturity.[33] Lawrence's autobiographical novel explores a similar subject with more substantial parental figures. Lawrence is more interested in the extended, living interaction between parent and child and, therefore, is not drawn to the situation of the orphan.[34] In Lawrence's version of the story, the mother is an active protector of the son. She can preserve him while he matures in the struggle against his father and—eventually—turns against her as well, claiming a fragile independence. Lawrence's

32. Charles Dickens, *David Copperfield,* chap. 1, p. 10.

33. Fleishman argues that in writing *David Copperfield,* Dickens, already a successful author in the middle of his career, is "outgrowing his child self-image and acquiring an adult identity, recognizing himself as a mature man who has grown beyond the children (of all ages) among whom he has lived." He suggests that in this novel Dickens begins to view childishness in adults as a defect, and to "regard his own youthful self as a chastisable young puppy, like David." This line of thinking tends to parallel my interpretation of Lawrence's relation to *Sons and Lovers* in my next chapter (*Figures of Autobiography,* 208).

34. Death in childbirth does not occur in Lawrence, but there are several instances of fathers abandoning families. In *The Trespasser,* in which the father commits suicide, and in *Aaron's Rod,* in which the father leaves to seek self-fulfillment in Italy, the emphasis is on the father's experience, not the child's. The one story in which a mother leaves her family, *The Virgin and the Gipsy,* is loosely drawn from the experience of Frieda Lawrence's children; it expresses scorn for the moralizing father and manipulative grandmother who raise the children in her stead. The mother's version of this story appears in *Mr. Noon.*

development of the oedipal situation may be said to begin where Dickens's leaves off.

Jane Eyre, like *David Copperfield,* is narrated by the orphan herself; yet it is a more naked study of a child's consciousness. This novel's emotional power has been generally underrated, and its distinction as a narrative of childhood largely overlooked. This misapprehension may be due to what Raymond Williams calls the male middle-class image of the governess (Jane Eyre's occupation) as a repressive, unfeminine, dowdy figure. That image has blinded many readers to the fact that, in concert with her sister Emily, Charlotte Brontë "remade" the novel so that intense feeling, even passion, could be directly communicated.[35] Because Jane Eyre is alone from the outset, this directness is enhanced. Unlike David Copperfield, who has his mother to himself for several years before she marries Murdstone, Jane has never known that which she lacks. Her tremendous resilience and vigorous independence of character make her a fictional ancestor of Lawrence's Anna and Ursula Brangwen.[36] Though Jane is older and more articulate than Anna, her outspokenness and sheer energy foreshadow what Robert Langbaum calls the "portrait of Anna as all light, motion, and incandescence."[37] Jane describes herself at age ten addressing her abusive guardian:

> That eye of hers, that voice stirred every antipathy I had. Shaking from head to foot, thrilled with ungovernable excitement, I continued: "I am glad you are no relation of mine; I will never call you aunt again as long as I live. . . ."
>
> Ere I had finished this reply, my soul began to expand, to exult, with the strangest sense of freedom, of triumph, I ever felt. It seemed as if an invisible bond had burst, and that I had struggled out into unhoped-for liberty.

When Jane Eyre looks back on these years, she does so with a sharp sense of distance traveled, but she avoids undue sentimentality or

35. Williams, *The English Novel,* 60–63.

36. Williams suggests that a fictional genetic line may be traced from Jane Eyre and Lucy Snowe through to Sue Bridehead, Ursula Brangwen, Tess of the D'Urbervilles, and Miriam Leivers. All these women (even Miriam, if we can ignore Lawrence's own indictment of her) are courageous and unconventional. In connecting the child character of Jane Eyre with the Lawrence children, I must add Anna to the list, for it is she who has the fiery spirit that little Jane exhibits, while it is Ursula who seems to have inherited Jane's adult determination (ibid., 63).

37. Robert Langbaum, *The Mysteries of Identity: A Theme in Modern Literature,* 308.

contempt toward her younger self. Here she recalls her affection for her doll:

> Human beings must love something, and in the dearth of worthier objects of affection, I contrived to find a pleasure in loving and cherishing a faded graven image, shabby as a miniature scarecrow. It puzzles me now to remember with what absurd sincerity I doated on this little toy, half fancying it alive and capable of sensation. I could not sleep unless it was folded in my night-gown; and when it lay there safe and warm, I was comparatively happy, believing it to be happy likewise.[38]

In contrast, the characteristic style by which George Eliot represents Maggie Tulliver in a similar scene is a detached, almost analytical one that often has the effect of condescending to the child:

> She kept a Fetish which she punished for all her misfortunes. This was the trunk of a large wooden doll, which once stared with the roundest of eyes above the reddest of cheeks; but was now entirely defaced by a long career of vicarious suffering. Three nails driven into the head commemorated as many crises in Maggie's nine years of earthly struggle.[39]

Although Eliot often invokes logical discourse and adult perspective to dissect the alogical working of a child's mind, this same relentless analysis makes Eliot an accurate observer of childish foibles.

Eliot's awareness of childish emotional perversity is unprecedented. There are marvelously realistic moments in the narrative of Maggie's childhood, most of them scenes of Maggie's humiliation told in painful detail, such as her self-administered haircut, or her misery that she has allowed her brother's rabbits to starve and that he will not forgive her. In the greater shape of Maggie's character, however, Eliot sometimes negates that realism with a romantic self-indulgence. Maggie is nine years old when the novel opens, so Eliot does not present her earliest childhood. One must take the author's Wordsworthian words for it that the scene of childhood becomes "the mother tongue of our imagination, the language that is laden with all the subtle inextricable associations the fleeting hours of our childhood left behind them."[40] While Eliot rhapsodizes beautifully about childhood, she shows her hand in the presentation: Maggie

---

38. Charlotte Brontë, *Jane Eyre*, chap. 4, pp. 31, 22–23.
39. George Eliot, *The Mill on the Floss*, book 1, chap 4, pp. 25–26.
40. Eliot, *Mill*, book 1, chap. 5, p. 38. If Eliot's metaphor is deeply Romantic, it nonetheless bears a notable functional similarity to Freud's notion of the unconscious memory imaged as a mystic writing pad as it has been isolated by Jacques Derrida in "Freud and the Scene of Writing."

and Tom "ate together and rubbed each other's cheeks and brows and noses together, while they ate, with a humiliating resemblance to two friendly ponies."[41] Humiliating to whom? one must ask. Since it cannot be to either of the children, it must be to Eliot, who one assumes is uncomfortably remembering her own childhood.

Maggie's most piteous moments are brought about by her enormous need for her brother's love and her consequent vulnerability to his caprices. Her childhood is so keyed to this need that her independent spirit is quite buried, as in the scene where she enjoys fishing with Tom: "She never knew she had a bite till Tom told her; but she liked fishing very much."[42] Jessie Chambers reports that Maggie was Lawrence's favorite heroine: "He could not forgive the marriage [sic: they are engaged] of the vital Maggie Tulliver to the cripple Philip."[43] Yet it is no surprise—submission to the male has limited Maggie's character from her earliest days of slavish devotion to her brother. In her spiritual submission to Philip and her physical submission to Steven, she splits that childish devotion into its common womanly forms.

If Lawrence was not satisfied with Eliot's treatment of Maggie, he nonetheless gained something valuable from *The Mill on the Floss*. In this novel he found, I believe, a model of autobiographical fiction set in a level of society that was not terribly different from his own. He also found a character, endowed with wit and natural independence, who must struggle against the obstructions of small-mindedness and venality to preserve her very soul. These models of setting and character were appropriate inspiration for his own autobiographical projects. Indeed, all three novels I have been discussing are loosely based on their author's lives, and all three authors—Dickens, Brontë, and Eliot—shared with Lawrence the circumstance of having been born outsiders to literary London. As a young man, Lawrence was anxious about the working-class background that made him different from those in the literary world. Though this anxiety was unfounded—Ford Madox Ford reported that he had "never anywhere found so educated a society" as among Lawrence's young friends in Eastwood[44]—a derivative striving after literariness hobbles Lawrence's earliest work. While *The White Peacock* has many autobiographical features, and *The Trespasser* introduces

41. Ibid.
42. Ibid.
43. Jessie Chambers, *D. H. Lawrence: A Personal Record*, 98.
44. Edward Nehls, *D. H. Lawrence: A Composite Biography*, 1:152.

a fluid notion of consciousness that is developed in his later work, Lawrence does not grapple with his own background until his third novel, *Sons and Lovers*. If at times Dickens and Brontë and Eliot are guided by the romance or sorrows of their own histories—becoming interested not in children as independent characters, but in themselves as children—they nonetheless convey the tremendous power of real emotional experience. In this way, novels like *David Copperfield, Jane Eyre,* and *The Mill on the Floss* offered Lawrence literary and intellectual precedents for making emotionally powerful fiction out of autobiographical material.

Lawrence's engagement with the subject of childhood owes much to the literature that formed the mother tongue of his imagination, but it also draws upon his experience with actual children. I will review this experience very briefly, because the basic information is all well known. Because of Lawrence's working-class upbringing and time spent at home with his mother, he was more in the presence of young children than were other major writers of the period. This experience made it impossible for him either to neglect or overromanticize them. His particular closeness to his mother made him especially mindful of the physical nature of motherhood and childhood. In "Brooding Grief," he recalls, "I was watching *the woman that bore me* / Stretched in the brindled darkness / Of the sickroom . . ."[45] Though the phrase I have italicized may be a cliché, these lines carry a particular awareness of his mother as life-giver that is more obstetric than sexual.

From 1908 until 1912 Lawrence worked as a public schoolteacher. His occasional distaste for his pupils, whom he taught in classes of forty-five or more, and his dislike of what the schools were doing to them are recorded in his short stories and in Ursula's teaching experience in *The Rainbow*. He was never comfortable with institutional endeavor, but while he was teaching in Croyden he did enjoy the little girls in the household where he boarded. He spent hours with them and wrote what he called, jokingly, "the first teething song," replete with allusions to Blake's little poem "Infant Joy":

> I cannot call her 'Sweet Joy' now—
> My wee squirrel—
> She is no longer two days old—
> 'Twas a tale soon told.
>
> And dark now is the sky that she came through
> —My white bird—

45. Lawrence, "Brooding Grief," in *Complete Poems,* 111.

Heavy with drops of first keen rain
—Tears for her pain.

There, press your hot red cheek against mine
—My own baby—
There, for the heat of it causes a smart,
Stinging down to my heart.

(*Letters,* 1:108–9)

In this bit of juvenilia, one finds the tension between sentiment and the realism that was to become more fruitful in Lawrence's later characterizations of children. While the expressions here are self-consciously conventional, there is an attempt to convey both the difficulty and the sweetness of caring for children.

Although Lawrence was quite devoted to the two little Jones girls while he lived in their home in Croydon, he did not look back on this middle-class family as a better model of family felicity than the Lawrence family.[46] From them he derived characters for his story "The Old Adam," including a small girl who is "a bacchanal with her wild, dull-gold hair tossing about like a loose chaplet . . . so abandoned to her impulses."[47] In a letter written from Austria a year after he had left Croydon, he declares, somewhat inexplicably, "Damn the Jones menage. Now, and only now, do I know how I hated it all. I still dream I must teach—and that's the worst dream I ever have. How I loathed and raved with hate against it, and never knew!" (*Letters,* 1:455).[48] In that passage, as in the disillusioned short stories of the Croydon period, "The Fly in the Ointment" and "A Lesson on a Tortoise," it is not by the schoolboys or Jones children that Lawrence feels defeated, but by his health, and by the job of teaching and his inability to affect anything through it: "I felt very tired, and very sick. The night had come up, the clouds were moving darkly, and the sordid streets near the school felt like disease in the lamplight."[49]

46. Keith Cushman, "Domestic Life in the Suburbs: Lawrence, the Joneses, and 'The Old Adam,'" 230.

47. D. H. Lawrence, "The Old Adam," in *Love among the Haystacks and Other Stories,* ed. John Worthen, 74.

48. Cushman, in his article on Lawrence's years with the Jones family, concludes, "Colworth Road had ultimately taught him that middle-class life was as stifling and constrictive as the working-class life he had emerged from," but adds that the story that he wrote near the end of his three years there is about sexual, not social identity. In the story, Severn, the character who is like Lawrence, "is more comfortable with the three-year-old [girl] than he is with either the teenaged maid or the little girl's mother" ("Domestic Life," 230).

49. Lawrence, "A Lesson on the Tortoise," in *Love among the Haystacks,* 20.

The memoirs of people who knew Lawrence, as well as his own notations regarding the children he knew, suggest that Lawrence made a point of befriending children throughout his life, though he was seldom a sentimental admirer of them. One child who knew Lawrence well, Harwood Brewster Picard, the daughter of Earl and Achsah Brewster, has reminisced about the days Lawrence spent with her family in Ceylon and Capri. She was eight years old at the time, and Lawrence sometimes singled her out to be his companion on walks. She felt, she says, "accepted not just as a child but as a person." He worried that she would grow up "too attached to her parents and was pleased when she was sent to school in England." Though he teased her about her doll, calling it "Swabina" because its porcelain face had been replaced by a dishrag, he also defended her wish to take her doll carriage back to Europe and even devised a way for her parents to pack it full of books.[50]

It seems ironic that a writer who thought so much about childhood, who worked as a schoolteacher, and in whom friends noted a particular fondness for children, did not himself have children. Little is known about why he had no children. In a letter written to Frieda in 1912, Lawrence mentions the possibility of an infant, making it clear that he does not wish them to use contraception:

> Never mind about the infant. If it should come, we will be glad, and stir ourselves to provide for it—and if it should not come, ever—I shall be sorry. I do not believe, when people love each other, in interfering there. It is wicked, according to my feeling. I want you to have children to me—I don't care how soon. I never thought I should have that definite desire. But you see, we must have a more or less stable foundation if we are going to run the risk of the responsibility of children—not the risk of children, but the risk of the responsibility. (*Letters,* 1:402–3)

An earlier insight regarding Lawrence's sentiments about fatherhood occurs in a dream he recounts (in French, perhaps to ensure that no one else read it) to his fiancée Louie Burrows in 1911:

> I dreamed that we were really married, and that you were giving birth to our first child. You were suffering greatly . . . I moved a little way off, and everything was dark. When I came back, you were recovering, you were smiling, and they showed me the child: a boy, very pretty and placid, with deep blue eyes. As soon as I had seen him, I was the one who had to disappear from the scene, and there was a dark shadow in my place. (*Letters,* 1:272, trans. Boulton)

50. Harwood Brewster Picard, "Remembering D. H. Lawrence."

The dreamer's fears about fatherhood, or perhaps about this marriage, are expressed in his dream that he will "disappear" if he has a son by Louie. This ambivalence seems to me to have a greater ring of truth than the comments by critics and admirers who have regretted that Lawrence did not have, or was not able to have, children. Philip Rieff, for example, says in his introduction to an edition of *Fantasia*:

> Lawrence's practical advice on the conduct of family life seems to me healthy; it is also sad, for . . . the love relation with his wife, Frieda, was childless. . . . because of his ambition to be an exemplar, his life, more than most, shows up its patches of familiar compromise. He was a second husband. His wife had already had her two [*sic:* she had three] children by a man whom she no longer loved—if ever she had. This preacher of family as well as conjugal passion never experienced, in his own childhood, that which he advocated. His own family example could only have taught him what it is he had to criticize, not, except by abstract negation, what to praise.[51]

This sympathy seems misguided to me, especially in its implication that Lawrence's wish to have children was blocked because Frieda already had children. Both this letter to Louie Burrows and Lawrence's well-documented jealousy of Frieda's longing for her children suggest that he was not eager to share his wife with children, even though the letter to Frieda suggests that they did not practice contraception. Lawrence was apprehensive and critical of the effect of motherhood on wives. In *The White Peacock* both Meg's and Lettie's marriages are profoundly debased when they choose their children over their husbands, while in "England, My England" Lawrence constructs Egbert's tragedy from similar materials. Judith Ruderman demonstrates in her book on the fiction of Lawrence's leadership period that "after 1920 or so, a central concern [of Lawrence's] is with the means of combating the 'devouring mother.' "[52] In his catalog of reasons Lawrence did not have children, Rieff argues that Frieda's not loving Ernest Weekley implies she would therefore not wish to have children by a man she *did* love. Others have suggested, perhaps more plausibly, that at age thirty-four Frieda was not eager to have children, or that Lawrence was infertile even before tuberculosis made him impotent. Jeffrey Meyers

51. Philip Rieff, Introduction to *Psychoanalysis and the Unconscious* and *Fantasia of the Unconscious,* xviii.
52. Judith Ruderman, *D. H. Lawrence and the Devouring Mother: The Search for a Patriarchal Ideal of Leadership,* 21.

cites evidence that Lawrence was made sterile by an illness he suffered at age sixteen.[53]

Whatever Lawrence's unconscious feelings about fatherhood
may have been, in at least one instance he was able to apply his
views about childhood to the difficult problem of Frieda and her
children. His belief in nurturing the independent spirit of every
child was such that, in a letter to Frieda's sister Else, he explains:
"Whatever the children may miss now, they will preserve their inner
liberty, and their independent pride will be strong when they come
of age. But if Frieda gave up all to go and live with them, that would
sap their strength because they would have to support her life as
they grew up. They would not be free to live of themselves—they
would first have to live *for her,* to pay back" (*Letters,* 1:486). This
argument has a self-serving aspect, but Lawrence spoke sincerely;
his own mother had demanded such sacrifices of him. Furthermore,
Lawrence's attitude was vindicated in the eventual friendships that
developed among Frieda, Lawrence, and her children, especially
Barbara, who was only ten when her mother eloped with Lawrence.

In his introduction to his collection of historical essays on the
child, William Kessen observes that the history of the study of children tends toward *re*discovery in which the same themes appear
with "remarkable regularity." He attributes this looping of ideas
about children to

> the discovery by philosophers, biologists, and psychologists of their
> own children; the study of child behavior began anew, fresh and en-
> thusiastic, with the birth of Doddy Darwin . . . Jacqueline Piaget . . .
> Each father saw his own child—that is, the child that his prejudice or
> theory would predict—but sharing a common object of observation
> bound these men of divergent times and opinions to a set of common
> problems.[54]

Kessen is specifically interested in nonliterary studies of childhood.
Oddly enough, several of the significant literary evocations of childhood have come from authors who did not have children of their
own: Emily and Charlotte Brontë, George Eliot, Henry James. Charles
Dickens and Mark Twain, who had numerous progeny as examples,
seem, nonetheless, to have drawn their child characters more from
their own memories of childhood. Perhaps our increasing knowledge of earlier women writers (some of them mothers) and the

53. Jeffrey Meyers, *D. H. Lawrence: A Biography,* 73.
54. Kessen, ed., *Child,* 1.

many mothers writing in our own century will come to belie these generalizations with more representations of children drawn from live models.

In Lawrence's case, though, the strength and uniqueness of his contribution to literature and thinking about childhood may even *owe* something to his childlessness. He allowed *Sons and Lovers* to absorb the materials of his own childhood. That absorption, together with his childlessness, may account for both his general lack of unwarranted sentimentality about children and his ability to view his child characters as individuals distinct from their parents. Thus, his effort to understand the relations of parents and children and the focus he placed upon childhood are all the more congruous with the rest of his art.

The salient fact, to my mind, is that from the early poems and fiction to *Lady Chatterley's Lover,* Lawrence rarely neglects to portray parenthood and childhood. In doing so, he revitalizes and modernizes the tradition of symbolically innocent child figures with domestic and psychological realism. His work makes a significant contribution to the troupe of child characters in the modern novel and deepens our imagination of what it may be like to be a child. The children in Lawrence are symbolic figures in a new mode, a mode I call visionary realism. This mode dispenses with the old opposition of innocence and corruption and, instead, expresses Lawrence's conception of the unique, pristine, individual soul and his concomitant idea of character in the novel as something deeper than ego or personality. Lawrence expands the term "consciousness" to encompass the nonmental *unconscious:* "The individual unit of consciousness and being which arises at the conception of every higher organism arises by pure creation, by a process not susceptible to understanding, a process which takes place outside the field of mental comprehension, where mentality, which is definitely limited, does not exist" (*PU,* 14–15). Lawrence's concept of consciousness is broader than George Eliot's mediator or Henry James's fine register of thought and feeling. It encompasses Dickensian dreamlike unconscious perceptions, the Brontës' emotional passion and attentiveness to nature, and something of Hardy's sense of forces larger than the self. Lawrence's unlimited definition of the self—"I, who am man alive, am greater than my soul, or spirit, or body, or mind, or consciousness, or anything else that is merely a part of me"—applies also to his conception of the child.[55]

55. D. H. Lawrence, "Why the Novel Matters," in *Study of Thomas Hardy,* 195.

As a beginning to commentary on Lawrence and the child, one can note the detail with which Lawrence observes and represents children and childish things. It is the same meticulous, physically delighted attention that he accords to flowers, animals, and even the details of housekeeping. Thus, in Lawrence's early novel *The Trespasser,* Siegmund watches his daughter Gwen—in fact, only her feet and legs—while he is on the verge of a breakdown:

> At about a yard from his chair she stopped. He, from under his bent brows, could see her small feet, in brown slippers nearly kicked through at the toes, waiting and moving nervously near him. He pulled himself together as a man does who watches the surgeon's lancet suspended over his wound. Would the child speak to him? Would she touch him with her small hands? He held his breath, and, it seemed, held his heart from beating. What he should do he did not know.
>
> He waited in a daze of suspense. The child shifted from one foot to another. He could just see the edge of her frilled white drawers. He wanted, above all things, to take her in his arms, to have something against which to hide his face. (*TR,* 190)

Even though Lawrence mixes up the names, ages, and number of Siegmund and Beatrice's daughters, they are not mere ciphers in the plot. The glimpses Lawrence gives of them are explicit and the intensity of their effect on their father is fully particularized: "As he watched them he hated the children for being so dear to him. Either he himself must go under, and drag on an existence he hated, or they must suffer" (*TR,* 51).

Yet, in his physical descriptions, Lawrence retains some striking features of the Christian symbolic child and the Romantic child. Like the bambino's in his painting *A Holy Family,* most of his literary children's heads are surrounded by an aureole that is, actually, their own fleecy, light-infiltrated hair. This hair may be described as thistledown, a mop of curls, or bronze dust, but it is never short, dark, or bristly, and it is seldom omitted. Pedro, the elder son of *The Plumed Serpent*'s Don Ramón, has hair that is "softer, more fluffy than his father's, with a hint of brown," and his brother Cyprian has the "fluffy, upstanding brown hair and the startled, hazel eyes of his mother" (*PS,* 353). While the illumination and softness of these children's heads suggest purity and beauty, Lawrence modifies these angelic features with details that bring the child back to earth. Thus, Anna Lensky's "glistening, fair hair like thistledown" sticks out in "straight, wild, flamy pieces" above the "odd little defiant look" that appears on her "face like a bud of apple-blossom" (*Rainbow,* 32–33).

Lawrence, the modern novelist in search of new forms for his prophetic moral vision, synthesizes and finally transforms two prominent strains in the history of the literary child by creating child characters who are neither innocent nor guilty.

Beyond Guilt and toward Visionary Realism
2 The Accomplishments of *Sons and Lovers*

Sons and Lovers tells the story of an artistically inclined young man growing up in a coal-mining village like Eastwood, with parents like Arthur and Lydia Lawrence. The fact that *Sons and Lovers* is a version of Lawrence's own childhood sets it apart from his later fictional portraits of childhood. The Lawrence character, Paul Morel, though probably the best-known child in Lawrence's oeuvre, does not possess the hard, vital individuality that is notable in the children of *The Rainbow*. The portentous role that *Sons and Lovers* plays in the history of the literary child is due, rather, to its probing of the dynamics of family psychology and sexuality, which reveals a struggle between parents over the souls of the children, and the guilt children may feel as a result.

In this autobiographical novel are embodied the two spirits that figure, though less obviously, in all of Lawrence's work, those of his mother and his father. Ford Madox Ford observed in a memoir of Lawrence, "Two beings may have looked out of Lawrence's eyes—a father-spirit who hoped you would put a little devil into him and a mother-spirit that dreaded that you would lead him outside the chapel-walks and persuade him not to wear flannel next his skin." As Ford also noted, those two beings, the force of his father and the force of his mother, "fought an unceasing battle" in Lawrence.[1] The extraordinary power of Lawrence's child characters stems in part from this battle, rooted in his childhood, and in part from his sometimes unconscious quest to translate those opposing forces into a single, imaginative vision. The conflict in Lawrence was, as Ford saw, unceasing and protean, more like guerrilla warfare than a tradi-

1. Nehls, *D. H. Lawrence: A Composite Biography,* 1:117.

tional battle. There were periods in Lawrence's life and work when the mother claimed the victory, others when the father won it. In *Sons and Lovers,* the mother spirit dominates. In the two novels that followed, *The Rainbow* and *Women in Love,* the two forces are most evenly—and most fruitfully—matched.

Even in his first novel, *The White Peacock,* Lawrence describes children with remarkable care and detail. Later, in *The Trespasser,* as we have seen, the love of Siegmund for his daughters significantly defines his character and renders his suicide more deliberate. But in *Sons and Lovers* the children become major characters, and Lawrence begins to convey a sense of what it is like to be a small child. The following scene, in which Paul is sent to collect his father's weekly pay, may seem reminiscent of Dickens in its cognizance of the physical sensations of being small and incompetent:

> Paul knew his turn was next but one, and his heart began to beat. He was pushed against the chimney-piece. His calves were burning. But he did not hope to get through the wall of men.
> "Walter Morel!" came the ringing voice.
> "Here!" piped Paul, small and inadequate.
> "Morel—Walter Morel!" the cashier repeated, his finger and thumb on the invoice, ready to pass on.
> Paul was suffering convulsions of self-consciousness, and could not or would not shout. The backs of the men obliterated him. Then Mr. Winterbottom came to the rescue.
> "He's here. Where is he? Morel's lad?"
> The fat, red, bald little man peered round with keen eyes. He pointed to the fireplace. The colliers looked round, moved aside, and disclosed the boy. (*SL,* 110)

There are surprisingly few such instances of this kind of direct presentation of the child's consciousness in *Sons and Lovers.* The reason for this scarcity is connected with the autobiographical nature of Lawrence's source material and—more particularly—with the extraordinary effort he made to render that material into an artistically successful novel. Although this novel may not be a strictly accurate portrait of Lawrence's childhood, it is—to some degree—a recognizable one. This recognizability tends to obscure the book's literary form and make it seem instead that the material of Lawrence's own childhood is laid open to inspection. Before *Sons and Lovers* was completed, Lawrence was so uncertain about his artistic handling of the personal subject matter that he invited others to scrutinize his manuscript at every stage. The history of these early conversations and decisions confirms the primacy of his relationship with his mother and suggests the ground upon which he raised the artistic structure of the novel.

As Lawrence began his first draft of "Paul Morel" in 1911, he and his friends were aware that he was tackling new and difficult material. His two previous books had not been so directly drawn from personal experience, and he was still grieving for his mother, who had died in December 1910. The subject of his family was inescapable for Lawrence; *Sons and Lovers* was his first explicit attempt to write about the mother-spirit and the father-spirit that resided in him. The opinions of his most influential early critics, Jessie Chambers and Frieda Weekley, are perceptive of the struggle for power that was going on in Lawrence's mind.

Jessie Chambers, who figures in the novel as Miriam, recalls that she read the first manuscript of "Paul Morel" and prodded Lawrence to revise it, advising him that "she was surprised he had kept so far from reality in his story . . . what had really happened was much more poignant and interesting than the situations he had invented." She hoped that he might "free himself from his strange obsession with his mother" if he could "treat the theme with strict integrity." When he did revise, taking out such melodramatic incidents as the killing of Paul's older brother by his father and making the psychological opposition between Miriam and Mrs. Morel more pronounced, Chambers was shocked by his treatment of her. She found that instead of overcoming his singular attachment to his mother by writing the story, he had handed her the "laurels of victory" over a scapegoat Miriam.[2]

Not long after his final break with Chambers, Lawrence left England with his future wife, Frieda Weekley. At this time, as he was rewriting "Paul Morel" again, he learned something about Freud and the Oedipus complex from Frieda. She led him to recognize that the relationship between Paul and his mother might be unhealthy. This new perspective prompted Lawrence to change the title from the single character's name, "Paul Morel," to *Sons and Lovers*. By leaving some ambiguity about whose sons and whose lovers are concerned, the final title reflects the layered perspectives and relationships that make up the novel. The tacit reference is, of course, to Gertrude Morel, whose sons are also her lovers. After he sent his revised manuscript to Edward Garnett, Lawrence wrote his too-much-trusted explanation of the book: "The old son-lover was Oedipus. The name of the new one is legion. And if the son-lover takes a

---

2. Chambers, *A Personal Record,* 198, 202.

wife, then she is not his wife, she is only his bed . . . and his wife in her despair shall hope for sons, that she may have her lover in her hour."[3] Years later Lawrence again contributed to the discussion by remarking that he "would write a different *Sons and Lovers* now; my mother was wrong, and I thought she was absolutely right."[4]

The personal debates that attended Lawrence's composition process tell us about the book's emotional history and the evolution of its particular form. Both women saw correctly that Lawrence intended to exalt his mother through the characterization of Mrs. Morel. Frieda's psychoanalytic interpretation of the story persuaded Lawrence to give the oedipal aspect stronger emphasis in his remarks than it receives in the novel. Whereas Jessie Chambers, her friendship with Lawrence already ebbing, was unable to acknowledge her own conflict with Mrs. Lawrence and was probably hurt by the novel's suggestion of such conflict. Ironically, the acknowledgment that Lawrence made after he met Frieda lends credence to the view of events that Chambers expresses in her memoir of Lawrence. The narrator of *Sons and Lovers* does indeed give the laurels of victory to Mrs. Morel/Lawrence, though there are many ways in which the novel undercuts its narrator. Psychoanalyst Selma Fraiberg suggests that in this novel Lawrence fails to "overcome the clinical drabness of mother-son love" and that "the tragedy of Paul seems a little commonplace to the modern reader who has ripened on the psychological novel." The insight she expresses in her response is one Lawrence could applaud: "Is the Oedipus complex, the clinical syndrome, material for tragedy? . . . A man in a novel who is defeated in his childhood and condemned by unconscious forces within him to tiredly repeat his earliest failure in love, only makes us a little weary of man; his tragedy seems unworthy and trivial."[5] But Fraiberg errs in assuming that the Oedipus complex is the whole subject of Lawrence's third novel with Paul as its tragic (anti-)hero. The mother's domination is apparent not only in its immediate influence on the child Paul/Lawrence, but more subtly in the specific form that Lawrence gave to the novel and in the narrative attitudes and ambiguities that pervade its texture. I will explore the latter aspect in the remainder of this chapter.

More than it is a record of his childhood, *Sons and Lovers* is

3. "Foreword to *Sons and Lovers*," in *The Letters of D. H. Lawrence*, ed. Aldous Huxley, 102.

4. Frieda Lawrence, *Not I, But the Wind . . .* , 56.

5. Selma Fraiberg, "Two Modern Incest Heroes," 647–48.

Lawrence's attempt to excuse or justify his origins, his youth, and, especially, to exonerate and eulogize his mother.[6] Lawrence conflates the autobiographical elements of his material with the more reliable and objectifiable structure of tragedy. Thus, the result of Lawrence's consultations about and rewriting of the novel is not simply the story of a young man growing up. The book's final form is an explicitly literary one—the tragic story of the life of Gertrude Morel. The growth, education, and precarious rising of the young man occur in counterpoint to the aging, gradual disillusion, and prideful decline of his mother. This concentration on the mother casts a chiaroscuro effect upon the child and adolescent character, sometimes obscuring him but at other times revealing him with a brightness and penetration that are peculiarly maternal. In other words, Paul remains his mother's boy throughout much of the novel, seen as his mother sees him.

Embedded in *Sons and Lovers* is a doubled narrative line: the son's story and the mother's story. It is, I believe, the intertwining of two stories, two sets of authorial intentions, and a variety of narrative voices that gives this novel its particular formal strengths and emotional cachet. The larger pattern of the novel is that of his *mother's life as Lawrence believed that she imagined it*. Two events that merge the son, Paul, with the mother demarcate the narrative time of the novel: her pregnancy with him, and his grief over her death, which Paul induces through an overdose of medicine to relieve her misery. Thus, the present tense of the novel is begun and ended by events that entail absolute involvement of the son's life in the mother's.

Within that larger pattern there are many instances—ranging from full scenes to telling choices of detail or language—in which the autobiographical impulse directs the narrative. Notice, for example, the shifting narrative voices and emerging consciousness that occur within the following brief scene from the opening chapter. Lawrence describes the feelings of Paul's older brother, William,

6. Daniel Weiss's study, *Oedipus in Nottingham,* is the classic statement of this view. Weiss argues, "Gertrude Morel moves through *Sons and Lovers* like a cry of pain. Her truth is valid only as she is an expression of her son's anguish. . . . Of the other characters it can be said that Lawrence is truly their creator, since they live in obedience to their own laws. But of Gertrude Morel he is merely the undertaker. . . . Her likeness is a magnificent death mask" (39). My reading, though it begins with a similar observation, takes a different tack from Weiss's, arguing that the perspective of Gertrude Morel governs much of the novel.

who at seven years of age is just old enough to be allowed to go to the wakes (parish festival) by himself. William had not expected Mrs. Morel to join him; when she does arrive, late, he presents her with two egg-cups he has won for her:

> He was tipful of excitement now she had come, led her about the ground, showed her everything. Then at the peep-show, she explained the pictures, in a sort of story, to which he listened as if spellbound. He would not leave her. All the time he stuck close to her, bristling with a small boy's pride of her. For no other woman looked such a lady as she did, in her little black bonnet and her cloak. She smiled when she saw women she knew. (*SL,* 38)

Most of this description is objective ("led her around the ground," "he listened as if spellbound"), but there is also a voice that can generalize about William's feelings, labeling them as "excitement" and "pride of her." In addition, there seems to be direct representation of William's consciousness in this view of his mother: "For no other woman looked such a lady as she did." The single transitional word, "for," identifies the source of William's pride in *his* judgment of the mother's appearance, and at the same time casts some doubt on the objectivity of the observation. That Mrs. Morel "smiled when she saw women she knew" is an observation by the narrator or William. In either case her smile suggests that she is also proud, either of her own appearance or of her boy's excitement. The above passage gives readers the initial impression that they are seeing what William sees. But the apparently simple omniscient point of view is actually a shifting one that produces a complex mosaic of perspectives. While the point of view superficially conveys William's consciousness, it more closely represents the mother's sensibility. The phrases "He would not leave her . . . he stuck close to her" in particular are infused with a pridefully possessive maternal attitude.

The technique, serendipitous above, is more distinct in a following passage: "And she went slowly away with her little girl, whilst her son stood watching her, cut to the heart to let her go, and yet unable to leave the wakes. . . . At about half-past six her son came home, tired now, rather pale, and somewhat wretched. He was wretched, though he did not know it, because he had let her go alone. Since she had gone, he had not enjoyed his wakes" (*SL,* 39). Here the previously noted narrative ambivalence develops into a statement that the child is not cognizant of the responses that are reported of him. Such awareness of the unconscious nature of feeling is a crucial element of Lawrence's handling of consciousness in his later novel *The Rainbow.* Here though, the boldness of the insight is undercut, I believe, by the narrative explanation that William felt wretched "because he had let her go alone." This interpretation of William's feeling must be ascribed to the mother, for no one else could make it. In writing such a line Lawrence identifies not with the child but with an idealized mother/son attachment that makes even a brief separation painful for the child. The phrase "his wakes" condescends to the child and must also be ascribed to the mother because it is she who dislikes and belittles the wakes. The preceding examples demonstrate how the dominant maternal attitude of the novel is woven into the seemingly innocuous and omniscient angles of Lawrence's narrative sentences. The child in these examples, drawn from the first chapter, is William; Mrs. Morel is eight months pregnant with Paul. Even before birth the unwanted second son is claiming a place in the family and usurping some of his older brother's privileges. It is the baby who wearies Mrs. Morel and keeps her from staying longer at the wakes. The complex mixing of perspectives in such a passage allows Lawrence to put Paul at the center of the story even when he is not actually present. William, though active in the scene, is supplanted by Paul through the mother's sentiments, while these in turn express Paul's unconscious desire to oust his brother. I cannot think of a preceding English novel, other than *Adam Bede,* in which a mother's feelings about an unborn child play such a definite role. Rivalry between the two brothers also appears in a section Edward Garnett deleted from the manuscript of *Sons and Lovers* in which William carries on while Mrs. Morel nurses Paul, says the baby "looks nasty," and asks his mother why she sings to a baby who cannot understand her.[7]

Everything in *Sons and Lovers* leans toward its center, which is the relationship of Paul Morel and his mother. Before his birth the embryonic consciousness seems to grow against the wishes of its mother.[8] She feels "wretched with the coming child. . . . She could not afford to have this third. She did not want it" (*SL,* 39–40). This pregnancy has brought Gertrude Morel the realization that her own life is finished: " 'What have *I* to do with all this? Even the child I am going to have! It doesn't seem as if *I* were taken into account' " (*SL,* 40). This quasi-feminist insight differentiates Mrs. Morel from other

7. Mark Schorer, ed. *"Sons and Lovers" by D. H. Lawrence: A Facsimile of the Manuscript,* 53.

8. "Is the foetus conscious?" Lawrence asks. "It must be since it carries on an independent and progressive self-development. . . . the foetus is not *personally* conscious. [It] is, however, radiantly, individually conscious" (*PU,* 18–19).

pregnant women in Lawrence's work—Lydia Brangwen, Alvina Houghton Ciccio, Connie Chatterley, and especially Anna Brangwen—who never think of protesting the impositions of motherhood. Gertrude believes she can only regain her self through her sons—"nothing else would happen for her—at least until William grew up." In fact, as Lawrence knew when he wrote, the older son, William, like his own brother William Ernest, would not survive to revivify the mother; that responsibility would fall to Paul, as it did to Lawrence himself.

The unborn child is a felt presence in the novel, responding to the mother's moods. One illustration of this connection is strangely violent. It occurs in the scene in which Walter Morel pushes and locks Gertrude out of the house. Responding to Gertrude's fury, "the child boiled within her" (*SL,* 59). At first, she walks in anger; then, both mother and baby are gradually calmed by the clear, moonlit night. "Boiling" recalls the scene in which the fight began:

> The kitchen was full of the scent of boiled herbs and hops. On the hob a large black saucepan steamed slowly. Mrs. Morel took a panchion, a great bowl of thick red earth, streamed a heap of white sugar into the bottom, and then, straining herself to the weight, was pouring in the liquor.
>
> Just then Morel came in. He had been very jolly in the Nelson, but coming home had grown irritable. . . . He entered just as Mrs Morel was pouring the infusion of herbs out of the saucepan. Swaying slightly, he lurched against the table. The boiling liquor pitched. Mrs Morel started back.
>
> "Good gracious," she cried, "coming home in his drunkenness!" (*SL,* 57)

The domestic peace, symbolized by the liquid Mrs. Morel pours into the womblike earthen bowl, is disrupted by the entry of the man. The figurative "boiling" of the fetus within Gertrude's body is like the lurching of the husband, a disruption in her orderly life. After she has walked in the garden for a while, Mrs. Morel loses herself in the scent of tall white lilies: "Except for a slight feeling of sickness, and her consciousness in the child, herself melted out like scent into the shiny pale air" (*SL,* 60). Curiously, Gertrude's consciousness "in the child" resists the swooning condition longer than does her personal self. Lawrence thus suggests that the mother's deep psychic need for this child is stronger than her egoistic needs. The concept of such a need serves a dual purpose: it gives the mother a motive for accepting the inevitable, and it comforts Paul/Lawrence, who would otherwise have to feel guilty for his very existence. The visionary moment eventually subsumes even her consciousness of the child: "After a time the child, too, melted with her in the mixing-pot of moonlight, and she rested with the hills and lilies and houses, all swum together in a kind of swoon" (*SL,* 60). Later, in her mirror, Gertrude "smiled faintly to see her face all smeared with the yellow dust of lilies" (*SL,* 62). Lawrence was probably given the kernel of this quarrel scene, including some directions for how to represent its effect on Paul's fetal consciousness, by his own mother. Jessie Chambers recalls that Lydia Lawrence once said to her: "I know why he hates his father. It happened before he was born. One night he put me out of the house . . . he's bound to hate his father."[9] According to Chambers, Mrs. Lawrence "bent her head with a strange smile" while delivering this opinion. This gesture seems to corroborate Lawrence's version of the smile to the mirror in *Sons and Lovers;* however, Chambers had read the novel before she composed her memoir. The secret smile seems to me a testimony of a new bond between the mother and this previously unwanted child. It is the confidential smile of a woman who has been unfaithful. This is the bond that governs the intricate dual structure of *Sons and Lovers,* the autobiography that becomes the mother's biography as well, but never lets go of itself.

In his study of the sources of Lawrence's creativity, Daniel Dervin reveals that the house in which the Lawrences lived before D. H. was born, the house she was locked out of, did not have a garden. Therefore, Mrs. Lawrence could not have communed with lilies in her own garden at that time. Dervin proposes that in adding the garden episode to his mother's story of being locked out, Lawrence allows Mrs. Morel "to undergo something on the order of a second impregnation, or pollination, by means of purely natural elements." This creates a family romance that replaces Paul's actual father with a kind of natural parthenogenesis.[10] Although Dervin does not mention this, the lilies reappear in the novel much later, still as an emblem of Paul's union with his mother.[11] When Paul, at age twenty-four,

9. Chambers, *A Personal Record,* 138.

10. Daniel Dervin, *"A Strange Sapience": The Creative Imagination of D. H. Lawrence,* 129.

11. In this second scene, the tall white lilies are referred to as "madonna" lilies, another common name for the Annunciation lily. Thus Lawrence would seem to be associating the event with the angel Gabriel's announcement of the Incarnation to Mary, Mrs. Morel with the virgin Mary, and Paul with the Christ child. Such associations, I believe, strengthen Dervin's reading, for the effect of the Annunciation is to replace suspicion of an earthly father with belief that the Holy Ghost is the father.

decides to break with Miriam, he is standing in the moonlight before "the rocking, heavy scent" of a "white barrier" of Madonna lilies. "They flagged all loose, as if they were panting. The scent made him drunk . . . the great flowers leaned as if they were calling" (*SL*, 355). Paul's drunken feeling answers the same call that his mother heard years before. Like her experience, Paul's is an abandonment of the self, though his receives the pejorative name of "drunk" while hers is more honorably "dizzy" and a "swoon." Then, noticing a "raw and coarse" scent in the air, Paul finds the "fleshy throats and dark, grasping hands" of the purple iris (*SL*, 356). The "brutal" iris seems to bring Paul to a resolution. As if to consummate the prenatal engagement his mother made by way of the lilies years before, Paul goes in the house and tells his mother that he will break with Miriam. The bond with his mother, signified by the lilies and fortified by the male sexuality Paul recognizes in the iris, triumphs over intruders. Lawrence's use of the lilies as a symbol for the attachment of Gertrude and Paul allows him to give dramatic and more general form to his mother's apparently preposterous notion that he learned to hate his father before birth. It puts the apocryphal story of early hatred in service of the novel's major theme, the relationship of mother and son.[12]

Just as the bond between Mrs. Morel and Paul is symbolically established before his birth, the parents' mutual alienation is represented in their inability to communicate after the baby comes. Walter is tired from work, where he has stayed late hacking at a piece of rock that blocks his next day's coal. At home, his laboring wife, "feeling sick to death," assumes he has stopped at the pub and wonders "What did he care about the child or her?" He barely acknowledges the neighbor's joylessly told news that his wife is "about as bad as she can be. It's a boy childt" (*SL*, 68). When he sees the child—"It was a struggle to face his wife at this moment"—he can think of nothing to say except "Bless him!" which makes Gertrude laugh because "he blessed by rote—pretending paternal emotion, which he did not feel just then" (*SL*, 69). She dismisses him, and he leaves the room. But Lawrence does not close the scene with that raw separation. Rather, he deepens the poignancy: "Dismissed, he wanted to kiss her, but he dared not. She half wanted him to kiss

12. Dorothy Van Ghent, in *The English Novel: Form and Function,* 256–57, and Mark Spilka, in *The Love Ethic of D. H. Lawrence,* 39–59, first drew attention to Lawrence's floral imagery. In a more recent essay, "For Mark Schorer with Combative Love: The *Sons and Lovers* Manuscript," Spilka calls such imagery a "relational sign," a phrase that is particularly apt (37).

her, but could not bring herself to give any sign. She only breathed freely when he was gone out of the room again, leaving behind him a faint smell of pit-dirt" (*SL,* 69). For a moment the relentless battle of father and mother is suspended, the sides are evenly weighted by the narrator, and yet nothing happens. The poignancy here comes, I think, from an autobiographical element. These sentences illuminate the difference between a fictionalized autobiographical childhood and a fictional childhood. The scene itself must be invented, for Lawrence could not have remembered it or known his parents' thoughts. As early as 1908, before he had kissed a woman on the mouth, Lawrence wrote, "Such a touch is the connection between the vigorous flow of two lives. Like a positive electricity, a current of creative life runs through two persons . . . a certain life current passes through them which changes them forever" (*Letters,* 1:99). Thus Gertrude and Walter's mutual—but separate—longing for a kiss expresses the author/child's own longing for a better welcome into the world, for not just a truce, but a "circuit of family love" to encircle the child (*FU,* 169).

It is not to be. The battle between the father-spirit and the mother-spirit, which Ford Madox Ford noted in Lawrence, is violently enacted by Walter and Gertrude Morel. While the narrator generally gives preference to Gertrude's position in these arguments, there are a few scenes that break away from the rest of the narrative and show Walter Morel standing clear, a man unto himself despite the narrator's assertion that he has "denied the God in him" (*SL,* 102). Nearly every critic who has written at length about *Sons and Lovers* cites the same two scenes as examples of Lawrence's involuntary tribute to his father: the scene in which Walter cooks his breakfast alone before the fire, and the one in which he and the children make fuses for the mine out of wheat straws. The second of these appears, like a penance, directly after the statement that "conversation was impossible between the father and any other member of the family" (*SL,* 102).

Such contradictions between what is shown and what is told about Walter Morel are multiplied by the ambiguities that are embedded in many of the narrative declarations about Gertrude and Walter Morel. The following statement occurs at the close of a brief episode in which Walter takes the youngest child, Arthur, into his arms after work. Because the father is covered with pit dirt, Gertrude wraps the boy in an apron to keep him clean. Nonetheless his face is smutted by his father's kisses, and Walter laughs joyfully, claiming he's a little collier. "These," the reader is told, "were the happy moments of her life now, when the children included the father in her heart" (*SL,* 86). Gertrude Morel has, in scene after scene, turned these children against their father and used them to comfort herself. "Lord, let my father die," Paul often prayed. Yet what is one to make of this curious assertion that Mrs. Morel is happy when "the children included the father in her heart?" It seems to me that Mrs. Morel is now able to admit her husband to her heart *only* when the children bring him there. It suggests that she would like him to be there but cannot admit him herself, or—more likely—that Paul/Lawrence wishes him to be there. It expresses, I think, Lawrence's nonoedipal desire for parents who love each other.

The comment about Gertrude's happy moments condescends to Walter and at the same time suggests that she still can be pleased by affection *for* her husband. It exonerates the children from blame in the debacle of the parents' marriage. Although Gertrude often says that if it were not for them, she could leave Walter, the scene's closing line suggests that the children are not the cause of their mother's unhappiness and may even be the means to her happiness. Lawrence's real understanding of family psychology shows in his language, which finds a way to admit the father, even though the author may intend to defend only his mother. In *Fantasia of the Unconscious* Lawrence remarks that a "child exists in the interplay of two great life-waves, the womanly and the male" (*FU,* 73). The theories of family relations that he articulates in *Psychoanalysis and the Unconscious* and *Fantasia of the Unconscious* are, Lawrence stresses, based on what he learned from writing novels. The theories are, indeed, a corrective to the mother-dominated attitude expressed by the narrative structure and voice in *Sons and Lovers.* While it sometimes seems in this novel that the crashing of the two life-waves is so extreme that the children are damaged by what ought to nourish them, in the long run the theory vindicates the indomitable spirit of the father that persists in *Sons and Lovers* despite the narrator's attempt to discredit it.

Lawrence's insistence that Paul Morel and his mother are victimized by the father and by their lower-class surroundings differentiates the vision of childhood in *Sons and Lovers* from that in *The Rainbow.* This insistence skews the author's vision of Paul. At this time it was still difficult for Lawrence to conceive of himself, and thus to portray Paul, as an independent being. Paul Morel satisfies his mother by becoming a clerk in Nottingham rather than going into the coal mines; however, his maturity and independence at the end of the novel are tenuous. A sense of the child as a victim of parentally generated psychological imbalances, along with the emphasis on his erotic connection with his mother, makes *Sons and Lovers* seem intractably Freudian. No complex novel of the high modern period has accommodated itself more comfortably to psychoanalysis. As we have seen, the theory that Paul loved his mother so much that he could never love another woman was first recorded by Lawrence himself.

Lawrence differs from Freud, however, in attributing no sexuality to the child himself. While Lawrence understands that the oedipal complex was caused by the child's incest craving, he mistakenly believes that Freud advocates tolerance or even indulgence of oedipal desire in order to prevent psychic damage from repression. Uncomfortable with—and perhaps offended by—Freud's emphasis on infantile desire as the disruptive force in the child's psychic development, Lawrence blames developmental failures on parents. Sons are preyed upon by mothers who are not spiritually fulfilled in their marriages; the sons' latent sexual desire is inadvertently awakened by the mothers' demands for spiritual sympathy.

When Lawrence constructs his psychology in *Fantasia,* he faults the parent who asks for a child's sympathy: "*Never* make a child party to adult affairs. Never drag the child in. Refuse its sympathy on such occasions. Always treat it as if it had *no* business to hear, even if it is present and *must* hear. . . . It is despicable for any one parent to accept a child's sympathy against the other parent. And the one who *received* the sympathy is always more contemptible than the one who is hated" (*FU,* 131). The sympathy that Mrs. Lawrence was still exacting from her son as he wrote *Sons and Lovers* prevented him from delineating the child Paul with the clarity so marked in his other child characters. The dual structure of the novel, with its interlaced perspectives and voices, brings about a kind of reflective portraiture which subsumes the individuals. This mirroring may be related to the difficulty, as Lawrence describes it in *Fantasia,* of perceiving one's parent as an independent being: "The portrait of the parent can never be quite completed in the mind of the son or daughter. As long as time lasts it must be left unfinished" (*FU,* 108). The degree to which the child is able to form a mental concept of the parent is an indication of the child's individuality. As the child's "dynamic relation" with the parent wanes, the child is able to see the parent more clearly as a separate being. In *Sons and Lovers,* as Mark Spilka shows, the dynamic polarity between Paul Morel and his mother increases rather than wanes up through the time of the mother's death.[13] Likewise, the continuing dynamism of Lawrence's relationship with his mother (a process that includes the writing of the novel itself) produces an extremely affecting and unusual document in the history of childhood, a eulogy that is the culmination of Lawrence's devotion to his mother.

The rendering of a child character seems to call for a sort of stereoscopic vision to be convincing, to eliminate the blinders of self-involvement or loyalty to only one parent. Dostoyevsky's unfinished *Netochka Nezvanova* provides an example. Just as in *Sons and Lovers,* the child's parents (in this case mother and stepfather) do not get along, and the child (somewhat like James's Maisie, but more feelingly) chooses between them. She turns against her mother, helps her stepfather steal her mother's household money, and runs away with him, abandoning the mother's freshly dead body. It is a phantasmagorical scene, worthy of Dickens in its dramatics. The father soon abandons Netochka as well, but she remembers him fondly until years later when she is disabused of her devotion by a man who knew him. From that informant's story and her own conjectures she realizes that she wronged her mother both in life and in memory. This double perspective—how she recalls feeling as a child, and how she feels now that her recollection has been reappraised—gives the character vividness and dignity. Paul Morel lacks those qualities because of his single-minded devotion to his mother and his aversion to his father.

The composing of *Sons and Lovers* was rather like a darkroom process in which Lawrence developed and tried to apply fixative to his photographs of his mother. In the following passage, for instance, he creates a diptych of interiorized portraits in which Gertrude and Paul consider each other. Each feels responsibility and guilt for the other's very existence. First Gertrude watches Paul, whose survival has defied her initial rejection of him:

> So after dinner he lay down on the sofa, on the warm chintz cushions the children loved. Then he fell into a kind of doze. That afternoon Mrs Morel was ironing. She listened to the small, restless noise the boy made in his throat as she worked. Again rose in her heart the old, almost weary feeling towards him. She had never expected him to live. And yet he had a great vitality in his young body. Perhaps it would have been a little relief to her if he had died. She always felt a mixture of anguish in her love for him.

Then Paul watches his mother:

13. Spilka, *Love Ethic,* 74–82.

He, in his semi-conscious sleep, was vaguely aware of the clatter of the iron on the iron-stand, of the faint thud, thud on the ironing-board. Once roused, he opened his eyes to see his mother standing on the hearthrug with the hot iron near her cheek, listening, as it were, to the heat. Her still face, with the mouth closed tight from suffering and disillusion and self-denial, and her nose the smallest bit on one side, and her blue eyes so young, quick, and warm, made his heart contract with love. When she was quiet, so, she looked brave and rich with life, but as if she had been done out of her rights. It hurt the boy keenly, this feeling about her that she had never had her life's fulfilment: and his own incapability to make up to her hurt him with a sense of impotence, yet made him patiently dogged inside. It was his childish aim. (*SL,* 105)

Those two portraits epitomize the attitude toward childhood that prevails in this novel. Though Lawrence does not use the Freudian word—*guilt*—a sense of guilty responsibility is present both in Gertrude's "weary feeling" toward Paul and in his "hurt" feeling because his mother has "never had her life's fulfillment." This guilt represents a possessive sentimentalizing, a distortion through over-personalizing, of the relationship between parent and child. Lawrence later came to advise, speaking in the persona of a parent, that "there must be in me no departure from myself, lest I injure the pre-conscious dynamic relation" (*FU,* 89). In the paragraphs I have just quoted there is more departure from the self than Lawrence would later approve, and it causes a distortion in the mental portrait each makes of the other. While each of the paragraphs from the ironing scene begins with realistic details—chintz cushions, small restless noises; the thud, thud of the iron, the hot iron near her cheek—they both shift into that imaginary perspective of the mother's life as he wished/believed that she imagined it. The images are deceptively clear because of the realistic regard of places and things that surround the characters, but Paul's sentiments are not convincing as a young boy's. A child would not notice that his mother looks young, though an adolescent might. The regret about her lack of life's fulfillment is also an adolescent's, and probably learned from the mother herself.[14] The re-creation of the mother's consciousness is bolder and more effective. While we are used to the assumption that

14. My judgment of the fictional representation here might be modified in consideration of Lawrence's own unusually strong nurturing impulse. Daniel Schneider concludes in *The Consciousness of D. H. Lawrence: An Intellectual Biography,* 4–8, that Lawrence spontaneously and precociously assumed responsibility for others. He suggests that the bouts of weeping that Lawrence's younger sister Ada reports were connected with his early sympathy for his mother's unhappiness.

a mother departs from herself for her children, Lawrence's inclusion of her weariness presages his later aversion to such sacrificial motherhood.

In fact, one can see that rebellion is already steeping within Lawrence's tribute to his mother. Lawrence's general championing of the character of Gertrude Morel encompasses a resentment that occasionally surfaces; this resentment is analogous to the respect for the father that emerges from the loathing of him. In later works Lawrence will direct his hostility against the whole citadel of passive-aggressive Victorian motherhood. For instance in 1928, he wrote that now "young men know that most of the 'benevolence' and 'motherly love' of their adoring mothers was simply egoism again, and an extension of self, and a love of having absolute power over another creature."[15] A tinge of this feeling is evident in the otherwise sympathetic episodes of Mrs. Morel's death. While Paul nurses his mother through the final stages of cancer, soothing her and calling her by pet names like "my pigeon," "my little," or "my love," she recounts to him the "things that had been most bitter to her" in her marriage. It seems that with these memories she wants to bind him to her and designate him to carry on her hatred of her husband; he feels "as if his life were being destroyed, piece by piece, within him" (*SL,* 455). Part of Paul seems to realize that her refusal to die is related to her possessiveness of himself, and that he must rebel against it. He tells Clara Dawes: " 'And she looks at me, and she wants to stay with me,' he went on monotonously. 'She's got such a will, it seems as if she would never go—never!' " (*SL,* 457). Thus Paul's admiration verges ever so slightly on hatred for this woman who will postpone death in order to increase her hold on him. When he decides to hasten her death by giving her all of her remaining morphia tablets in a single dose, he and his sister "both laughed together like two conspiring children. On top of all their horror flickered this little sanity" (*SL,* 464). What is the sanity? Is it just that Paul and Annie can still laugh like children? That euthanasia is a sane alternative to such horrible suffering? While it is both of those, it is also that rebelling against the relentless will of his mother, even killing the body that maintains that will, is a sane action for Paul. This act has, indeed, the natural sanity that Lawrence respects in children, for it expresses simultaneously the self's desire for independence and a sympathetic connection with another person.

The death of the mother by the son's hand represents, also, the

15. Lawrence, "The Real Thing," in *Phoenix,* 199.

silencing of the narrative voice that has wished to dominate the story. Without the certainty that that voice has held for him, Paul is nearly extinguished himself: "On every side the immense dark silence seemed pressing him, so tiny a spark, into extinction, and yet, almost nothing, he could not be extinct." He literally whimpers his mother's name in the darkness, but of course her voice is gone, intermingled in the "vastness and terror of the immense night" (*SL,* 492). Lawrence himself summarized the end of his novel incorrectly, telling his editor that Paul is "left at the end naked of everything, with the drift toward death" (*Letters,* 1:477). This voice expresses again *the mother's life as Lawrence believed that she imagined it.* Without her, this voice would have us believe, the son is nothing. But the narrative voice with which even Lawrence himself speaks in his letter is not the only voice in the novel. The actual ending belongs to the dissenting party, to the voice of another storyteller who wishes to fabricate not his mother's story, but his own. It tells us that Paul "would not give in. Turning sharply, he walked toward the city's gold phosphorescence. His fists were shut, his mouth set fast. He would not take that direction, to the darkness, to follow her. He walked towards the faintly humming, glowing town, quickly" (*SL,* 492).

The text of *Sons and Lovers* is, then, like the palimpsest of attitudes that make up any living relationship; it contains much that Lawrence constructed about his own prehistory, much that he would eventually disclaim, and much that he was never aware of. Psychoanalytic insistence that the intimate mother-son relationship depicted in *Sons and Lovers* is unhealthy may blind us to the auspiciousness of that intimacy for Lawrence's exploration of other relationships in his later novels. The mother, who feeds her baby and cares for its body, Freud argued, is "the first and strongest love-object and the prototype of all later love relations—for both sexes."[16] The intensified closeness and sense of victimization that Lawrence shared with his mother is, Alfred Kazin points out, the source of Lawrence's style and pride, and the primary source of his belief that his mission as a novelist is to show "the perfected relation between man and his circumambient universe." Later, in novels that were not based so directly on his own life, Lawrence was able to explore relationships that occur between less victimized, more strongly expressive individuals. Of Lawrence's relationship with his

16. Sigmund Freud, "An Outline of Psycho-Analysis" in *The Standard Edition of the Complete Psychological Works,* 23:188.

mother, which culminated in her death and the writing of *Sons and Lovers,* Kazin concludes: "Ever after Lawrence was to try to re-create this living bond, this magic sympathy, between himself and life. He often succeeded. "[17] We must attribute Lawrence's vision of the novel as the "perfect medium for revealing to us the changing rainbow of our living relationships"[18] to the anxious and perhaps perverse love of Lydia Lawrence for her son, and to the closeness she demanded from him.

By writing a novel about his own childhood, Lawrence achieved a complex vision of family life that then enabled him to create the vital, independent child characters (like *The Rainbow*'s Anna Brangwen) who are free of Freud's less auspicious vision of life. Anna's initial unhealthy dependence on her mother is much like Paul Morel's chronic dependency on his. However, Anna's stepfather is the kind of father that Lawrence lacked, one who is able and willing to participate in family dynamics to create the balance of dependence and independence necessary for the child's psychic growth. Lawrence's developing ability to convey complex family relations, which resulted in *The Rainbow*'s visionary realism, may be noticed in *Sons and Lovers* as he transforms traditional symbolism into psychologically incisive representations. Most of Lawrence's descriptions of young children contain the same iconographic detail: ringlets of golden hair. One would expect an author as attentive to physical reality as is Lawrence to realize that not all children have such hair. Nonetheless, he persists in endowing his children with this particularly Victorian figuration of innocence, a sort of halo made by nature. Early in *Sons and Lovers* this unlikely hair becomes an integral, though fairly conventional, symbol when Walter Morel cuts one-year-old William's curls, an act that becomes the "spear through the side of [Gertrude's] love for Morel" and an emblem of the parents' struggle for influence over the children (*SL,* 51). Later in this same novel, in a passage that foreshadows the style of *The Rainbow,* Lawrence folds new layers of meaning into an apparently conventional use of hair and blood as symbols for innocence and sacrifice. In his drunken fury over a kitchen accident, Morel has thrown a drawer at Gertrude and cut her forehead; "sickened with feebleness and hopelessness of spirit," he inspects the wound: "He was turning drearily away, when he saw a drop of blood fall from the averted wound into [Paul's] fragile, glistening

17. Alfred Kazin, "Sons, Lovers, and Mothers," 32.
18. Lawrence, "Morality," in *Study of Thomas Hardy,* 175.

hair. Fascinated, he watched the heavy dark drop hang in the glistening cloud, and pull down the gossamer. Another drop fell. It would soak through to the baby's scalp. He watched, fascinated, feeling it soak in; then, finally, his manhood broke" (*SL,* 77). Here the child's hair is surely representative of his innocence, and the drop of blood that stains it is the corruption of the unhappy marriage that obtrudes into the child's defenselessness. But the static symbolic code of the scene is forced into another mode by the statement that Morel *feels* the blood soak into the baby's scalp. The code is then turned another notch by the juxtaposed assertion that "then, finally, his manhood broke." By thus using the scene to describe the breaking of Walter Morel's manhood, Lawrence allows the complexity of the family drama to supersede conventional analysis and makes it difficult to gauge the narrator's sympathy. The apparently conventional symbolism of innocence and evil is expanded by the dynamics of the sentence: Walter feels compelled to watch the blood soak to the scalp, and then his manhood breaks. Lawrence tells us by this novelistic juxtaposition of seemingly unconnected events not only that the dripping blood violates the baby's innocence, but also that the sight of this blood demolishes Walter Morel's naive belief in his manhood, his simple notion that having the power to order his wife to prepare his supper constitutes manhood. Lawrence demonstrates, that is, that the family psychology is in constant flux, a "changing rainbow of living relationships." Baptized by his father in his mother's blood, the baby Paul becomes his mother's child, and his father's emasculator. But the drama is not finished.

"What of this child?" Gertrude Morel asks before she tells her husband to get her something to bind her bleeding forehead.[19] The answer may be that, not only for this child, who is a version of Lawrence, the version that absorbs his suffering and frees him of it, but for every child in Lawrence, the old symbolism will not mean quite what one expects it to mean. In modifying iconic child fea-

19. In chapter 1 of Luke, where the Annunciation is recounted (see note 10 to this chapter), occurs the question "What then will this child be?" posed by Zacharias about his son John (the Baptist). Zacharias, able to speak for the first time since he was struck dumb by the angel Gabriel for his disbelief, answers his own question by prophesying that his son will "go before the Lord to prepare his ways." Gertrude Morel's question, "What of this child?" (77), goes unanswered by the child's humiliated father. Perhaps it is for Lawrence, the emerging master of himself and his art who "sheds his sicknesses in books," that Paul Morel prepares a path toward personal health.

tures such as the halolike hair, Lawrence draws upon the heritage of
the spiritually symbolic child and yet naturalizes the child by plac-
ing him in ordinary domestic circumstances and involving him
fully in novelistic relations. Scenes such as this one in *Sons and
Lovers* are the workshops in which Lawrence learned the skills that
enabled him to create the visionary realism of *The Rainbow.*

The technical, structural, and symbolic traits that create the
mother-son knot show that even here, even in this autobiographically rooted and psychoanalytically shaped vision of the family,
Lawrence is moving toward the critique of Freud and the development of his own theory of family structure that emerge in *The Rainbow* and *Fantasia of the Unconscious.* The depth and diversity
with which he explores childhood as a subject in itself there, and his
later return to the subject in other guises and forms, indicate a lifelong fascination with the origins of character in childhood and a
conviction that child consciousness is worth recovering.

The Potency of Childhood

3 Birth and Childhood as Metaphor, History, and Salvation

While many novelists have written autobiographical novels that include their early years, most have then abandoned the narrative of childhood. Good novelists, literary cliché assumes, go on to consider more mature subjects. A practical reason for this is obvious: having used up the material of their own early years, they have little to say about childhood. Yet, in *The Rainbow* Lawrence goes beyond the subject of himself as a child, and beyond the sharp, background sketches of children used in the two novels that preceded *Sons and Lovers.* He creates children who are major characters in their own right and reexamines the "circuit of family love" (*FU,* 169) as an arrangement for nurturing children.

In 1913, Lawrence began both his life with Frieda and a novel called "The Sisters." At that time his interest in childhood and the family was galvanized by two forces: his new conviction that marriage should be the arena in which men and women struggle for relationships and self-knowledge, and his experience of changes that occur in a family as characters develop modern consciousness. The depiction of children in "The Sisters" thus becomes crucial to Lawrence's central effort to regard character in new, visionary terms. As he worked on this new novel, which would become two books, *The Rainbow* and *Women in Love,* Lawrence said, "It is *very* different from *Sons and Lovers:* written in another language almost. . . . I shan't write in the same manner as *Sons and Lovers* again, I think: in that hard, violent style full of sensation and presentation" (*Letters,* 2:132).

In this new work Lawrence deepens his consideration of the imagery and significance of childhood, both as a literary idea and as a key to the nature of adult human beings. Adopting the familiar

56

metaphor of birth for vital changes in a life as the major structuring image within the novel, he then allies the metaphor with rare clarity to the act of women in childbirth. To create the Brangwen family's first generation, Lawrence reaches back to the early years of Tom and Lydia, revealing their childhoods as essential influences on their adult characters. In both cases what is revealed is also an achievement in the literary reimagining of childhood. For Tom Brangwen, Lawrence draws upon the tradition of the child as enigmatic, inarticulate being, and then allows Tom's maturity to develop out of the experiences of his childhood. In the story of Tom's wife, Lydia Lensky, Lawrence invokes on the spiritually healing properties of childhood. In so doing, he both recovers the romantic conception of innocence and advances it beyond guilt, as we know it from the Freudian model of psychic development, toward a more direct connection between childish impulses and their adult expression.

The Rainbow's children are striking in their realism and their individuality. Nevertheless, in apparent contradiction of this realistic mode, Lawrence recalls and revitalizes a tradition of idealized, romantic conceptions of childhood and parenthood in which the stages of procreation and childhood become symbols for the journey of life. For example, this passage about the pregnant Anna Brangwen, taken in isolation, makes no concessions to realism and seems to belong, rather, to a dated mythology of contented motherhood: "She was a door and a threshold, she herself. Through her another soul was coming, to stand upon her as upon the threshold. . ." (*Rainbow,* 182). This image, like many others in Lawrence, leaps out from the realistic surface of the chronicle and yet is not fully detached from it: the soul on the threshold is, after all, a future heroine of another novel, Gudrun of *Women in Love.* More immediately, she is the first of the "storms of babies" that will eventually drive Ursula to seek an identity separate from her mother's. The forward movement of the narrative thus undercuts the traditional impulse of the particular image.

It may seem surprising that Lawrence invokes what seem to be traditional images of childhood more in *The Rainbow* than in his first three (and generally less experimental) novels. The explanation may lie, as I suggested in my previous chapter, in Lawrence's acceptance of his parents' unsatisfactory marriage, his overcoming of childhood guilt, and his eventual transcendence of this background through his relationship with Frieda and confidence in his writing. The three early novels present children as a problem: the married men of *The White Peacock* virtually lose their wives to their chil-

dren. Only slight hope is offered in the closing images of the pregnant Emily, who seems to have found domestic repose—not ser-
vitude—in farm life with her husband, Tom. In *The Trespasser,*
Siegmund, long estranged from his wife, can find no way to recon-
cile his own longing for independent life with his obligation to his
children, whereas in *Sons and Lovers* only the death of the mother
begins to free the son from her all-encompassing, jealous love.

In *The Rainbow* Lawrence revitalizes the old themes of family
loves and jealousies by attending to families not as social and psychological problems but as the raw materials of ordinary life, part of
the donnée of his fiction. He chronicles not the deaths of families
but the episodes through which they survive. In contrast to much
modern literature that focuses on the solitary life, Lawrence scrutinizes pregnancies, parents, and children over several generations
in his presentation of the development of modern consciousness. Of
the metaphors Lawrence elaborates to structure these themes in *The
Rainbow,* birth is ubiquitous. While a literary connection between
beginning and birth is so natural that it disdains comment, what is
startling in Lawrence is his insistence on the literal, linking the
metaphorical cycles of psychic birth and rebirth with actual pregnancies and deliveries. This arcing out of the realistic event into
transcendent meaning is a characteristic that Frank Kermode notes
with special reference to the union of the historical (social and
political conditions in England) and the apocalyptic (the *Dies Irae*
theme) in *Women in Love.*[1] Together the domestic realism and
mythical symbolism in *The Rainbow* form a pattern of birth imagery that serves—rather than the conventional bildungsroman form—
Lawrence's newer conception of the novel as a testing and exposure
of relationships among people and their "circumambient universe."

Lawrence's apparent knowledge of actual births, and his perception that birth is a time when deeper nature reveals itself, gives
substance to his development of birth as a metaphor. In *The Rainbow* the metaphor is used for the continuing effort of characters to
become themselves, an effort that cannot be completed for more
than a moment before it must be begun again. Anna Brangwen's
pregnancies are imbued with cosmic significance while Lydia's are
tinged with self-involved melancholy. Both are quite different from
the pregnancies of Gertrude Morel. The expectant Gertrude feels
resigned and guilty about the coming of each of her three younger
children: "She felt, in some far inner place of her soul, that she and
her husband were guilty . . . she would make up to it for having

1. Frank Kermode, "D. H. Lawrence and the Apocalyptic Types," 128–51.

brought it into the world unloved" (*SL*, 74). Even the animistic experience that Gertrude, pregnant with Paul, undergoes in the garden seems motivated more by physical and emotional misery than by the transcendent possibilities of pregnancy. In *The Rainbow,* birth is dramatized as more than an event in a woman's life, and yet Lawrence's treatment of the event itself gains in realism from his setting of it within richly layered meanings.

I do not know of another English novelist, man or woman, who includes so many confinements in his or her novels. Lawrence wrote during an unusual time in the history of childbirth; the topic would have been quite unacceptable in literature of the Victorian period, when men, even husbands, were generally not welcome in the birthing room. Widow Ivy Bolton's recollection of her husband in *Lady Chatterley's Lover* expresses a common attitude: "The way he sat when my first baby was born, motionless, and the sort of fatal eyes he looked at me with, when it was over! I had a bad time, but I had to comfort *him*. . . . I don't believe he had any right pleasure with me at nights after. . . . I always blamed his mother, for letting him in th' room. He'd no right t'ave been there. Men makes so much more of things than they should, once they start brooding" (*LCL*, 169–70). The subject was natural to Lawrence not only because he was close to his mother and grew up when home birth was still common, but also because the event of birth fascinated him and urged upon him its momentousness. Childbirth is, Lawrence says when he has Tom Brangwen visit his laboring wife, "an extreme hour." Because the labor occurs at home, Tom is free to visit his wife, though he does not assist her (as Will assists Anna): "She looked at him as a woman in childbirth looks at the man who begot the child in her: an impersonal look in the extreme hour, female to male" (*Rainbow,* 77). With that diction—"extreme hour"—usually reserved for death, Lawrence recognizes the gravity of childbirth as an event that can be little influenced by human will. At the same time, he begins to tease a new meaning out of the old one he has suggested; the birthing time is significant not only in its joining of life and death, but also in its revelation of the quality of relations between wife and husband. Thus, the fact that Lawrence is one of the first novelists to include deliveries becomes significant within his larger vision.[2] The variety of attitudes that people express dur-

2. Shortly after Lawrence's time, anesthesia and new medical procedures made the subject rather inaccessible. Maternity ward scenes that occur in *Ulysses* and *The Adventures of Augie March* seem to be included more for their value in the encyclopedic coverage of Dublin and Chicago than to convey any

ing childbirth follows a bell curve from the earlier to the later novels, with the greatest exchange of unconscious knowledge between parents-to-be occurring in *The Rainbow.*

In *Sons and Lovers* Walter Morel must have his supper before he goes upstairs to see Gertrude in childbed. When he does go, the mood for both of them is one of helpless exasperation with an intruder, followed by an ineffectual desire to kiss that neither can act upon. In *The Lost Girl* Lawrence shows the brutal, degrading laboring of poor women whom Alvina Houghton attends as a maternity nurse; these women do not seem to care that they suffer or that they behave badly, and this is what degrades them. In *The Rainbow* he shows Will and Anna, the second generation, going through labor hand in hand with an absence of fear that might have inspired later twentieth-century proponents of unanesthetized labor. Lawrence, however, finds something distastefully servile, even emasculating, about Will's participation. It is Tom and Lydia who are the purest embodiment of a theme; Lawrence tells us that Tom, though thinking of owls and his own childhood, is unconsciously "elsewhere, fundamental[ly] . . . with his wife in labour" and filled with knowledge of the origin of the child in his own body: "He and she, one flesh, out of which life must be put forth. The rent was not in his body, but it was of his body. On her the blows fell, but the quiver ran through to him, to his last fibre" (*Rainbow,* 71). Yet the look that Lydia and Tom exchange, and that Lawrence approves, stresses their difference: it is "an impersonal look, in the extreme hour, female to male" (*Rainbow,* 77). Lawrence's preference for the impersonal look over the fleeting sentimentality of Gertrude and Walter Morel or the hearty teamwork of Will and Anna may seem antediluvian in an era that emphasizes communication and empathy, but it is not mean spirited. It depends upon his absolute distinction of male and female. The birth moment between Tom and Lydia (whose marriage

---

particular interest in the actual births. In European literature, naturalistic description of births (and all body functions) is more common, as in *Anna Karenina* and in Zola's *Pot-Bouille.* Only in recent years have descriptions of birth scenes begun to appear in American fiction. Larry Woiwode, "Firstborn," reprinted in *The Best Short Stories 1983,* ed. Anne Tyler (Boston: Houghton Mifflin, 1983), 285–316; L. D. Clark, "The Journey," in *Cross Timbers Review,* 5.1 (Spring 1988): 16–23; and Pamela B. Culver, "Evolution," in *Iowa Woman,* 7.4 (December 1987): 18–19 are examples from what seems to be an emerging genre. Nancy Sorel surveys accounts of childbirth in fiction in "A Look at 'Noble Suffering,'" *New York Times Book Review,* January 26, 1986, 1; her *Ever Since Eve: Personal Reflections on Childbirth* collects historical and fictional birth accounts.

is literally between foreigners) embodies Lawrence's notion of character at the elemental level, the level beneath all the allotropic expressions of personality.[3]

Peter Balbert's welcome attention to the rhythms and imagery in this novel tends to disengage the birth imagery from the events of birth, finding the imagery to be Lawrence's significant accomplishment. Balbert describes the novel as a long birthing scene: "*The Rainbow* describes the efforts of three generations of Brangwens to be born—that is, to escape to a meaningful freedom by ridding themselves of all restrictions to their organic being, and thus providing for the unhampered expression of their essential selves." Yet Balbert argues that Lawrence's "concern with generations and inherited qualities" in this novel is a "concession to the Victorian novel" because for Lawrence the events from birth to young adulthood are "mere steps before the more difficult birth" into conscious being. Balbert's interpretation is typical of a critical tendency to divide and conquer *The Rainbow* by calling its realistic episodes throwbacks to Lawrence's early period and its introspective passages forerunners of the form of *Women in Love*. Thus Balbert discounts the scenes that do not occur in what he calls the "introverted" style:

> Lawrence regards the periods of natural birth, early childhood, or young adulthood as mere steps before the most difficult birth—"the passionate struggle into conscious" being that Lawrence mentions in the foreword to *Women in Love*. Though those formative periods signify rites of passage, they are not visualized by Lawrence in the conventional celebratory terms which progressively relate the individual's coming of age

3. Marguerite Beebe Howe offers the best explanation that I have found of Lawrence's metaphor of allotropy for the human personality: "Allotropy is the property chemical elements have of existing in several forms. The two Lawrence uses most are carbon and water. Water, for example, occurs in the novels first as a liquid, then is transformed into a vapor (the rainbow), and ultimately into a crystal (snow). . . . Allotropy becomes the main metaphor in Lawrence's next ego theory, and determines the structure of *Women in Love*. . . . In *The Rainbow* certain characters [Will, Baron Skrebensky, Anton Skrebensky, young Tom Brangwen] are unmistakable instances of negative allotropy, an unvital inorganic hardening. . . . The marsh and the rainbow stand at the fluid, volatile end of the allotropic spectrum, which is akin to vitalism" (*The Art of the Self in D. H. Lawrence*, 33–34). Good as Howe's analysis is, she misses a connection in using the metaphor of allotropy primarily to interpret other symbols, rather than also applying it directly to interpretation of the characters. Tom, Lydia, Anna, and Ursula all exhibit positive allotropy in the fluidity of their development from childhood to adulthood (and also as adults).

as a fairly predictable process of maturity that can be described with a
telephoto lens . . . the periods are not really "visualized" or romanticized at all by Lawrence; they come under such close analytic scrutiny
that the outer world of countryside and politics is shut out for thirty or
forty pages at a time in *The Rainbow* in favor of an introverted concern
with his character's developing consciousness.[4]

Balbert's analysis disregards many visualized and even romanticized scenes representing character's formative periods. Although
these "steps" of childhood and young adulthood in *The Rainbow* are
not exactly conventional or always celebratory, neither are they per-
functory or prefatory. Rather, the novel's generational structure and,
particularly, its emphasis on relations between generations inten-
tionally revitalize a Victorian convention and use it richly in service
of the Lawrentian self. The births and childhoods of Tom, Anna, and
Ursula Brangwen are more than a prelude to their struggles for consciousness. The many scenes devoted to childhood episodes could be
quite tedious if they were not integral with character development
and with Lawrence's exploration of consciousness. While Lawrence
shows what Balbert calls "regressive concern with . . . inherited
qualities," this concern does not diminish the emphasis he places on
the absolute individuality of each character. For instance, both Anna
Lensky Brangwen and her daughter Ursula, when each is age twelve,
shun contact with common people. That similarity gives greater significance to differences in their later actions, particularly to Anna's
decision to protect herself within her own matriarchy and Ursula's
persistence in becoming a schoolteacher. Furthermore, Lawrence's
replication of traits from one generation to another is not a regressive
conception of character such as one finds in Fielding or Thackeray,
when the discovery of the true birth of Tom Jones or Henry Esmond
ratifies the hero's surprisingly good character, or even in Thomas
Hardy or Émile Zola, in whose works weaknesses are handed down
through the generations. Rather it is part of Lawrence's effort to
examine both the inherited behaviors and the modern struggle to
break from them into conscious being.

Lawrence does attend to and visualize the actual formative periods of human lives—birth and childhood—closely depicting and
enacting certain passages that are, for him, significant. These passages are, in fact, the conventional ones: pregnancies, births, school
enrollments, marriage proposals, weddings, but Lawrence does not

4. Peter Balbert, *D. H. Lawrence and the Psychology of Rhythm: The
Meaning of Form in "The Rainbow,"* 20–21.

imbue them with predictable sentiment. He gives them a different emphasis from that of previous novelists by exploring their universality as much as their peculiarity, and thus appropriating them for his concern with the states of being that lie beneath realistic fiction's characteristic level of social intercourse. For instance, the birth of Ursula Brangwen is significant as just that—the birth of a first child, one who is destined for an important role in the novel. The ancillary reflections about the meaning of this birth that occur have to do with how Anna and Will feel about the baby, or about themselves as parents. By contrast, Dickens uses the description of a birth as an opportunity to reveal an unusual family event. While newborn Paul Dombey is left near the hearth to toast like a muffin, the reader learns that his mother is dying, that his sister is considered "a piece of base coin that couldn't be invested," and that his father is a monomaniac. In *David Copperfield,* Dora's miscarriage is described metaphorically by David and becomes yet one more instance of his child-wife's inability to become a woman: "I had hoped that lighter hands than mine would help to mould her character. . . . It was not to be. The spirit fluttered for a moment on the threshold of its little prison, and unconscious of captivity, took wing." Similarly, in George Meredith's *The Ordeal of Richard Feveral,* while the infant Richard Feveral lies asleep in his cot, his cuckolded father sobs silently, dropping tears that the nursemaid can see and count onto the child's bed. In a scene such as Meredith's or Dickens's the baby is the occasion, but the adult is the subject. The style defines the author's sense of humor or pathos, not the child's character. The muffin simile or the fact that Sir Austin's tears are countable distracts the reader from the babies themselves.[5] Lawrence exploits similar situations to show that individual characters, including children, experience complex emotions while the scene itself goes on quite normally—no one dies, or runs off with another man, or uses the child as a liaison for forbidden assignations. There is no infant mortality and no death in childbed because Lawrence is not interested in the condition of dying or orphaned children. Rather he is concerned with the inner growth of living children within the complex web of ordinary family relations.

   In other words, the distinction that Balbert makes between the conventionally visualized rites of passage and the Lawrentian introverted concern with the developing consciousness, and that be-

5. Dickens, *Dombey,* 13; *David Copperfield,* 553; George Meredith, *The Ordeal of Richard Feveral,* 15.

tween the mere steps toward birth and the more strenuous birth
into being, is specious. Lawrence has neither suppressed the conventional occasions nor trivialized them; he has, rather, placed them
in a larger landscape, one where the winds rush by in many directions, taking with them the consciousnesses of characters who are
nonetheless undergoing ordinary events with apparently ordinary
outcomes. What Lawrence accomplishes here as elsewhere is a consecration of the ordinary.

Lawrence devised a language of consciousness for his adult characters, but to formulate the nature of being in children, he relied on
scenes. Perhaps that is why Daniel Schneider, in his otherwise comprehensive study *D. H. Lawrence: The Artist as Psychologist,* joins
previous Lawrence critics in virtually ignoring the characters' childhoods, even though, like Balbert, he is guided by the belief that the
desire to attain individual being is central to Lawrence's conception
of character. Schneider argues that in *The Rainbow* Lawrence makes
a scientific project of identifying the "more or less invariant patterns of psychic interaction" that are exhibited by various characters in their quest to "come into being."[6] Still, I find that the induc-
tive nature of Lawrence's psychology of the child resists conforming
to a pattern. While both Anna and Ursula Brangwen rebel against
their fathers, the differences in their modes of rebellion and in their
fathers' responses seem sharper to me than do the similarities. The
theory to be induced from the tremendous variety of child behavior
in Lawrence's novels is that each child is ontologically unique. Lawrence exhibits this uniqueness by detailed mimetic and dramatic
rendering as well as by interiorized psychological analysis: Tom
cannot read his favorite poems for himself. Anna comes to her parents' bed on their wedding morning. Tom must undress Anna when
no one else can. Ursula tries to set potatoes for her father and cannot
please him. Gudrun is at the bottom of her grammar school class. All
of these telling threads are woven into the whole of the novel's
fabric; thus, the ordinary materials of a child's life are significant in
Lawrence's study of psyche.

This consecration of the ordinary accompanies a new awareness
of the psychology of children in *The Rainbow,* where Lawrence
attends to the childhoods of several invented characters as no English novelist before him had done. This novel was the first he composed entirely after his exposure to contemporary European psychoanalytic thought; and I think his concentration on childhoods

6. Daniel Schneider, *D. H. Lawrence: The Artist as Psychologist,* 148.

that are unlike his own owes something to that exposure. When Freud applied the historical model to the development of the individual psyche, as Darwin had applied it to the development of the species, he opened new territory for the novelist. While the psychoanalyst retrieves his patient's childhood through analysis, the novelist—realizing the importance and variety of the early years—is free to invent a childhood for his character. Evidence suggests that Lawrence had little familiarity with Freud's ideas when he composed *Sons and Lovers*. It was through Frieda Weekley and her friends in Germany and Ascona that he became acquainted with psychoanalytic thought. The influence of Frieda on revisions of *Sons and Lovers* is well known, as is her spoof of the novel, "Paul Morel, or His Mother's Darling."

Whether through a reaction to psychoanalytic ideas, or through the healing of his oedipal fixation that occurred as he wrote *Sons and Lovers*, Lawrence became more critical of his mother and more defensive of his father in the years following publication of *Sons and Lovers*. Without the disturbing struggle against parental influence, Lawrence was able, in *The Rainbow*, to study relations within families that are not obviously pathological. In doing so he creates three of the most memorable children in the modern English novel: Tom Brangwen, Anna Lensky Brangwen, and Ursula Brangwen. It is difficult to describe his presentation of these children within their families in the usual vocabulary of prose stylistics. Particularly, Lawrence's relaxed handling of point of view results, in many passages, in an evenhanded representation of family emotions, seeming to encompass the child's perspective without entering the child's consciousness. Lawrence, one recalls, is the novelist who cautioned his kind against putting their thumbs in the pan through intrusive narrative. Mikhail Bakhtin offers a valuable term for discussing Lawrence's characteristic narrative mobility. Bakhtin emphasizes, as Lawrence himself did, the ability of the novel to include more of life than any other genre, a characteristic that Bakhtin analyzes with the linguistic notion of *polyglossia*.[7] Such polyglossia occurs in many

7. Mikhail Mikhailovich Bakhtin, *The Dialogic Imagination: Four Essays*, 3–40. The applicability of Bakhtin's theories to Lawrence's works was first proposed by Avrom Fleishman in "He Do the Polis in Different Voices: Lawrence's Later Style." Wayne Booth, in *The Company We Keep: An Ethics of Fiction*, 445–46, suggests that "double-voiced" narration occurs in Lawrence's work earlier than Fleishman claimed, giving examples from *The Rainbow* and *Women in Love*. In Chapter 2, I noted a similarly complex use of free indirect discourse in *Sons and Lovers*.

domestic scenes in *The Rainbow* for which it is difficult to identify any perspective that is maintained with Jamesian consistency. One has the sense of participating in the individual experiences of several characters and of hearing several voices. Lawrence's method of interweaving points of view and voices results in something that might be called a *familial* point of view. The method is especially noticeable in the earlier sections of *The Rainbow* that present the childhoods of Tom and of Anna, whereas Lawrence is more concerned to establish a private, interior effect for Ursula's consciousness.

Tom Brangwen, who becomes the novel's patriarch, is first presented as a boy, the fourth son of Alfred and his wife, who are "two very separate beings, vitally connected, knowing nothing of each other, yet living in their separate ways from one root" (*Rainbow,* 15). These primordial parents, so briefly described, have a model Lawrentian marriage; their connected separateness suggests Rupert Birkin's image of marriage four generations later in *Women in Love:* "an equilibrium, a pure balance of two single beings:—as the stars balance each other" (*WL,* 148). Lawrence gives a three-paragraph sketch of two of Tom's elder brothers (the eldest merely "ran away early to sea, and did not come back," *Rainbow,* 15) before settling his attention on Tom. These passages seem gratuitous, as if Lawrence felt obligated to populate the household. But with Lawrence's description of Tom, it becomes apparent that Tom's place in the configuration of the family is a *problem.* As the youngest son, he is his mother's favorite and the companion of his sisters. As it was for Paul Morel, the favored child's position is a mixed blessing:

> [His mother] roused herself to determination, and sent him forcibly to a grammar school in Derby when he was twelve years old. He did not want to go and his father would have given way, but Mrs. Brangwen had her heart set on it. Her slender, pretty, tightly-covered body, with full skirts, was now the centre of resolution in the house, and when she had once set upon anything, which was not often, the family failed before her. (*Rainbow,* 16)

Tom is the object of his mother's ambitions by default. Her older sons have disappointed her: Alfred, whose mistress will one day stimulate a revitalization of Tom and Lydia's marriage and whose son will marry Anna, is a boy who "in spite of his dogged, yearning effort . . . could not get beyond the rudiments of anything, save of drawing" and becomes a "rigid, a rare-spoken, almost surly man." Frank, as a child "drawn by the trickle of dark blood that ran across the pavement from the slaughterhouse," becomes a butcher, drinker, and "noisy fool" (*Rainbow,* 15–16). So the child of her heart is Tom. Gertrude Morel, for all her possessiveness, had judged Paul's talents correctly when she sent him to grammar school instead of to the pit. Tom's mother, with similar motives, judges wrongly: "So Tom went to school, an unwilling failure from the first" (*Rainbow,* 16).

Tom is twelve years old, endowed by Lawrence with an inarticulate understanding of himself that opposes his mother's idea of what he should be. He is a victim of what Lawrence, in *Fantasia of the Unconscious,* calls "ideal bullying": Mrs. Brangwen attempts to mold Tom into her idea of a gentleman. In the panoramic opening section of *The Rainbow,* Lawrence observes the desire of the generic Brangwen woman to make her children—"at least the children of her heart"—the equals of the vicar's or curate's children who, she decides, are superior to her own because of "knowledge," "education and experience"—"not money, nor even class." People like the squire and the vicar represent, to the Brangwen women, "the wonder of the beyond." Rhetorically Lawrence circles the question of whether education and experience can make people better than others. It is a question that the novel as a whole attempts to answer by exploring the coming into being of the three generations. Lawrence focuses first on Tom. Of the three generations of children, Tom is the most limited by his upbringing and also the least conscious of the forms of limitation. He is rather like Paul Morel but without Paul's ability to turn sensitivity into words, or to use words for evasion. *Fantasia*'s criticism of motherhood explains what Lawrence meant by the equivocal phrase "children of her heart." These are the children who are loved too sympathetically, whom the mother reconceives in her imagination to the distortion of their own being: ". . . more dangerous is ideal bullying. Bullying people into what is ideally good for them. . . . to impose *any ideals* on a child as it grows is almost criminal. It results in impoverishment and distortion and subsequent deficiency" (*FU,* 90). As a consequence of his mother's wish to make a gentleman of him, Tom becomes increasingly confused about who he is. Lawrence describes Tom's experience at school from a point of view that is more or less Tom's own, but painfully infused with the school world's opinions of him: "When it came to mental things, then he was at a disadvantage. He was at their mercy. He was a fool. He had not the power to controvert even the most stupid argument, so that he was forced to admit things he did not in the least believe. And having admitted them, he did not know whether he believed them or not; he rather thought he did" (*Rainbow,* 17). Mrs. Brangwen's error in sending Tom to grammar school combined with the demands of the curriculum for concentration and abstract thinking—"he had an instinct for mathematics, but if this failed him, he was helpless as an idiot" (*Rainbow,* 18)—teach Tom only to have a "low opinion of himself . . . that his brain was a slow, hopeless, good-for-nothing. So he was humble" (*Rainbow,* 17).

In *The Rainbow* Lawrence does not make a villain of either the school or the mother who sends Tom there. Like much that happens in the first section of the novel, Tom's education seems inevitable, beyond moral debate. Although Tom fails to learn, the grammar school becomes used to him, "setting him down as a hopeless duffer at learning, but respecting him for a generous, honest nature" (*Rainbow,* 18). Rather than castigate anyone, Lawrence is content to show that Tom's other aspects more than compensate for his academic weakness. His "feelings were more discriminating than those of most boys, and he was confused. He was more sensuously developed, more refined in instinct than they" (*Rainbow,* 17). Tom's superiority of feeling is both "mechanical" (meaning, apparently, that he can do things with his hands) and emotional. When a teacher reads "Ulysses" or "Ode to the West Wind" aloud, Tom's "lips parted, his eyes filled with a strained, almost suffering light . . . [he] was moved by this experience beyond all calculation, he almost dreaded it, it was so deep" (*Rainbow,* 17). Yet when Tom attempts to read these poems himself, "The very fact of the print caused a prickly sensation of repulsion to go over his skin . . . his heart filled with a bursting passion of rage and incompetence. He threw the book down and walked over it and went out to the cricket field. And he hated books as if they were his enemies" (*Rainbow,* 18). Tom comes to hate all books because they represent what Lawrence elsewhere calls mental consciousness.[8] In *Fantasia* he restates the objections to schools that Tom feels but does not articulate: "We talk

---

8. Rousseau tells of his early habit of staying up all night with his father reading romance novels left by his deceased mother, with the result that he "had conceived nothing . . . had felt the whole" and acquired an "extravagant, romantic notion of human life" (*Confessions,* 4–5). In both Rousseau's and Tom's cases, this ability to feel is considered a virtue by the author. Yet it is significant of the difference between genres and authors that Rousseau, telling the tale of himself, gives it a quixotic aspect, while Tom's experience is anchored in the quotidian details of a dreary classroom. Furthermore, Tom's bifurcation is not between romance and reality, but between hearing sounds and reading words. If there is a gulf between romance and reality for Lawrence, it is one that is navigated often by most of his characters.

about education—leading forth the natural intelligence of a child. But ours is just the opposite of leading forth. It is a ramming in of brain facts through the head, and a consequent distortion, suffocation, and starvation of the primary centres of consciousness. A nice day of reckoning we've got in front of us" (*FU,* 128). The shift in Lawrence's emphasis between Tom's story and *Fantasia* indicates both that Lawrence's hatred of formal education has intensified in the years between the writing of the two books and that Lawrence is, after all, conscious of the requirements of genre. Tom is a fully conceived character, not an instance in a diatribe. The four pages describing Tom's schooling sculpt his character—he has an almost mute but powerful presence even as a youth, even in a setting that makes him feel incompetent and ignominious. It is impressive that Lawrence can make so convincing a figure of Tom primarily by describing him negatively (his inability in school) and by *not* seeking sympathy for him or damning the school. Instead Lawrence seems to offer it as a measure of Tom's soul that he has suffered without being fatally damaged:

> He was glad to leave school. It had not been unpleasant, he had enjoyed the companionship of the other youths, or had thought he enjoyed it, the time passed quickly, in endless activity. But he knew all the time that he was in an ignominious position, in this place of learning. He was aware of failure all the while, of incapacity. But he was too healthy and sanguine to be wretched, he was too much alive. (*Rainbow,* 18–19)

The statement that Tom is too sanguine to be wretched is followed immediately by "Yet his soul was wretched almost to hopelessness." Lawrence, of course, invites us to make a distinction between Tom's feeling soul and his physical and social presence. Dualistic conceptions of individual being are so familiar to Lawrence's readers that one can easily be inattentive to them. This potentially confusing characterization of Tom as a boy who can suffer intensely within and yet outwardly enjoy his companions adds clarity to his adult character. His attraction to foreigners, for instance, expresses the same longing to go beyond himself that he felt when hearing the poetry of Tennyson and Shelley.

While Lawrence undertakes a difficult task in endowing a character with a sensitive but inexpressible consciousness, he has the advantage of tradition when he begins with the character as child. Reinhard Kuhn, in his study of children in Western literature, points out that in both ancient and modern representations of the "enigmatic" child, the child's linguistic deficiency often symbolizes the virtual impossibility of communication between children and adults. Kuhn adds that the enigmatic child is rarely the focus of a story because at best "the writer can recapture only the disappearing echo of his faint voice."[9] With Tom, Lawrence revises this tradition by allowing Tom to keep his silence but still investigating his consciousness and thereby keeping him in the center of the story. Tom is a masterful representation of a character who, like Fanny Price in Austen's *Mansfield Park,* is able to "exert silence."[10] His childhood is essential to Lawrence's reconception of the relation of society and the self. Tom's feeling self is partially thwarted by the attempts of his grammar school to teach him to think abstractly; yet—more important—in Tom the resources for salvaging the self are also found in childhood. The richness of possibility found in the individual child is the hallmark of Lawrence's vision of the child. It separates him from both the Romantic notion of the child as a morally free and superior being, and the naturalistic or Freudian analysis of the child as the victim of social buffeting. While Tom's mother becomes the agent of social distortion, Tom is granted the capability to partially resist that distortion and then to incorporate ambivalence into the self and to triumph over opposing influences.

Before he begins grammar school, Tom has a "child's deep, instinctive foreknowledge of what is going to happen to him" (*Rainbow,* 16–17). More importantly, he also has a deep, instinctive knowledge of who he is. In his introduction to his translation of Giovanni Verga's novel *Mastro-don Gesualdo,* Lawrence chastises Verga for not granting his protagonist "any spark of heroic consciousness," and instead attempting to pour his own great consciousness into a limited character. "A hero," Lawrence argues, "must be a hero by the grace of God, and must have an inkling of the same."[11] Tom Brangwen, like Gesualdo, is an inarticulate rustic; but Brangwen has the capacity to feel that which Verga's *verismo* techniques could not grant to Gesualdo. The feeling soul that Lawrence

9. Reinhard Kuhn, *Corruption in Paradise: The Child in Western Literature,* 61.

10. The phrase is applied to Fanny by Mary Ellmann in *Thinking about Women,* 206 n. It has been brought to my attention by Eugene Robert Minard's unpublished paper "Fanny Price: The Still Center of *Mansfield Park,*" in which he concludes, "While Edmund is older and more learned than Fanny, he sees much less, is something of a blunderer. Fanny is more interesting than he; she, after all, has contrived a self out of the practice of self-effacement" (11).

11. Lawrence, "*Mastro-don Gesualdo,* by Giovanni Verga," in *Phoenix,* 227.

describes for Tom sets him apart as an individual when he might otherwise blend into the pastoral ambience of the early pages of the novel. Though he cannot speak his feelings, he is born, as Lawrence believes everyone is, with "an unanalyzable, indefinable reality of individuality . . . an individual nature incomprehensibly arise[n] in the universe, out of nowhere" (*PU*, 14).

The confusion and wretchedness Tom feels in his soul, then, are not the result of his being inarticulate or ignorant. They are signs of his early effort to assimilate the ambitions imposed upon him by his mother and by the education she chooses for him. By the time Tom leaves school these conflicts, brought about by the mother's "love-bullying," have created in Tom a condition something like the one Lawrence describes in *Fantasia:* "Instead of leaving the child with its own limited but deep and incomprehensible feelings, the parent, hopelessly involved in the sympathetic mode of selfless love, and spiritual love-will, stimulates the child into a consciousness which does not belong to it, on the one plane, and robs it of its own spontaneous consciousness and freedom on the other plane" (*FU*, 151). This limbo encompasses Tom until he engages his being in the struggle of marriage with Lydia Lensky. Moreover, Lawrence presents Tom's first encounters with Lydia in terms that connect clearly with his youthful dilemmas. When Tom first sees Lydia on the road, he reflects: "She had passed by. He felt as if he were walking in a far world, not Cossethay, a far world, the fragile reality. He went on quiet, suspended, rarefied. . . . He moved within the knowledge of her, in the world that was beyond reality" (*Rainbow,* 29). Is this not the world of poetry which had once eluded Tom's mental grasp? And when he has seen Lydia a second time and learned her name and a hint of her history from his pub mates, Tom feels

> that here was the unreality established at last. He felt also a curious certainty about her, as if she were destined to him. It was to him a profound satisfaction that she was a foreigner.
> A swift change had taken place on the earth for him, as if a new creation were fulfilled, in which he had real existence. Things had all been stark, unreal, barren, mere nullities before. Now they were actualities that he could handle. (*Rainbow,* 32)

Lydia appears to Tom as a living embodiment of the ideas he was unable to grasp in school. Her foreignness makes her attractive; her womanhood makes her accessible. Once Tom has recognized in Lydia his elusive reality, certain earlier episodes seem less inchoate. In school, for instance, Tom had loved a boy who was frail and consumptive, but clever—like Lawrence himself. Tom admired this boy but felt mentally inferior to him: "the two had had an almost classic friendship, David and Jonathan, wherein Brangwen was the Jonathan, the server." But "the two boys went at once apart on leaving school." Lawrence does not even give this other boy a name, but says, "Brangwen always remembered his friend that had been, kept him as a sort of light, a fine experience to remember" (*Rainbow,* 19). The wistful, glancingly erotic tone of this passage, the weighty "always," and the fineness of the episode in Tom's memory are touchstones for his quest after the "beyond" about which he feels so confused and inarticulate.

In the years between school and Lydia's appearance, another foreigner attracts Tom's admiration; he is the escort of a girl who blithely seduces Tom and affords him his first pleasurable experience of sex. Unable to pull himself away from the girl, he stays on at the hotel where they met, observing her and the "other fellow" with fascination, and lingering after dinner to smoke and talk about horses with him. Tom's secret sharing of the girl has made him feel related to this man. The phrase "other fellow" in Tom's mind suggests that Tom feels sensually equal to him despite his intense feeling that the other man represents the world beyond himself: "He was transported at meeting this odd, middle-aged, dry-skinned man personally. The talk was pleasant, but that did not matter so much. It was the gracious manner, the fine contact that was all." This fineness of contact links this encounter with Tom's "fine experience" of the school friend whom he feels he lost because "the other's mind outpaced his." When Brangwen speaks with the foreigner he again feels mentally inferior: "They talked a long while together, Brangwen flushing like a girl when the other did not understand his idiom" (*Rainbow,* 25). Thus he becomes a child again, enraptured by the sound of poetry, but intimidated by its written words and the fluency they require.

Most critics neglect the complexities of Tom Brangwen's nature, perhaps because of the pastoralism of *The Rainbow*'s early settings. They tend to regard the novel's first generation as a sort of baseline of innocence and unconsciousness. There are elements of unacknowledged homosexuality connected with Tom's vague, passionate fascination with the foreign world of schools and intellect. Repetitions of language and feeling link Tom's wish to please his mother by seeking a place in the world beyond Marsh Farm; his love for the fine, frail, clever boy at school; and his pleasure in making love to a woman who accompanies a fine, gracious man who comes from that world beyond—literally (and Tom's mind is very literal) a foreigner. Tom's feeling of mental inferiority, from which derives his wretchedness of soul, guides him into situations in which he can

feel equality with the objects of his sexual desire. His homoeroti-
cism, though unrecognized by him, contributes to the pleasure he
takes in the girl at Matlock, because with her he takes briefly the
position of the "other fellow." Even though the girl has turned to
Tom for an afternoon's pleasure, Tom is intrigued by "how the foreigner treated the women with courteous contempt, as if they were
pleasing animals" (*Rainbow,* 24). In all of this Tom seeks a way
outside himself. When he returns to his room, he lies "staring out at
the stars of the summer night, his whole being in a whirl. What was
it all? . . . What was there outside his knowledge? How much? . . .
Where was his life, in that which he knew or all outside of him?"
(*Rainbow,* 25). And the next day, after leaving the hotel early to
avoid seeing "any other visitors":

> His mind was one big excitement. The girl and the foreigner: he
> knew neither of their names. Yet they had set fire to the homestead of
> his nature, and he would be burned out of cover. Of the two experi-
> ences, perhaps the meeting with the foreigner was the more significant.
> But the girl—he had not settled about the girl.
> He did not know. He had to leave it there, as it was. He could not sum
> up his experiences. (*Rainbow,* 26)

After this encounter, Tom remains in a limbo of daydreams and
sexual fantasies, liquor and self-loathing, wondering, "Did he, or
did he not believe that he belonged to this world of Cossethay and
Ilkeston? There was nothing in it he wanted. Yet could he ever get
out of it?" (*Rainbow,* 28). Years, apparently (he is said to be twenty-
eight when he meets Lydia), pass for Tom in this sort of protracted
childhood and unfocused adolescence. He has wrongfully inherited
the predicament of the Brangwen women: longing for the "spoken
world beyond," a logos that eludes him, rather than remaining content with the "blood-intimacy" of men.

Having considered the sexual and mental ambivalence that Tom
acquired in childhood, and his tentative and frustrated early attempts
at relationships outside of the "homestead" of his nature, one sees
that Lydia Lensky is the ideal person upon whom his disparate desires can resolve. She is, first of all, female and alone—he may marry
her and bring her into *his* life. She will not immediately burn him
"out of cover" because he need not measure himself against her mentality as he did with the boy at school or the foreign man. Yet, she *is*
foreign, from the "spoken world beyond," and she possesses the fine
quality that Tom associates with the world beyond:

> There was a fineness about her, a poignancy about the way she sat and
> held her head lifted. She was strange, from far off, yet so intimate. She

was from far away, a presence, so close to his soul. She was not really there, sitting in Cossethay church beside her little girl. . . . She belonged to somewhere else. He felt it poignantly, as something real and natural. But a pang of fear for his own concrete life, that was only Cossethay, hurt him, and gave him misgiving. (*Rainbow,* 32)

Lydia represents the articulate world from which Tom feels himself excluded, and yet her language is Polish, which Tom could not expect to understand. Furthermore, with her, Tom can imaginatively repeat the triadic relationship he had with the couple at Matlock, legitimately this time because the first husband, the small foreign man, is dead.

So marriage for Tom Brangwen becomes a resolution of childhood tensions. The life on Marsh Farm, the legacy of generations of Brangwen men, is maintained; yet the desire of his mother to make a gentleman of him is also fulfilled through his marriage to a woman who is "fine," a born aristocrat. Although this reading goes against the usual Lawrentian view of marriage as a passage into a greater fulfillment and unprecedented possibilities of being, I think it accurately presents the roots of the dynamic of that fulfillment. Lydia and Tom do have a successful marriage, though it does not encompass the difficult areas of modern consciousness that Birkin and Ursula must tackle. Individually Tom does not reach any greater development of being. His ignoble death, by drowning while he is too drunk to save himself, shows how weak was his hold on the level of being he achieved with Lydia. Nonetheless, the qualified success of the marriage soothes the mental wretchedness Tom acquired in childhood. When the marriage begins to atrophy in its early years, Lydia uses her power of speech (now in English) to express their problems, flabbergasting Tom: "He stared in wonder at his own wife as she told him his own heart so callously. And he was indignant. What right had she to sit there telling him these things? She was his wife, what right had she to speak to him like this, as if she were a stranger?" (*Rainbow,* 88). When finally Tom is able to answer Lydia's speech, her need, her desire, permitting himself to reach toward "the reality of her who was just beyond himself," he does so silently, with his body: "She was beyond him, the unattainable. But he let go his hold on himself, he relinquished himself, and knew the subterranean force of his desire. . . . He began to approach her, to draw near" (*Rainbow,* 90). This new consummation in which Tom feels blinded and destroyed is a passage to freedom, and the language echoes the Gospels: "losing himself to find her, finding himself in her." Perhaps it's still obvious, but one must remember that Lawrence is describing coitus here, not only making metaphors for the state of Tom's soul—it was for scenes such as this one that the book was banned. Thus Lawrence invests the spirit in the body and attempts to erase the mentally derived distinction between the two. After this new baptism and confirmation, Lydia's foreignness is neither a threat to him nor an object of desire in itself, but rather a bit of memory and unfulfilled possibility: "He did not know her any better, any more precisely, now that he knew her altogether. Poland, her husband, the war—he understood no more of this in her. . . . But he knew her, he knew her meaning, without understanding" (*Rainbow,* 91).

This consummation remains a permanent point of reference in the novel. Fifteen years later, as he struggles with Anna over her engagement, Tom exclaims to himself: "What had he known but the long, marital embrace with his wife! Curious that this was what life amounted to! At any rate it was something, it was eternal" (*Rainbow,* 120). Most readers may be eager to accept this oxymoronic, self-belittling, and, at the same time, ennobling summation from a man who was once unable "to sum up his experiences." Yet, what does it mean to say, in one breath, it was *something,* it was *eternal?*

The naiveté of Tom's expression bespeaks Lawrence's continual effort to bind the worldly, the "something," with the spiritual without resorting to the intellect. And, seen from the perspective of Tom's early years, this marriage does indeed conjoin the worldly and the spiritual; his longing for the eternal is embodied in his wife. Unlike the argument-racked marriages of couples who attempt to express their feelings—Anna and Will Brangwen, Ursula and Rupert Birkin, or Harriet and Richard Somers (in *Kangaroo*)—this marriage appeals because it is little disturbed by discussion.

For many Lawrence readers, the marriage of Tom and Lydia is mythical, a satisfying primitive image from the childhood of thought, where intellection is bypassed, the sacred ancestral line begun. Like childhood, it is romanticized and smoothed out in memory. After the great consummation that ends chapter 2, Lawrence leaves Tom and Lydia alone to become the first parents of the rest of *The Rainbow.* The marriage relation, once achieved, subsides into the novel's prehistory, becoming the preverbal experience of a new main character.

While for Tom marriage is an arena in which he unconsciously resolves or escapes from childhood dilemmas, for Lydia it is a confirmation of recovery from the sufferings of her youth and first marriage and a retrieving of some of the happier moods of her childhood. In devising the scheme of *The Rainbow* and especially in rewriting the first two generations in greater detail,[12] Lawrence could have conveniently omitted Lydia Lensky's recollections of her childhood. Would it not have served his purposes as well to let her remain a stranger who comes into being only when Tom decides to "make her his life"? In choosing to fill in her history Lawrence provides himself with an opportunity to explore the conventional theme of a child as savior. He does this in two ways: by making Anna an agent for her mother's survival, and by making Lydia's reconnection with *her own* childhood a crucial link to her retrieval of her self and her readiness for a future with Tom.

In the early chapters of *The Rainbow* Lydia is saved by her daughter, who here takes on a role common within the Romantic view of childhood, that of the redemptive child who reconciles the past with the present.[13] Like the Christ child, Florence Dombey, Little Dorrit, and Silas Marner's Eppie, Anna is a child-angel who saves the errant or despairing adult from herself. In Poland, Lydia lost her two children to diphtheria. She blames herself for their loss because "as if drugged" she had followed her husband in his revolutionary work, "like a shadow, serving, echoing," often leaving the children behind. Then, away from their homeland, Paul Lensky, mad with loss and poverty, begins to die as well.[14] In London, Lydia nurses Anna into life as Paul slips into death:

12. Charles Ross shows in *The Composition of "The Rainbow" and "Women in Love": A History,* 26–31, that Lawrence probably created the Brangwen generations in reverse order, adding in the third draft known as "The Wedding Ring" more than two hundred pages about the childhood of Ella (as Ursula was then called), and then adding another 140 autograph pages about Anna's childhood and Lydia and Tom's marriage to the final draft, which was then called *The Rainbow.* In the introduction to the Cambridge edition of *The Rainbow,* editor Mark Kinkead-Weekes states that the third version of the novel (known as "The Wedding Ring") contained "all three generations, though the earlier stories must have been considerably attenuated" (xxvii). This process of working backward into family history reflects Lawrence's version of Prospero's aphorism: "We are such stuff as our grandmother's dreams are made on" ("The Dream of Life" in *The Princess and Other Stories,* 158). In creating Ella/Ursula, Lawrence must have been compelled by his sense of generational influence to seek out the dreams that had formed her modern being.

13. Kuhn, *Corruption in Paradise,* 52.

14. Joseph Conrad's short story "Amy Foster" (first published in 1903) treats a similar situation, that of a Polish emigrant who is shipwrecked and washed ashore on the English coast. Conrad's Yanko, after living in England for several years, terrifies his English wife by shouting at her in Polish to bring him a drink of water; she runs off and leaves him to die of a heart failure that the English doctor-narrator suggests is more than physical. It seems likely to me that this story, as well as Conrad's own situation, may have suggested the Lensky characters to Lawrence.

He was wasting away. Already when the child was born he seemed nothing but skin and bone and fixed idea. She watched him dying, nursed him, nursed the baby, but really took no notice of anything. A darkness was on her, like remorse, or like a remembering of the dark, savage, mystic ride of dread, of death, the shadow of revenge. When her husband died, she was relieved. He would no longer dart about her. (*Rainbow,* 50)

Lawrence describes Lydia's despair spatially and visually, as a movement in darkness. One small light in this darkness is the needfulness of the baby: "She walked without passion, like a shade, tormented into moments of love by the child" (*Rainbow,* 50).

Lydia is kept alive by the presence and dependency of Anna; even so, life is an assault, a torment to Lydia's soul. Her state of mind is something like the one Sylvia Plath portrays in a hospital patient who has received an unwelcome gift of flowers: "The tulips are too red in the first place, they hurt me. / Even through the gift paper I could hear them breathe / Lightly, through their white swaddlings, like an awful baby."[15] Unlike Plath, Lawrence will not send his character so far into despair as to find the idea of a baby "awful." Though Lawrence does not refrain elsewhere in his work from making a mother an emotional devourer of her child, he never does confront the possibility that the child may at times be appalling to its mother. Perhaps the absence of this attitude can be attributed to some residual Romanticism in Lawrence about the natural relation of mother and children rather than to knowing choices in characterization. When the unresisting Lydia is sent by the Anglican Church to work for an old rector in Yorkshire, childhood becomes a giver of unsought renewal in a second way: "This [move] was the first shake of the kaleidoscope that brought in front of her eyes something she must see" (*Rainbow,* 51). This tormenting insistence of life which demands response from Lydia has a dual relation to childhood: the physical world she feels forced to see reminds her of *her own* childhood and then, in turn, causes her to attend to Anna, her child. The passages that describe Lydia's gradual, painful reawakening to life are long, and the imagery that relates vision, memory, and childhood is pervasive, but a few excerpts will illustrate the patterns that interest me here: "And then, she was sent away into the country. There came into her mind now the memory of her home where she had been a child. . . . It hurt her brain, the open country and the moors. . . . Yet it forced itself upon her as something living, it

15. Sylvia Plath, "Tulips," in *The Collected Poems,* ed. Ted Hughes, 160–61.

roused some potency of her childhood in her, it had some relation to her" (*Rainbow,* 51). Childhood, in such passages, is the particular realm of a spontaneous will to live that is sometimes dissipated in the process of growing up. When the Yorkshire landscape reminds Lydia of the land where she was a child, it seems also to force her to remember her childhood and her once spontaneous will to live; and this remembering then renews her vitality and enables her to experience Anna:

> There was a strange insistence of light from the sea, to which she must attend. Primroses glimmered around, many of them, and she stooped to the disturbing influence near her feet, she even picked one or two flowers, faintly remembering in the new color of life, what had been. All the day long, as she sat at the upper window, the light came off the sea, constantly, constantly, without refusal, till it seemed to bear her away, and the noise of the sea created a drowsiness in her, a relaxation like sleep. Her automatic consciousness gave way a little, she stumbled sometimes, she had a poignant, momentary vision of her living child, that hurt her unspeakably. Her soul roused to attention. (*Rainbow,* 51)

The circularity and luminous quality of Lawrence's style here serve to render Lydia's tortuous recovery from depression. Though landscape, memory, and the vision of Anna force Lydia into moments of awareness, she returns into darkness several times, becoming herself childlike, while, as in the following image, her child becomes a parent: "Her fingers moved over the clasped fingers of the child, she heard the anxious voice of the baby, as it tried to make her talk, distraught" (*Rainbow,* 51–52). In another passage Lawrence uses birth itself as the metaphor for recovery. Lydia, like an unborn baby, "could not bear to come to, to realise. The first pangs of this new parturition were so acute, she knew she could not bear it. She would rather remain out of life, than be torn, mutilated into this birth, which she could not survive" (*Rainbow,* 53). Notice that in this passage Lydia seems to be *both* the laboring mother and the fetus. Lawrence so accurately understands the biological wish for birth and the resistance to it that his metaphor may seem confused; whereas, in effect, he is evoking the desire and resistance of Lydia's old self to give birth to a new self, and the equally ambivalent need and disinclination of that new self to be born.

Anna, the return of crocuses and the planting of pea flowers, the sight of thrush's eggs in the nest, and finally—crucially—the appearance of Tom Brangwen pull Lydia back into life. The metaphor of the new self arising from the old (like the phoenix) establishes an identity between gestation and death, which are both unconscious states. Lydia's long periods of depression are deathlike, dark, but—as it turns out—also restorative, preparatory to her resurrection. The image Lawrence evokes to mark her certain return to consciousness again links childhood with light: "She felt like somebody else, not herself, a new person, quite glad. But she knew it was fragile, and she dreaded it. The vicar put pea-flower into the crocuses, for his bees to roll in, and she laughed. Then night came, with brilliant stars that she knew of old, from her girlhood. And they flashed so bright, she knew they were victors" (*Rainbow*, 53).

The account of Lydia's return to health despite her conscious resistance, the victory of the desire to live over her will to death, provides an instance of the difference between Lawrence's and Freud's views of the workings of the unconscious. Though he misunderstood Freud's conception of the unconscious by identifying its content as solely the repressed material of sexual life—"Nothing but a huge slimy serpent of sex, and heaps of excrement, and a myriad repulsive horrors spawned between sex and excrement" (*PU,* 5)[16]—Lawrence did not doubt the existence or importance of unconscious impulses. For his own more sanguine idea of the unconscious, he often preferred the word *soul* or used *conscious* and *unconscious* and *consciousness* with overlapping meanings. "The Freudian unconscious," Lawrence wrote, "is the cellar in which the mind keeps its own bastard spawn. The true unconscious is the well-head, the fountain of real motivity" (*PU,* 9). In his representation of Lydia Lensky's return to ordinary, conscious life, Lawrence links the central realms in Freudian analysis of the unconscious: gestation and childhood, death, and sexual transfiguration.

The needful presence of Anna and the insistent spring renewal of nature have forced Lydia to reencounter her own childhood and then to grow up again. Lawrence suggests here a psychology that permits healing by way of a return to childhood. It differs radically from psychoanalytic procedure. Childhood is sought as a source of direct renewal, a realm in which the healthful balance of sympathetic and independent impulses may be discovered, rather than as a locale where repressed complexes may be disentangled. Gaston Bachelard has expressed a similar faith in the salutary powers of images from childhood: "beyond all family history, after going beyond the zone of regrets, after dispersing all the mirages of nostalgia, we reach an anonymous childhood, a pure threshold of life,

---

16. The breeding between sex and excrement suggests the engendering of Death by Satan upon Sin in *Paradise Lost,* 2.746–809.

original life, original human life. And this life is within us . . . a dream (*songe*) brings us back to it. The memory does nothing but open the door to the dream (*songe*)." Bachelard argues that the use of the concept of childhood innocence lies in the "application" of it to complex adult lives. Lydia's childhood is not the forgotten cause of her depression; it is clear that the deaths of her husband and two children and her separation from Poland were enough to traumatize her. What she finds in her childhood is not the origin of neurosis, but rather a pure vitality, an unwearied, uncorrupted enthusiasm for life—what Bachelard calls "a principle of deep life, of life always in harmony with the possibilities of new beginnings"—that has been held in abeyance by her later sorrows.[17] Once she has reconnected with her own past by retrieving certain childhood memories and done so with concurrent awareness of her English environment, Lydia may find fulfillment in adult expressions of unconscious desires, sexuality and motherhood.

It is important to recognize that Lawrence brings Tom Brangwen into Lydia's world only after she has begun consciously to acknowledge some vitality in herself. Although with this vitality has come confusion about her social position in England, she does not feel drawn to Tom for the security he can provide. Quite the contrary— her aristocratic pride opposes union with a farmer, but is overridden by her attraction to his youth, "the steady livingness of his eyes." Tom is the immediate focus of her new wish to live, but he is not the source of it:

> She was aware of people who passed around her, not as persons, but as looming presences. It was difficult for her to adjust herself. In Poland, the peasantry, the people, had been cattle to her, they had been cattle that she owned and used. What were these people? Now she was coming awake, she was lost.
>
> But she had felt Brangwen go by almost as if he had brushed her. She had tingled in body as she had gone on up the road. After she had been with him in the Marsh kitchen, the voice of her body had risen strong and insistent. Soon, she wanted him. He was the man who had come nearest to her for her awakening. (*Rainbow*, 53–54)

Awakening to true desire in Lawrence entails, as J. Temple has shown, a regaining of innocence: "Only in the accidental stirring of desire, can the 'self-possession' of adults be discarded and replaced by a

---

17. Gaston Bachelard, *The Poetics of Reverie: Childhood, Language, and the Cosmos,* 124–25.

tenderness which is poignantly related to childhood innocence."[18] This innocence involves a shedding of adult contingencies and a recovery of childlike receptivity to life. Thus Lydia Lensky's imaginative return to her Polish childhood has prepared her to overlook the awkwardness of her position in England and to accept, against her conscious will, but without guilt, the desire for Tom that has arisen in her.

18. J. Temple, "The Definition of Innocence: A Consideration of the Short Stories of D. H. Lawrence," 109.

"The Father Spark"
4 Anna Brangwen and the Struggle for Harmony

In *The Rainbow*'s Anna Lensky Brangwen, Lawrence renders the vitality that he admires in Cézanne's paintings. In my introduction I compared Lawrence's own accomplishment in the literary depiction of children to Cézanne's in still lifes as an attempt to "let the apple exist in its own separate entity, without transfusing it with personal emotion . . . to shove the apple away from him, and let it live of itself."[1] Lawrence accomplishes this "shoving away" of Anna by displaying the child's mind without probing it. The style by which he achieves her "unanalysable, indefinable reality of individuality" (*PU,* 14) is unusual within *The Rainbow.* Rather than intruding into Anna's consciousness through either interior monologues or authorial metaphors, he favors dramatic scenes and narration from external perspectives.

Ironically, this emphasis on the externals of Anna's life produces the impression that she, preeminently among Lawrence's child characters, has an independent existence. Lawrence's depiction of Anna is enhanced by his different treatment of Ursula Brangwen, the main child figure of the novel's second half. The narrator infiltrates the consciousness of Ursula from babyhood. Sentences like these keep us just outside Anna's consciousness: "And a new fear shook the child from the sound of his voice. She cried mechanically, her eyes looking watchful through her tears, in terror, alert to what might happen" (*Rainbow,* 73). They are very different from these about Ursula: "Her soul, her consciousness seemed to die away. She became shut off and senseless, a little fixed creature whose soul had

1. Lawrence, "Introduction to These Paintings," in *Phoenix,* 567.

82

gone hard and unresponsive. The sense of her own reality hardened her like a frost" (*Rainbow,* 207).

Lawrence also accentuates the childhood of Anna by his arrangement of events within the account of Tom and Lydia Brangwen's first year together. This crucial year is broken into three sections that one may envision as a triptych within the chapter entitled "They Live at the Marsh." First in this triptych comes a panel recounting the marriage of Tom and Lydia. David Cavitch, adapting Lawrence's own remarks, advisedly calls the style "futuristic"— generalized narration that softens "the lines which separate one personal identity from another" while the "matrix of human consciousness flows from person to person."[2] The opposing panel, from the same time period, depicts Anna's move from absolute dependence on her mother to a more difficult and strange, but also liberating, relationship with her stepfather. This section is written in the more objective style I noted in my previous paragraph. The center and resolving panel (in the narrative, a concluding scene) of this triptych is the one known to Lawrence critics as the birth night or barn scene. In this intense, vivid episode the family's emotions are shaken out and recombined: The child accepts the father. The mother confirms her new marriage by delivering Tom's child. Tom acknowledges his responsibility—and comes to feel a connection among his own childhood, his paternity, and the "swift, unseen threshing of the night" (*Rainbow,* 77). From the emotional vortex of that night, Anna begins to participate in a world beyond Marsh Farm, eventually becoming free in her own being and moving toward independence.

Anna's vitality and vibrancy are initially expressed by her striking fleece of blonde hair and dark eyes, which Lawrence mentions almost every time she appears. As I noted in Chapter 1, Lawrence

2. David Cavitch, *D. H. Lawrence and the New World,* 39–43. Lawrence used the term *futurism* in his letter of June 5, 1914, quoting from Filippo Marinetti's manifesto for the short-lived futurist movement in literature, which calls for celebration of speed and aggressiveness in modern life along with destruction of museums, libraries, and other strongholds of tradition. The notion of futurism becomes a bit more interesting when adopted by Italian visual artists; they focus on "dynamism" and offer such ideas as this one of Umberto Boccioni's: "a galloping horse has not four legs; it has twenty." In preserving Lawrence's term, Cavitch is able to emphasize both the intended newness of Lawrence's style in the novel (a "bright book of life" for the future) and the problems that accompany attending to character that is mobile rather than static.

gives most of his fictional children angelic features, but combines them with realistic details that belie the suggestion of spiritual innocence. Anna's hair and face are quite lovely, reminiscent of Blake's chimney sweep, whose hair "curl'd like a lamb's back" before it was shaved, or of his charity children's clean, innocent faces with "radiance all their own" in "Holy Thursday." Lawrence (like Blake) immediately follows the conventionally angelic image with details that bring Anna back to earth. He uses an example of fierce behavior that will be an important element in the marriage of Tom and her mother: "It was a child with a face like a bud of apple-blossom, and glistening fair hair like thistle-down sticking out in straight, wild, flamy pieces, and very dark eyes. The child clung jealously to her mother's side when he looked at her, staring with resentful black eyes" (*Rainbow*, 32). By assigning feelings of jealousy and resentment to the goldenfleeced child, Lawrence insists upon the connection of spirit and flesh, and on the connection between a figurative language that glorifies the child and the literal language that describes natural behavior. Yet Lawrence would not deny the spiritual element or destroy the icon that represents it. Configured as such a duality, Anna also represents both hope and strife, the English future and the Polish past. She is destined to be a reminder of the exotic element that has joined the earthy Brangwen family, especially in her maintenance of a connection with the Skrebenskys, a liaison that will eventually bring Anton Skrebensky into the story as Ursula's first lover.

Just as Anna's appearance brings with it the iconography of innocence, so the setting for her childhood draws upon the conventional associations of pastoral literature. They suggest that the rural life fosters harmony in human lives. The events that make up what I have called the triptych of "They Live at the Marsh" take place within the shelter of the idyllic Marsh Farm that Lawrence describes in *The Rainbow*'s lyrical prologue. The "blood-intimacy" between men, animals, and soil at Marsh Farm is repeated in the relations of parents and children, who seldom find reason to be fatefully divided against one another. In creating Anna's childhood, Lawrence invents an edenic version of childhood. In this version, strife leads to resolution rather than to increased consciousness and new strife, as it does for Paul Morel and even Ursula Brangwen, whose circumstances and experiences are closer to Lawrence's own. In the first half of *The Rainbow* the two generations are so simply and fruitfully intertwined that telling the story of one implies that of the other. The pastoral imagery is not undercut as immediately in *The*

Rainbow as the iconography of innocence is. Eventually the growth of consciousness in the characters and growth of industrialism in England do distort the peace and natural vitality of Marsh Farm into imitations of themselves such as the "harvest supper" wedding of the farmer Fred Brangwen. This event is devised not by the farmer himself, but by his fiancée, who has studied morris-dancing at teachers' college, and by his brother Tom, a "cynical Bacchus" who works in London.

While Lawrence evokes the traditions of Christian symbolism, pastoralism, and Romanticism, they are secondary to the struggle into being that goes on within each member of the Brangwen family against that evocative background. Since the lives of Tom, Lydia, and Anna are deeply connected, their stories are difficult to separate. Considering the amount of criticism that has been produced about Tom and Lydia—as individuals and as a couple—it is surprising that little of it focuses especially on Anna as a child.

To remedy this neglect, one must see that, instrumental as Anna is in the creation of an idyllic family life at Marsh Farm, her most important role is to be herself. When Lawrence introduces her, she is just four years of age and coming into a difficult verbal consciousness, attempting to use words to gain possession of the world. After she has found a red button on the ground near Tom Brangwen's foot, she retreats to her mother: " 'Mother, I may have it, mayn't I?' came the child's proud, silvery tones. 'Mother'—she seemed always to be calling her mother to remember her—'Mother'—and she had nothing to continue now her mother had replied 'Yes my child.' But, with ready invention, the child stumbled and ran on 'What are those people's names?' " (*Rainbow*, 33). So although Anna's growth is in some ways a subplot in the history of Lydia's relationship with Tom, at the same time it is the history of the novel's pivotal figure, she who is the linchpin that connects the three generations. What Henry James said of his conception of *The Portrait of a Lady*, that it is a wonder "how absolutely, how inordinately the Isabel Archers, and even much smaller female fry, insist on mattering,"[3] is a discovery made again by Lawrence. For Anna Lensky insists very much on mattering, and she does so at a younger age than did Isabel Archer or even Maisie Farange. Though James himself is an essential writer in the history of literary children, I wish to distinguish his own achievement from Lawrence's. James never took for his perceiving consciousness or for his main character a child younger than Maisie,

3. Henry James, *The Art of the Novel*, 49.

who is six when her ordeal begins. Other memorably young characters such as Morgan Moreen of "The Pupil," Nanda Brookenham of
The Awkward Age, Nora of *Watch and Ward,* and Verena Tarrant of
The Bostonians are nearer adolescence when James takes them up.
A more subtle difference between James and Lawrence is one of
attitude toward children; Lawrence lacks the sense James expresses
in the preface to *What Maisie Knew* of the child as a particularly
useful pawn in the game of novel-making: "the child becoming a
centre and pretext for a fresh system of misbehavior . . . there would
be the 'full' irony, there the promising theme into which the hint I
had originally picked up would logically flower."[4] James's sense of
the child as a "case" to be manipulated is even more determining of
his attitude toward Miles and Flora in *The Turn of the Screw.* Of
course, James speaks of most of his characters who register consciousness as "cases," so I am only saying that he makes no exception for his child characters. James does achieve a more acute reflec-
tion of social and moral ironies than does Lawrence with his
children, though Lawrence's irony in "Rocking-Horse Winner" has a
Jamesian feel to it.

I find James's statement about "smaller female fry" prophetic of
Lawrence's accomplishment with child characters. By examining
The Rainbow's well-beloved first generation from Anna's perspective I hope to reveal much that has not been noticed about the style
with which she is characterized and the nature of her relationships
with her parents, particularly with her stepfather. The involvement
of Anna in their marriage is unique even in Lawrence's work. While
in *The White Peacock, Sons and Lovers, The Trespasser,* and *Aaron's Rod* and a number of the short stories, children are victims in
bad marriages, in *The Rainbow* Lawrence makes the child a benefi-
ciary of a successful marriage. And, once that marriage achieves
stability in its reconsummation after two years, it becomes her heritage as Lawrence turns his focus to the growth of Anna. Thence, it
must be seen that, to echo James's pronouncement again, the child
not only matters, but she matters in a particularly Lawrentian way, a
way that reveals how one character touches the very being of another and how one generation becomes the next.

Lawrence makes manifest the rhythms of unconscious growth in
his child characters. He shows, for instance, that taking on even a
kindly parent may be as difficult as losing parents was for all of
those orphans in the Victorian novels. The relationship that devel-

4. Ibid., 143.

ops between Anna and her stepfather is as deep and complex as any connection between two people in Lawrence's fiction. At the time he composed *The Rainbow,* Lawrence was able to depict fatherhood as he had not done before and would not do as thoroughly again. In this novel the conventional stepfather, that threatening, looming, menacingly sexual figure known best as Mr. Murdstone, becomes a full-bodied, sexually alive, sometimes sexually confused, and also gentle, loving influence on the child.

Anna Lensky is a lively figure in the background from the first time Tom sees her mother, well before the marriage. Initially she is more conspicuously receptive to Tom than is her mother. While Lydia seems to ignore him, Tom effortlessly gains the four-year-old girl's confidence by his "native good humour." When he is giving the two of them a ride in his carriage, the "child huddled close to him, as if for love, the mother sat very still" (*Rainbow,* 39). Sitting between the two adults, Anna is both a buffer and a link. As I noted in Chapter 3, Anna's early childhood has been lonely. She has often had to draw love from her mother rather than simply receive it, as promised in the myth of ideal childhood. Her expression of her need for love to Tom helps him overcome his shyness with her mother. Anna's unsatisfied need for closeness has marked her infancy; it is a corollary of her mother's deracination and depression, enfolded in the history of her mother's immigration and widowing.

The extent to which Lawrence realizes the abnormality of Anna Lensky's infancy may be gauged from the descriptions in his psychological essays—phrased in his own electro-biological vocabulary—of the polar connections between mother and baby. At their solar plexuses, he states, the two express an instinct toward unity, each finding the whole world, including the (m)other, a part of the self. At the lumbar ganglion, however, each feels independent of the other and separate from the rest of the world. Of this early relation the goal is "perfected individuality." For the child to attain that individuality he or she must first experience a balance of union *with* and independence *from* the mother:

> If we could only realize that all through life these are the two synchronizing activities of love, of creativity. For the end, the goal, is the perfecting of each single individuality, unique in itself—which cannot take place without a perfected harmony between the beloved, a harmony that depends on the at-last-clarified singleness of each being. . . .
> So the child. In its wonderful unison with the mother it is at the same time extricating itself into single, separate, independent existence. The

one process, of unison, cannot go on without the other, of purified severance. (*PU,* 22)

Judged by this standard, the infancy of Anna Lensky has been severely deficient. It seems that Lydia, with her "long blanks and darknesses of abstraction," rarely talks to her baby or looks into her face—"She heard the anxious voice of the baby, as it tried to make her talk, distraught" (*Rainbow,* 50, 52). Facial and vocal interaction between mother and child, as Heinz Kohut and others have since shown, encourages the infant's paradoxical development of union with and independence from the mother. At the age of four, when Anna becomes a central figure in the novel, she is "incomprehensibly" jealous of her mother, yet willing to snuggle up to Tom's "bigness" when she feels desolate. According to Tilly, the Brangwen family servant, Anna is "bewitched." She seems to have a kind of capricious, gratuitous independence that is not founded upon a durable sense of self: "Happy she never seemed, but quick, sharp, absorbed, full of imagination and changeability" (*Rainbow,* 65). In comparison with Lawrence's model in the essays, Anna's connections with her mother have been disrupted, stunted, and crossed because of her mother's inability to respond fully as either a sympathetic nurturer or an independent opposite. Anna's crying, Lawrence says in a remark that is reminiscent of Thomas Hardy's emblematic boy in *Jude the Obscure,* Father Time, is "heartrending . . . her childish anguish seemed so utter and timeless, as if it were a thing of all the ages" (*Rainbow,* 66).

Anna's lack of a living father, until her mother's marriage to Tom, is also an impoverishment, according to *Fantasia,* where Lawrence insists upon the importance of a father's influence:

> To an infant the mother is the whole universe. Yet the child needs more than the mother. It needs as well the presence of men, the vibration from the present body of the man. . . . They do not need the actual contact, the handling and caressing. On the contrary, the true male instinct is to avoid physical contact with a baby. It may not need even actual presence. But, present or absent, there should be between the baby and the father that strange, intangible communication, that strange pull and circuit such as the magnetic pole exercises upon a needle, a vitalistic pull and flow which lays all the life-plasm of the baby into the line of vital quickening, strength, knowing. (*FU,* 73)

Unlike the blood-connected but physically absent father described in *Fantasia,* Tom Brangwen takes interest in Anna from their first meeting, entertaining and charming her while carrying on a rather austere courtship with her mother. At first Anna responds easily, as when she "huddled close to him as if for love" in the wagon. Here she seems to be instinctively seeking the parental warmth she lacks. After the wedding, though, it suddenly becomes clear that Anna is, after all, used to the simple, isolated relationship with her mother.

In the scene just preceding his proposal of marriage, Tom sees Lydia and her daughter as Madonna and Child, apparently sufficient unto themselves and blessed with illumination. Sheltering a bouquet of daffodils from the wind, Tom watches the pair through the frame of the window:

> He saw her seated in the rocking chair with the child, already in its nightdress, sitting on her knee. The fair head with its wild, fierce hair was drooping towards the fire-warmth, which reflected on the bright cheeks and clear skin of the child, who seemed to be musing, almost like a grown-up person. The mother's face was dark and still, and he saw, with a pang, that she was away back in the life that had been. The child's hair gleamed like spun glass, her face was illuminated till it seemed like wax lit up from the inside. The wind boomed strongly. Mother and child sat motionless, silent, the child staring with vacant dark eyes into the fire, the mother looking into space. (*Rainbow,* 42)

Lawrence's emphasis on the aureole quality of Anna's hair, the repetition of the definite article with the words "mother" and "child," and the omission of any personal names increase one's sense that this scene, lit by the hearth and framed by the window, borrows its iconography from the Bethlehem nativity. But, when Lawrence made his own painting entitled *A Holy Family* he included the father prominently in the composition and placed the child slightly farther back as an observer of his parents.[5] Like the father in Lawrence's painting, Tom must enter the apparently closed circle of Lydia and her child, accepting—as Joseph does in marrying Mary— the mystery of Lydia's previous life and Anna's parentage. Tom waits outside, "suspended, looking at the wild waving of the trees in the wind and the gathering darkness. He had his fate to follow, he lingered here at the threshold" (*Rainbow,* 42).

The scene Tom views through the window is a necessary prologue to his entrance. It silently dramatizes Tom's sense of himself as a seeker approaching the unknown by turning him into a watcher at the window, aware of Lydia's Polish past and fascinated by her

---

5. See *Paintings of D. H. Lawrence,* ed. Mervyn Levy, or D. H. Lawrence, *Ten Paintings.* The painting is on exhibit by its owner, Saki Karavas, at the La Fonda Hotel in Taos, New Mexico.

foreignness. "Behind her," he thinks later as he moves to consummate their union, "there was so much unknown to him. When he approached her, he came to such a terrible painful unknown" (*Rainbow,* 56). But when Anna starts at the sound of the wind shaking the house, and her mother, to comfort her, begins singing a Polish lullaby, Anna interrupts in a "high, complaining, yet imperative voice: 'Don't sing that stuff, mother; I don't want to hear it.' The singing died away. 'You will go to bed,' said the mother" (*Rainbow,* 42). Anna protests and asks that her mother tell her a story instead. After Lydia has finished, she will carry Anna up to bed and Tom will knock on the door to make his proposal. When Lydia wants to give and receive comfort, she sings a Polish song that Anna, already separating herself from her foreign history, dislikes. (Tom can hear it, oddly enough, through a closed window on a windy night.) Irritation with Anna and the telling of the story (presumably in English, though Tom does not hear this) bring about Lydia's reengagement with the present.

In refusing the Polish song, Anna virtually invites Tom to overcome his awe of their foreignness and share his Englishness with them. Lydia finishes the story and rises, lifting the child. Outside, Tom has already imagined himself added to the scene, making a sort of animal breeder's evaluation of his future wife: "She must be strong, to carry so large a child so easily." Tom identifies himself with the child, agreeing that Lydia should abandon her old "stuff." He wants her to begin, with him, a new episode in her life: "Along with the child, he felt a curious strain on him, a suffering like a fate" (*Rainbow,* 43).

The strain Tom and Anna both feel is "the resistance and the fight with something unseen," the desire to seek it and the fear of seeking it (*Rainbow,* 43). Yet Tom does cross the threshold and marry the strange woman. Such a decision reveals how, in *The Rainbow,* Lawrence works out the dynamics of the relation between men and women, and children as well, in terms that transcend his own history and the version of it he recorded in *Sons and Lovers.* Even after his marriage, Tom has periods of jealousy and anger when he is amazed and outraged by Lydia's strangeness and apparent self-sufficiency—when he could "smash her into regarding him" (*Rainbow,* 62)—and in these periods he often turns to Anna.

Lawrence places great emphasis on the wedding itself as a significant event for Anna. The wedding morning marks the beginning of a series of episodes that are out of strict chronology with the rest of the narrative.[6] Within the chapter titled "They Live at the Marsh," Lawrence recapitulates the early months of Tom and Lydia's marriage. Previously told from within Lydia's and Tom's consciousnesses, the relationship is now discussed from a perspective that is sympathetic to Anna while only rarely penetrating her consciousness. This chronologically redundant section dramatizes the process of Anna's coming to terms with Tom through a series of scenes that emblematically explores Anna's sexual impulses and personal identity. Although she and her mother seem to have resided at Marsh Farm for some brief time preceding the wedding (*Rainbow,* 55) her possessiveness is aroused when her mother, on the wedding night, begins sharing Tom's bed. Awakening to find that her mother is not nearby, Anna comes to their closed bedroom door in her anxious search. Tom opens the door and confronts the child's "black eyes staring round and hostile":

> "I want my mother," she said, jealously accenting the "my."
> "Come on then," he said gently.
> "Where's my mother?"
> "She's here—come on."
> The child's eyes, staring at the man with ruffled hair and beard, did not change. The mother's voice called softly. The little bare feet entered the room with trepidation.
> "Mother!"
> "Come, my dear."
> The small bare feet approached swiftly.
> "I wondered where you were," came the plaintive voice. The mother stretched out her arms. The child stood beside the high bed. Brangwen lightly lifted the tiny girl, with an "up-a-daisy", then took his own place in the bed again.

6. Peter Balbert's essay "'Logic of the Soul': Prothalamic Pattern in *The Rainbow*," in Peter Balbert and Phillip Marcus, eds., *D. H. Lawrence: A Centenary Consideration,* reads the novel as "A virtual hymn . . . to the spirit of marriage" and shows that Lawrence "never seriously considers, throughout these years of turmoil [before his marriage to Frieda], any compromise in his stress on *legal* status." Thus, for Balbert, both the novel and the biography testify to "the conservative impulse in Lawrence that is at the heart of his most apocalyptic doctrines; it reflects a sensibility inclined toward traditional forms of worship, stability, and passion, even though he wishes to transmute and invigorate the forms" (47). Balbert does not explicate the scenes of Tom and Lydia's wedding and wedding morning, but his thesis lends support to my argument that Lawrence's odd arrangement of events in chapter 3 throws weight on the wedding—as a legal embodiment of the choice of the soul (as Balbert emphasizes) or as a significant event to the child (as I wish to emphasize).

> "Mother!" cried the child, as in anguish.
> "What, my pet?"
> Anna wriggled close into her mother's arms, clinging tight, hiding from the fact of the man. (*Rainbow*, 64)

Unconsciously Anna senses that the new bond that exists between her mother and Tom threatens her. Before, Tom was an outsider, a man like the two vicars in whose houses her mother had worked, and Anna was her mother's only vital human tie. Later in the day when Lydia attempts to answer Anna's protest she relies on an abstract (yet, to Lawrence, elemental) prescription that "All women must have a husband," which has little meaning to Anna, who has not experienced a family before. Tom's response is more placating, but necessarily skirts the real question. Such discussion only frustrates Anna further because she cannot herself articulate the nature of her jealousy:

> "*Why* do you sleep with *my* mother? My mother sleeps with me," her voice quivering.
> "You come as well, an' sleep with both of us," he coaxed.
> "Mother!" she cried, turning, appealing against him.
> "But I must have a husband, darling. All women must have a husband."
> "And you like to have a father with your mother, don't you?" said Brangwen.
> Anna glowered at him. She seemed to cogitate.
> "No," she cried fiercely at length, "no, I don't *want*."
> And slowly her face puckered, she sobbed bitterly. He stood and watched her, sorry. But there could be no altering it. (*Rainbow*, 65)

The word "want," italicized by Lawrence, lacks either a direct object or an infinitive to complete it; it is a primitive reply that shows that Anna's wanting and not wanting refer to everything, to all the world with which her relations seem so uncertain. Of course, Lawrence could have specified the nature of Anna's jealousy if he had chosen to do so. He had available the vocabulary for states of the soul, including its sexual impulses, that so frequently describe Tom and Lydia. In electing not to put words in Anna's mind, Lawrence seems to honor Anna's inarticulateness and to abide by his own dictum in *Fantasia of the Unconscious:* "Never have ideas about children—and never have ideas *for* them" (*FU,* 115). Nonetheless he does convey the unconscious dimension of Anna's being and the crucial nature of these events for her development. These passages about family sleeping arrangements anticipate Lawrence's heavier use of symbols to manifest the unconscious in *Women in Love* (and again one recalls that the first part of *The Rainbow* was nearest to the later novel in order of composition). By locating this opening scene of Anna Lensky's metamorphosis into Anna Brangwen in the parental bed, that icon of the primal scene, Lawrence reckons with the libidinal energy of the child and brings childhood into the modern period. Lawrence implies the sexual element in family emotions when Anna's dispossession of her mother occurs in the same place as Tom and Lydia's sexual possession of each other. Thus the "high bed" becomes a sort of Lawrentian high altar for the rites of family life. Although Anna grieves for the loss of her mother as a sleeping companion, she is invited to join her parents in bed in the morning—"There's room for you as well," he said. "It's a big bed enough." Such freedom was denied children by writers of child-care manuals in the Victorian period (Anna Lensky is born in 1864)[7] as well as by most, including the liberal Dr. Benjamin Spock, in the twentieth century. Nonetheless, Lawrence makes statements about children and sexuality in *Fantasia* that seem naively inadequate to this scene between Tom, Lydia, and Anna. In that essay he denies that children have the sexual feelings toward their parents that he reveals in his fiction. He says, for instance:

> Sex—that is to say, maleness and femaleness—is present from the moment of birth, and in every act or deed of every child. But sex in the real sense of dynamic sexual relationship, this does not exist in a child, and cannot exist until puberty and after. True, children have a sort of sex-consciousness. Little boys and little girls may even commit indecencies together. And still it is nothing vital. It is a sort of shadow activity, a sort of dream-activity. (*FU,* 137)

Lawrence the polemicist limits his definition of sex to simple ascription of gender at one extreme, and to erogenous activity at the other. Where he insistently differed with Freud, and hence also mistook some of the sources of power in his depiction of children, was about the middle area of sexuality, in which there is a love object but no specifically genital activity ("little indecencies"). Lawrence's dismissal of children's sexuality as "dream activity" suggests a connection that he refused to make, and refused to accept when Freud made it: that "dream-activity" has a sexual content.[8] The motiva-

7. "Chronology of *The Rainbow*," in *The Rainbow,* ed. Mark Kinkead-Weekes, 489.
8. In *Fantasia,* Lawrence also discounts Freud's valuation of dream material, finding in it rather than the royal road to the unconscious, a sort of street-sweeping activity that removes the dead garbage of the preceding day from the nerves and blood, occasionally and by accident sweeping an image into the

tion underlying Anna's response to finding her mother sleeping with Tom Brangwen comes from the unconscious area that Freud calls sexual and that Lawrence, despite his keen sense of the passional impulses of children, does not. If we believe that there is such a thing as infantile sexuality we need look only as far as the relationships of Anna and her mother or Ursula and her father to see that Lawrence also knew it, even if he refused to call it by that name.

While the sexual feelings of children in Lawrence's fiction are apparent, it does not necessarily follow that this sexuality demands a psychoanalytic interpretation. If one attempts to fill the blanks in the sources of Anna's feelings, it is conceivable that Anna is a surrogate oedipal Lawrence, playing the boy's role as she is drawn toward the mother's bed and jealous of the father. It is more plausible to me, though, to interpret Anna's attachment to her mother as a part of the pre-oedipal, dyadic phase that has simply been exacerbated and extended by the isolation of her early years.[9]

Daniel Dervin, though his approach to Lawrence is Freudian, emphasizes the creative aspect of sexual growth when he initiates his study with the intention of discovering "how an artist becomes," and finds that Lawrence's "imaginative resources were able to tap into that zone behind time [first and second years of life] when primary love may account for the sustaining sources of creativity and threatened maternal loss."[10] In his detailed analyses of specific cruxes in Lawrence's life and novels, Dervin concludes that Lawrence's unusually acute sense of his own early childhood was a salutary phenomenon for his art: "Applied to Lawrence (in contrast, say, to Kafka), creativity is more analogous to therapeutic working through than to catharsis, more akin to self-emergence than to cir-

---

mind; these images are "the heterogenous odds and ends of images swept together by the besom of the night-current, and it is beneath our dignity to attach any real importance to them" (*FU*, 193–94). Nonetheless, in "The Fox" (written in 1918) Nellie March's dreams of the fox foreshadow her attraction to Henry Grenfel (D. H. Lawrence, "The Fox," in *Four Short Novels*).

9. Judith Ruderman discusses the importance of unresolved pre-oedipal tensions in Lawrence's works. In *D. H. Lawrence and the Devouring Mother* she shows that the desire to escape the "enveloping, encroaching female parent—the trespasser par excellence—lay behind his distaste for democracy, mass man, humans in the aggregate" that is expressed in the books he wrote after the war (30), while in her more recent work, "Orality and Animality in *The White Peacock*," she argues that the desire to return to the womb is evident in several characters in that early novel. In *The Rainbow* one may see both these attitudes toward the mother, sometimes in combat with each other.

10. Dervin, "*Strange Sapience*," 9.

cular self-repetition, and so in the long run favoring maturity over the tenacious lures of childhood or the recurring grips of disease."[11] Dervin's analysis of the creative use Lawrence made of his own childhood suggests how it is that Lawrence came to be the renovator of the holistic view of childhood, growth, and adulthood represented earlier by Rousseau and Wordsworth. By choosing emerging self over self-repetition, Lawrence is able to imagine—as Wordsworth did—childhood as a continuum through which the child becomes adult rather than as a succession of static psychological conditions.

This emphasis on the living process of childhood does not overlook the painfulness of it. Giving up her exclusive hold on her mother, Anna "was curiously, incomprehensibly jealous of her mother, always anxiously concerned about her. . . . Yet as a rule, Anna seemed cold, resenting her mother, critical of her" (*Rainbow,* 65). Her unhappy possessiveness of her mother is matched by the alternately receptive and resistant attitudes she exhibits toward Tom. Even in natural families, when a child spends the majority of his or her time with the mother, the father is a welcomed change, an emotional refreshment, but his unfamiliarity to the child makes him not quite trustworthy. Anna quite easily accepts Tom as a sort of visiting uncle (another reminder of the treatment she might have received from the vicars), and yet she does not accept him as her mother's husband: "He was easy with her, talking to her, taking her to see the live creatures, bringing her the first chickens in his cap, taking her to gather eggs, letting her throw crusts to the horse. She would easily accompany him, and take all he had to give, but she remained neutral still" (*Rainbow,* 65). Anna's apparent neutrality masks, I think, "the silent, hidden misery of childhood" (*Rainbow,* 208) that Lawrence describes so much more explicitly in Ursula, a generation later, when she is about the same age. Lawrence is less categorical about Anna's internal struggle than he is about Ursula's. He uses details from daily farm life to convey the nuances of how relations develop between her and Tom rather than exhaustive sequences from within their minds. In the following case, Anna's ambivalence toward her mother's marriage is expressed by her anger at the farm geese and tested by her wish for them to accept her. The scene is presented as it is heard by Tom:

> "You're naughty, you're naughty," cried Anna, tears of dismay and vexation in her eyes. And she stamped her slipper.

11. Ibid., 9–10.

"Why, what are they doing?" said Brangwen.

"They won't let me come in," she said, turning her flushed little face to him.

"Yi, they will. You can go in if you want to," and he pushed open the gate for her.

She stood irresolute, looking at the group of bluey-white geese standing monumental under the grey, cold day.

"Go on," he said.

She marched valiantly a few steps in. Her little body started convulsively at the sudden, derisive Can-cank-ank of the geese. A blankness spread over her. The geese trailed away with uplifted heads under the low grey sky.

"They don't know you," said Brangwen. "You should tell 'em what your name is."

"They're *naughty* to shout at me," she flashed.

"They think you don't live here," he said.

The scene completes itself when Tom overhears Anna calling to the geese:

"My name is Anna, Anna Lensky, and I live here, because Mr. Brangwen's my father now. He *is,* yes he *is.* And I live here." (*Rainbow,* 66)

Lawrence rarely veers from surface description or adult points of view in such episodes from Anna's childhood. A possible exception would be the line "a blankness spread over her" in the scene just quoted, but even this might be construed as a facial expression. Yet the scene he uses in place of such description conveys a psychological event with perfect clarity. In the episode of Anna and the geese, Lawrence confidently assumes that this incident is adequate to portray the child-self; when Anna Lensky tells the poultry "Mr. Brangwen's my father now," the reader is supposed to believe it too. The credibility of the dialogue is further enhanced by the fact that Anna makes the assertion when she thinks Tom does not hear her. Though he adopts a conventional association of little girls with poultry, Lawrence makes an important revision: while, according to Anita Schorsch, Victorian educators "saw in ducks, chickens, and other barnyard animals a natural way to stimulate benevolence in the child" because of the birds' quiet dependency,[12] Lawrence makes the encounter with the noisy geese into a trial from which Anna emerges with a new identity.

Robert Langbaum calls attention to a crucial means by which Lawrence conflates the spiritual and the physical. He notes, "When

---

12. Schorsch, *Images of Childhood,* 123.

Lawrence uses animals in his fiction, he moves from people to animals to gods as a way of moving from the ordinary to the archetypal or mythical self, then back to a reconstructed individuality that oscillates between animal and god."[13] In this novel, while the use of animals is less clearly symbolic than in later works like *Women in Love* or "The Fox" or *St. Mawr*, true relations are often discovered in the presence of animals, and—more significantly—the true self partakes of both the gods and the animals. For instance, Tom Brangwen realizes that he must marry Lydia Lensky while he is sitting up with the ewes at lambing time. Lawrence again juxtaposes the human world with the animal in the history of Anna's acceptance of Tom as her father.

It is a small perversity of childish behavior that Anna tells the geese, but not Tom himself, that Mr. Brangwen is her father now. Such telling moments together with technical control of the realistic mode, which we seldom credit to *The Rainbow*, give us a view of the child "shoved away," as Lawrence said of Cézanne's apples, without the interpretive screen of authorial metaphors and verbalized consciousness to which authors—including Lawrence himself—ordinarily turn to probe the mind of a child. Henry James, for instance, who first thought of restricting the narration of *What Maisie Knew* "to what the child might be conceived to have *understood*," soon decided that his "subject strangled in that extreme of rigour" and allowed himself to "stretch the matter to what my wondering witness materially and inevitably *saw*."[14]

In holding himself to his task James achieves a remarkable child. Still, Maisie and indeed all of James's children differ from Lawrence's, it seems to me, in that James grants them a special condition of innocence that allows them to "see" more truly than most adults, and yet to be victimized through their lack of corruption. Despite Henry James's interest in the consequences of her growing consciousness, Maisie exists within a discourse that is explicitly a literary game. A kind of secret code allows the adult reader to understand what the innocent child sees but does not recognize: adulterous sexuality in *What Maisie Knew*, manipulative greed in "The Pupil." The child remains James's and our plaything because the game for him and for us is always to break the code of what the child sees into what we understand. Lawrence respects the child as a separate human being, perhaps different from adults in her perceptions, but

13. Langbaum, *Mysteries*, 266.
14. James, *The Art of the Novel*, 145.

neither an inferior creature nor a moral superior. Like Tom himself, Lawrence's style is " . . . careful of her, careful to recognize her and to give [itself] to her disposal" (*Rainbow*, 66–67).

Lawrence's respectful style is finely calibrated to show how farm life and Tom himself heal and transform Anna's soul. Her intense attachment to her mother, which has been a source of pain and distorted emotion to her because of Lydia's unresponsiveness, is now countered by the fecund atmosphere of the farm. Tom, having largely satisfied his own craving for distant, foreign, conscious knowledge in his marriage to Lydia, becomes a part of the farm. The first movements Anna makes toward him are toward the farm's impersonal fecundity rather than toward the individual man. Such an impersonal attraction is in keeping with Lawrence's intention of finding what the character "*is*—inhumanly, physiologically, materially—according to the use of the word: but for me, what she *is* as a phenomenon (or as representing some greater, inhuman will), instead of what she feels according to the human conception" (*Letters*, 2:183). Making a rare venture into her consciousness, Lawrence describes how Anna moves within the shelter of Tom, almost as if he were a warm chair by the hearth: "And gradually, without knowing it herself, she clung to him, in her lost, childish desolate moments, when it was good to creep up to something big and warm, and bury her little self in his big, unlimited being" (*Rainbow*, 66). Even when Anna is nearly grown up, just before she meets Will, she maintains this consciousness of Tom as an almighty natural force: "The only man she knew was her father; and, as he was something large, looming, a kind of Godhead, he embraced all manhood for her, and other men were just incidental" (*Rainbow*, 100).

Although Anna's relationship with her stepfather has many peaceful moments, it has, nonetheless, the sexual pattern that Lawrence described for all emotional and creative developments: "every natural crisis in emotion or passion or understanding comes from this pulsing, frictional to-and-fro, which works up to culmination."[15] In tracing the development of the relationship of Tom and Anna, Lawrence incorporates a similar to-and-fro movement into the rapid shifting of scenes and moods. Thus, the conflict on the wedding morning is followed by the appeasement of the geese. Anna's nestling in Tom's large being is followed by a nonsensical but earnest exchange of name-calling:

15. Lawrence, foreword to *Women in Love*, 486.

Brangwen, good-humoured but impatient, spoiled by Tilly, was an easy blusterer. If for a few minutes he upset the household with his noisy impatience, he found at the end the child glowering at him with intense black eyes, and she was sure to dart forward her little head, like a serpent, with her biting:

"Go away."

"I'm *not* going away," he shouted, irritated at last. "Go yourself—hustle—stir thysen—hop." And he pointed to the door.

The child backed away from him, pale with fear. Then she gathered her courage, seeing him become patient.

"We don't live with *you*," she said, thrusting forward her little head at him: "You—you're—you're a bomakle."

"A what?" he shouted.

Her voice wavered—but it came—

"A bomakle."

"Ay, an' you're a comakle."

She meditated. Then she hissed forward her head.

"I'm not."

"Not what?"

"A comakle."

"No more am I a bomakle."

He was really cross. (*Rainbow,* 67)

The intensity of Anna's moods suggests the distortions of her infancy and the drama of her sudden immersion in a new life with new people; however, the rapid shifting of moods—"She was curiously hard, and then passionately tender-hearted" (*Rainbow,* 67)—is both natural for her age and a quality evinced by Lawrence's successful adult characters. Lawrence's great capability to envision the scene as the child would—and yet without sentimental indulgence—is the remarkable thing here. The mood shifts noted by an adult are not sudden to the child, who, until the age of five or so, lives in a perpetual present tense. In *Fantasia* Lawrence describes the push-and-pull development of a child from dependence to independence in terms of sympathetic and voluntary fields of consciousness. In the following example he describes how a child learns to walk, a twofold action analogous to Anna's effort to learn to live at the Marsh: "The motion of walking, like the motion of breathing, is twofold. First a sympathetic cleaving to the earth with the foot: then the voluntary rejection, the spurning, the kicking away, the exultance in power and freedom" (*FU,* 86). Anna engages in the cleaving and spurning with each of her parents; the pattern is not simple, but its general direction is, I think, toward equilibrium (not stasis) in balanced movement. Her response to her mother remains intense and sensitive because Lydia herself has been unstable:

But always in the child was some anxious connection with the mother. So long as Mrs Brangwen was all right, the little girl played about and took very little notice of her. But corn-harvest went by, the autumn drew on, and the mother, the later months of her pregnancy beginning, was strange and detached, Brangwen began to knit his brows, the old, unhealthy uneasiness, the unskinned susceptibility came on the child again. (*Rainbow*, 68–69)

"Unskinned susceptibility" is the key to Anna. She needs the security, the covering (material and spiritual) that Tom offers, but she is afraid to trust anyone but her mother—who has herself been unreliable. To a great extent the relationship that develops between Tom and Anna is a response to the mother's attitude toward Anna. Critic Lydia Blanchard observes that as a mother Lydia Brangwen remains aloof from her children; Blanchard offers the following explanation:

Lydia . . . is so self-contained that there is little overt demonstration of her love for Anna. Lydia's role is primarily one of protector for her child, a role stemming in part at least from her own precarious background . . . Having lost two children, she cuts herself off from any strong demonstration of love to Anna. Anna's response is first a fierce period of jealous battling with the step-father for what there is of her mother's affections.[16]

Although Blanchard is correct that Anna battles for her mother's affections, I have already cited several passages illustrating that Tom is quite invulnerable to Anna's attack and thus there is no battle line to be drawn.

It seems to me that the strongest hours of Tom's being may be detected in his supposedly tangential relations with Anna during the first year of his marriage. Were he to allow the child to undermine his confidence by her jealousy, she would damage the entire family's emerging balance. Denied a focus for her jealousy, Anna instead careens rather wildly between moods and people.

Tom's reply in the exchange quoted below may seem crude to us. Our modern romanticism would have us believe that children should be protected from hearing about social and economic inequality, but Tom's remark is the kind of nonmental, pragmatic response that Lawrence recommends. It would not do for him to grovel before Anna by speaking of his love and solicitude for her. Rather, he must "forget utterly that there is such a thing as emotional reciprocity. But never forget [his] own honour as an adult individual towards a

16. Lydia Blanchard, "Mothers and Daughters in D. H. Lawrence: *The Rainbow* and Selected Shorter Works," 80–81.

small individual. It is a question of honour, not of love" (*FU*, 115). Lawrence's own laconic comment, "So they drew nearer together," confirms the rightness of Tom's attitude:

> "My mother *doesn't* live here."
> "Oh, ay?"
> "I want her to go away."
> "Then want's your portion," he replied laconically.
> So they drew nearer together. (*Rainbow*, 67–68)

For Anna the most important relationship, it will turn out, is this one with her stepfather, Tom Brangwen. When his dead body is brought to her home years later, she knows that he "had been to her the image of power and strong life"; in death he has still "the majesty of the inaccessible male" (*Rainbow*, 232–33).

Anna's resentment of Tom, their bantering together, and her gradual acceptance of him bring them to a personal attachment during Lydia's pregnancy. During these months, Tom feels "like a broken arch thrust out sickeningly from support." As a result, "to the little girl for her sympathy and her love, he appealed with all his power to the small Anna. So soon they were like lovers, father and child" (*Rainbow*, 62). In *Fantasia* Lawrence vehemently opposes any kind of demanding personal relationship between parent and child. Yet Tom, as we already know from his sensitive, honorable treatment of Anna during the first months of his marriage, is anything but a vulturine man turning upon an innocent female child to satisfy his repressed sexual desires. Rather, he and Anna are the bewildered members of a family without their linking member. Lydia is unable to do other than depose both of them in order to concentrate on her struggle to accept the child in her womb: it "needed so much life to begin afresh, after she has lost so lavishly" (*Rainbow*, 63). Once the baby Tom is born, Lydia is more content and less haunted by old fears from her life in Poland. Although husband and wife resume their sexual relations, an aloofness remains between them that lasts for two years until Lydia brings about a glorious reconsummation of the marriage. It is during this two-year period, when Anna is five and six years of age, that the crucial intimacy between Tom and Anna unfolds. Several critics, particularly Peter Balbert, have noted incestuous undertones in their relations and yet found themselves—rightly—uncomfortable with the term *incest*. Balbert, adopting Lawrentian diction, speaks of Tom's "dangerously sympathetic relationship with his stepdaughter."[17]

---

17. Balbert, *Psychology of Rhythm*, 42.

What are we, then, to make of the statement, which has been something of a red alert for many critics, that Tom and Anna were "like lovers"?

At least in part because of that phrase, the relationship of Tom and his stepdaughter Anna has received more critical attention than that of any other parent-child pair in Lawrence's novels except Paul and Gertrude Morel—which is to say that a handful of critics have devoted a few paragraphs to the subject.[18] Balbert, in his seminal study of form and rhythm in *The Rainbow,* writes: "Anna and Ursula's first task, as both metaphorical embryos and young children, will be the severance of the corrosive contacts with their fathers."[19]

For Anna the close involvement with her father is anything but corrosive. The eventual effect on Anna of the larger, more balanced family constellation that results from her mother's marriage and birth of little Tom is that she

> ceased to have so much anxiety for her mother . . . at last her little life settled on its own swivel, she was not more strained and distorted to support her mother. She became childish, not so abnormal, not charged with cares she could not understand. The charge of the mother, the satisfying of the mother, had devolved elsewhere than on her. Gradually the child was freed. She became an independent, forgetful little soul, loving from her own centre. (*Rainbow,* 79)

Elaborating upon Tom's reliance upon Anna's affections, Balbert finds that the relationship between Anna and Tom is "dangerously sympathetic":

> Between periods of his emasculated, "clipped-arch" condition, and the baptism to another life described above [the reconsummation, *Rainbow,* 90], Tom compensates for the strained relationship with his wife by establishing a dangerously sympathetic relationship with his stepdaughter Anna. With the achievement of relative stability between Tom and Lydia, Anna is relieved of her pressures as surrogate wife, and she looks up to see a miniature rainbow.[20]

---

18. George H. Ford, *Double Measure: A Study of the Novels and Stories of D. H. Lawrence,* 141; Langbaum, *Mysteries,* 308–9; Balbert *Psychology of Rhythm;* F. R. Leavis, *D. H. Lawrence: Novelist,* chap. 3; Richard Swigg, *Lawrence, Hardy, and American Literature,* chaps. 5–6. Only Balbert scrutinizes the relationship carefully. Swigg has marvelously suggestive comments on both Anna and Ursula Brangwen as well as on Winifred Crich. The other writers pay homage to the beauty of the barn scene, and Langbaum comments somewhat more extensively on its naturalness and lack of sentimentality.

19. Balbert, *Psychology of Rhythm,* 20.

20. Ibid., 42–43.

Thus we must ask whether the relationship between Tom and Anna is a dangerous one that requires severing, or whether, as I shall argue, a therapeutic one that transforms itself when Tom and Anna's need for it is lessened.

Both George H. Ford and Mark Spilka identify a tendency of modern literature to prefer the sexual and fear the sentimental in literary treatments of children. Ford regrets that modern readers can better appreciate a Lolita than a Little Nell and praises the "sureness of touch in [Lawrence's] portrayal of fathers and daughters. . . . the trifling incidents as well as the major encounters of such relationships are presented with insight and tenderness." Ford is quick to defend Lawrence from the charges of sentimentality, also frequently leveled against Dickens, that seem to lurk about any literary representation of the young. Ford relates an anecdote about a friend of his who was disturbed by his daughter's forthcoming marriage. When his friend asked Ford what he could read to help him with his difficulty, Ford recommended chapter 4 of *The Rainbow*. The friend was relieved and comforted to find his own feelings so well described. Ford concludes that Tom's attachment to Anna is perfectly normal. Spilka also uses Little Nell and Lolita as examples in his argument that while the Victorians were guilty of repressing sexuality, our culture is guilty of repressing domestic tenderness. In both cases, Spilka claims, there is "the same fear of sexual and emotional personhood in adult women. . . . The chief difference between the old and new versions of this regressive myth is that Nabokov's narrator denies the little girl's affective innocence . . . until the final pages." Nabakov's attitude, Spilka argues, is a "form of reverse sentimentality." Perhaps fear of sentimentality may also be understood as a reason for emphasizing incest motives in the relationship of Tom and Anna.[21] I think the issue is more complex than Ford suggests, but not as alarming as Balbert's terms "dangerously sympathetic relationship" and "surrogate wife" would imply.

Lawrence himself always firmly resisted the concept of an incest motive in children. He believed, though, that the incest wish is an aberration caused by the parents, particularly mothers (such as his own and Gertrude Morel) who demanded too much spiritual and sentimental response from their children and thus prematurely awakened their sexual responses:

21. Spilka, "On the Enrichment of Poor Monkeys," 176–77; Ford, *Double Measure*, 141, 144.

Instead of leaving the child with its own limited but deep and incomprehensible feelings, the parent, hopelessly involved in the sympathetic mode of selfless love, and spiritual love-will, stimulates the child into a consciousness which does not belong to it, on the one plane, and robs it of its own spontaneous consciousness and freedom on the other plane. (*FU,* 151)

Lawrence maintained that mothers who seek a spiritual love relationship with their children inevitably produce a premature and wrongly directed awakening of the child's sexual circuit and "derangement" of the natural systems of consciousness, promoting a "false relation" between parent and child that is a masquerade of adult love. In fact, the mother in such cases actually "bullies" the child while seeming to idealize love. Incest is, then, a logical result of an excessively sympathetic relation between parent and child. Like Freud's, Lawrence's theoretical discussion focuses on the problem as it involves adolescent boys. Neither author is helpful on the subject of female oedipalization, and, unfortunately, Lawrence never had an opportunity to react to Freud's earlier seduction theory. Certainly the incestuous exploitation of sons by mothers that Lawrence describes sounds more threatening than the fictionally enacted situation between Anna and Tom, or even that between Ursula and Will. Each of these daughters is emotionally and sexually formed by her relation to her father, but I would not say either is crippled by him.[22] Quite the contrary, in Anna's case. Anna's sexual and maternal confidence as an adult are probably the result of the strong individuality she maintained in her relations with her stepfather, combined with her mother's aristocratic temperament and spiritual aloofness. Anna's scorn for her husband and his spiritual longings, her compulsion about motherhood, bespeak not a failure as a wife, but rather a failure of the world to challenge a woman of her quality.

The drama of Anna's childhood, then, does not support a Freudian model. Her attraction to Tom must be seen in terms of the family dynamics, of the confluence of relationships between the four family members. Thus, Anna's unfixed nature and Lawrence's understanding of family relationships require that Lawrence see her from a variety of angles. Lighted from this variety of angles, she becomes, as it were, a prism that creates the rainbow of her energetic, unformed being. By using this prismatic style of characterization Law-

22. Lawrence did, however, develop the theme of a daughter damaged by an oversympathetic connection with her father in a late short story, "The Princess," in *The Princess and Other Stories* (1925).

rence avoids potentially sentimental commitment to the child's point of view that results from many first-person accounts of family disruption. In *Jane Eyre* or *David Copperfield,* for instance, the threatening aspect of the adult environment is effectively—and wonderfully—enhanced by the author's restriction to David's or Jane's perspective. But Lawrence's hope for the novel opposes the personal, particularly the personal that refers to the writer's "specific case." He rejects the precious and the exaggerated in favor of "genuine relationships—which are always *new.*"[23] Robert Langbaum, praising Lawrence for avoiding sentimentality in "the most beautiful account of father-daughter love [Tom and Anna's] and the most beautiful portrait of a child in the English novel" notes the quality of "energy" that Lawrence evokes in the creation of Anna. Lawrence avoids sentimentality, Langbaum argues, because he "pitches the child's life at the appropriate phase of identity; he treats her as a kind of energy. Sentimentality comes from treating as individual and rational emotions that are impersonal and generated by external forces."[24]

While the energy Anna exhibits is not personal in the sense of emanating from a well-defined ego, it is assuredly individual. Lawrence's avoidance of sentimentality in the portrait of Tom and Anna owes as much to her separate, individual being, which persists at her core, resisting sentimentalization *despite* the effects of external forces upon her, as it does to Lawrence's understanding of her child's sensibility—what Langbaum calls pitching her at the right level of identity. Langbaum's notion of Anna as a "kind of energy" helps explain the commensurate insistence and volubility of her presence. There *is* something impersonal about her emotions in that they exist at a level deeper than that of the social intercourse between personalities.[25]

In *The Rainbow* Lawrence is weaving a great many strands of consciousness into the family pattern and asking the reader to at-

23. Lawrence, "Morality and the Novel" (first version), in *Study of Thomas Hardy,* 242.

24. Langbaum, *Mysteries,* 308–9.

25. Robert Langbaum, in "Lawrence and Hardy," calls attention to Lawrence's achievements in the analytical study of the unconscious, and finds that Lawrence expanded upon and attempted to complete Thomas Hardy's movement away from social reality in the novel and toward a deep psychological mode. Lawrence, Langbaum points out, wrote his "carbon identity" letter on the same day he announced his "Study of Thomas Hardy." The roots of Lawrence's transition from a realistic to a mythical mode, Langbaum convincingly finds, are in the work of Hardy.

tend to all of them with almost equal attention—or, at any rate, to be willing to shift attention and moral support fluidly from one character to another. Harry T. Moore, taking the germ of his idea from Lawrence's June 5, 1914, letter to Edward Garnett, makes a valuable comparison of Lawrence's repetitive prose style within sentences to both the painting technique of "simultaneism" used by some futurists and cubists and Henry James's "law of successive aspects."[26] Lawrence adopts a similar approach to the figure and character of Anna. Using the repetitive style within the larger framework of paragraphs and chapters, he presents her first as a witness to her mother's courtship, then as a focal point of the marriage within the complex web of relations involving her mother, Tom, Tilly, and even the farm animals. It is impossible to make a judgment on the relations of Tom and Anna, for instance, without considering the influences, past and present, of other characters on each of them.

This simultaneous effect becomes most evident in the barn scene. Although much that is important in this episode does not occur in the barn, the epithet appropriately emphasizes the revisionary nature of this Lawrentian nativity scene, wherein light focuses not on the mother and infant but on the father and stepchild. The whole household figures in this climactic night of the birth of young Tom, as each member of it confronts the urgent necessity of birth. Lawrence no longer takes his time with each family member—now all the characters are orchestrated together. The central event occurring upstairs but always present in everyone's mind is Lydia's labor; with this physical event, nothing can be compromised. The confinement imposes on Anna an incomprehensibly absolute separation from her mother. She has never before, not even on the wedding morning, been forbidden her mother's company. The laboring mother's cries alternate with Anna's refrain of panic, "I want my mother," a cry that is repeated an irritating nine times in the scene.

Everyone has seen children display such useless persistence, often over very trivial desires or incidents. Here Lawrence combines a realistic portrayal of the common temper tantrum with the symbolism of childbirth. That, I think, is the genius of this scene. Though the cause of woe is always real enough to the child having an hysterical attack, a trivial event as cause would belittle Anna to the reader. The gravity and urgency of this occasion validate Anna's feeling at the same time that they display the futility of it. Tom's

26. Harry T. Moore, "The Prose of D. H. Lawrence," in Harry T. Moore and Robert L. Partlow, eds., *D. H. Lawrence: The Man Who Lived,* 246.

response is stern and angry, but it is not gratuitous because he too is feeling extraordinary emotions about the ensuing birth. Thus, Tilly's kindhearted, reasonable efforts fail before the angry, unconscious, but appropriate actions of Tom. The sound of his voice introduces a new rhythm to the tedious counterpoint of Lydia's moan and Anna's shriek:

> "You must come and be undressed," he said, in a quiet voice that was thin with anger.
> And he reached his hand and grasped her. He felt her body catch in a convulsive sob. But he too was blind, and intent, irritated into mechanical action. He began to unfasten her little apron. She would have shrunk from him, but could not. So her small body remained in his grasp, while he fumbled at the little buttons and tapes, unthinking, intent, unaware of anything but the irritation of her. Her body was held taut and resistant, he pushed off the little dress and the petticoats, revealing the white arms. She kept stiff, overpowered, violated, he went on with his task. And all the while, she sobbed, choking:
> "I want my mother." (*Rainbow*, 73)

Quite understandably and predictably, critics have emphasized the rapelike quality of this scene. Ford observes its similarity to William Carlos Williams's short story "The Use of Force," noting that the action in Williams's story is represented as a "violation, almost a rape."[27] Balbert offers a more detailed and more psychoanalytically influenced reading of the scene and of the entire relationship between Tom and Anna. He argues that it "is essential *not* to disapprove of Tom as he rips off her clothes—and tears her from her mother's womb. . . . The scene is awesome and brutal . . . but it is not perverted and not even 'sensual' except in the obvious way that many intimate moments between father and daughter have the healthy momentum of sexual inter-play."[28] Balbert rightly justifies Tom's behavior and defends his frustration; nonetheless, the language of his very defense of Tom slants his interpretation toward rape. He quotes the words and phrases that diminish Anna and brutalize Tom—" 'little apron', 'small body', 'little dress'—all of it 'grasped', 'pushed', and 'violated' by a father"—and neglects terms that work the other way, to suggest the resistant strength and consequent annoyance of Anna and the helplessness of Tom's anger: "he too was blind," "he fumbled"; "the irritation of her," "her body held

27. Ford, *Double Measure*, 142.
28. Balbert, *Psychology of Rhythm*, 46.

taut and stiff." Nothing in Lawrence's diction is as strong as Balbert's "he rips off her clothes," and the word "violate" is used by Lawrence to describe Anna's feeling more than Tom's intention.

What I wish to suggest here is that the image of rape is very near to mind for Lawrence, Ford, Balbert, and every other reader *not* because this scene is like a rape (with overtly sexual content) but rather because a rape and this scene are alike in their anger. In *Against Our Will,* Susan Brownmiller argues that rape is a deeply violent crime, not primarily a sexual act, directed against women by men who, for complex and often well-disguised reasons, hate women. With this adjustment of perception, one may recognize in the powerfulness of the undressing scene a reference to some essential offense in the attempt of the child to hold herself separate from her surroundings (recalling that her resistance began before Tom had even entered the room, in a struggle with Tilly).[29]

The conflict that develops, then, is between Anna's *will* to be independent (expressed, ironically and characteristically, as a wish to be with her mother when she chooses to be) and Tom's will to be the master of his strangely foreign, female household (and hence of himself). Lawrence describes Anna: "The child was now incapable of understanding, she had become a little, mechanical thing of fixed will. She wept, her body convulsed, her voice repeating the same cry." The paralyzed willfulness of Anna's condition is emphasized by the near-repetition of those phrases three paragraphs later: "She stood, with fixed, blind will, resistant, a small, convulsed, unchangeable thing weeping ever and repeating the same phrase" (*Rainbow,* 73–74). The recurring words describing Anna in this scene are from a vocabulary that opposes life and connotes Lawrence's disapproval: "automatic," "wincing," "panic-stricken," "back to the wall," "sobbed distractedly," "mechanical," "maddening blindness of the voice," "stiff, denying body."

I have said that Anna, in contrast with Lawrence's definition of the well-balanced individual, is out-of-kilter, veering without control between overdependence and stubborn independence, particularly in relation with her mother. In *Psychoanalysis* Lawrence finds the manifestation of the infant's "asserted isolation" in the

---

29. Another reply to those who interpret the scene as a rape (and rape as a primarily sexual act) may be borrowed from Lawrence's statement at the beginning of attack on Freud: "We are bound to admit that an element of sex enters into all human activity. But so does an element of greed, and of many other things" (*FU,* 59).

scream and the stiffened back, both elements of Anna's behavior in the scene under discussion. In that essay Lawrence observes:

> Nothing acts more directly on the great primal nerve-centers than the screaming of an infant, this blind screaming negation of connections. It is the friction of irritation itself. Everybody is implicated . . . When a child screams with temper, it sends out from the lumbar ganglion the violent waves of frictional repudiation . . . The little back has amazing power once it stiffens itself. In the lumbar ganglion the unconscious now vibrates tremendously in the activity of sundering, separation. (*PU,* 23)

Anna's stiff, mechanical, screaming denial of interference is part of her resistance to incorporation in the Brangwen world. This psychological interpretation is undergirded by the fact that Anna's desire for her mother is literal as well as symbolic. Most children wish for their mothers at moments of anxiety; the fact that her anxiety arises from being told she may not see her mother, whose moans she can hear plainly, only complicates and strengthens her wish. When Tom comes downstairs, she briefly looks to him to intercede between her and Tilly, but he is not much aware of her:

> "I want my mother," she quavered.
> "Ay, she's badly," he said mildly, unheeding.
> She looked at him with lost, frightened eyes.
> "Has she got a headache?"
> "No, she's going to have a baby."
> The child looked round. He was unaware of her. She was alone again in terror.
> "I want my mother," came the cry of panic.
> "Let Tilly undress you," he said. "You're tired."
> There was another silence. Again the cry of labour.
> "I want my mother," rang automatically from the wincing, panic-stricken child, that felt cut off and lost in a horror of desolation. (*Rainbow,* 72)

It is a moot question, but one wonders whether Anna might have bypassed hysteria if Tom had seized her conscious attention a moment earlier. Instead, he sits "stiff" in his chair, "his brain going tighter. . . . aware only of the maddening sobbing" (*Rainbow,* 73).

By recrossing the room, Tom assumes new authority, literally taking on a task that he probably has not performed before: undressing the child, and symbolically taking charge of himself and his home. It is important to recognize that in doing so, he directs his anger usefully rather than to spanking or otherwise abusing Anna. I would argue, despite the underlying analogy to rape that the read-

er's mind may suggest, that Tom does not betray his essential kind-
ness even in the roughest parts of the scene. While Tom's feelings
are violent with anger, his actions are not:

> He lifted one foot after the other, pulled off slippers and socks. She
> was ready.
> "Do you want a drink?" he asked.
> She did not change. Unheeding, uncaring, she stood on the sofa,
> standing back, alone, her hands shut and half lifted, her face, all tears,
> raised and blind. And through the sobbing and choking came the
> broken:
> "I—want—my—mother."
> "Do you want a drink?" he said again.
> There was no answer. He lifted the stiff, denying body between his
> hands. Its stiff blindness made a flash of rage go through him. He would
> like to break it.
> He set the child on his knee, and sat again in his chair beside the fire,
> the wet, sobbing, inarticulate noise going on near his ear. (*Rainbow,* 74)

Then, with an alternation of feeling that Lawrence believed essential to any true culmination of emotions, Tom becomes passive in his
anger. He withdraws himself and sits in a "daze," a "torpor" with
Anna still crying on his knee: "A new degree of anger come over
him. What did it all matter? What did it matter if the mother talked
Polish and cried in labour, if this child were stiff with resistance,
and crying? Why take it to heart?" (*Rainbow,* 74). What happens to
Tom in these passages, what changes occur in his being? He has
suffered masculine helplessness before the fact of his wife in childbirth—a feeling that the event has nothing to do with himself. Then
he has, in the unconsciousness of anger, taken over the chore of
getting Anna into her nightclothes without being able to calm her.
Now, as he sits in a daze, his anger gone beyond caring, he links and
dismisses Anna's and her mother's cries: both foreign to him, both
beyond him. Finally in those moments of torpor, he seems to gather
himself together. When he emerges, it is as if he does so from the
other side of himself. In Lawrence's terms, he now acts from his
sympathetic rather than his voluntary centers. He merges with
Anna in the nurturant mode rather than opposing his will to hers.
His instinct and the requirement of caring for his livestock guide
him to the right action:

> His voice was queer and distant and calm. He looked at the child. She
> was beside herself now. He wanted her to stop, he wanted it all to stop,
> to become natural.
> "Come," he said, rising to turn away, "we'll go an' supper-up the
> beast."

He took a big shawl, folded her round, and went out into the kitchen for the lantern.

"You're never taking the child out, of a night like this," said Tilly.

"Ay, it'll quieten her," he answered.

It was raining. The child was suddenly still, shocked, finding the rain on its face, the darkness.

"We'll just give the cows their something-to-eat, afore they go to bed," Brangwen was saying to her, holding her close and sure. (*Rainbow*, 74–75)

Leo Bersani speaks of "self-cancelling expressions" in Lawrence's language: "A first term is never erased; but all thought that might use that term as a point of departure is paralyzed by the juxtaposition of another term which gives us an unthinkable phrase ["physical mind"]. . . . The narrative continues, but it thus manages to suggest its own arrest." This "enforced stillness" of thought represents spiritual stillness in a character.[30] Such a spiritual hiatus seems to occur in Tom during the interval he sits with Anna on his lap. Tom is neither more nor less himself in either his angry (voluntary) or his gentle (sympathetic) minutes. Anna begins to come out of her hysteria when Tom brings her out of the house—out of the range of her mother's labor and into the soothing rhythms of the farmyard. While adopting the conventional association of children with animals, Lawrence once again transcends the cliché. In fact, it appears that he searches out common experiences in order to transcend them, to show how the prosaic contains and reveals the profound. In doing so he creates impressionistic sensory images, so the reader has no doubt that this particular child is *literally* affected by the change of surroundings: "There was a trickling of water into the butt, a burst of rain-drops sputtering on to her shawl, and the light of the lantern swinging, flashing on a wet pavement and the base of a wet wall. Otherwise it was black darkness: one breathed darkness" (*Rainbow*, 75).

Lawrence gives us, as it were, real cows in an imaginary barn. The barn is imaginary because it is, for the length of this episode, the pastoral world of literary convention, a world apart from human time and struggle against natural elements: "Outside there was the driving rain, inside the softly-illuminated stillness and calmness of the barn." Anna recovers her composure and becomes able to see outside herself again: "The child, all wonder, watched what he did.

---

30. Leo Bersani, *A Future for Astyanax: Character and Desire in Literature*, 162–63.

A new being was created in her for the new conditions" (*Rainbow,* 75). As Tom feeds the cows while carrying Anna, Lawrence continues to re-create the sounds and movements of the bovine environment, making the reader somewhat more conscious of these than Tom would be, even though ostensibly they are his observations. The detailed nature of the sensory description is directed toward an outsider, someone like Anna herself, and the reader's experience is like the child's. The rhythm of Tom's movements and "a contented, soothing sound, a long snuffing as the beast ate in silence" (*Rainbow,* 75) assist the precocious Anna in subsiding into her natural, childish self. Langbaum overstates the case when he says that "attuned to the rhythm of the cows breathing, [Tom and Anna] seal a union with each other through their pantheistic sense of the One Life," yet he is correct in pointing out, "Once again we see the pattern of rootedness and transcendence—the sound of the god rising from the sound of the animal."[31] For Lawrence, the god resides in the true self, and so the connection with the god may be achieved through recovery of one's child-self.

Even Tom, absorbed by the peace of the animals feeding, moves in a reverie toward childhood: "He looked down at the silky folds of the paisley shawl. It reminded him of his mother. She used to go to church in it. He was back again in the old irresponsibility and security, a boy at home." Lawrence counterpoints Tom's reverie with Anna's relaxation into sleep, displaying the new correspondence between their two natures: "As she sank to sleep, his mind became blank" (*Rainbow,* 76). The logical fallacy of *ad hoc ergo propter hoc* here becomes the emotional truth. Tom and Anna are here meeting one another in the kind of balanced relation that Lawrence later described for the true family, "a group of wireless stations, all adjusted to the same, or very much the same, vibration . . . [in a] long strange *rapport,* a sort of life-unison" (*FU,* 72).

In this scene Tom and Anna find, however briefly, a "true pole of magnetic rest in another human being" (*PU,* 45). Even with its pastoral element, the episode is not, for Tom, an escape from manliness or responsibility. Rather, it is a respite that strengthens him to return to his wife. As he carries Anna to the house and puts her in bed in "the room he had had before he married . . . he remembered what it was to be a young man, untouched" (*Rainbow,* 77). Thus Tom puts himself—the child he used to be—to sleep. The remembered sound of the owls that used to frighten Tom as a boy now becomes a

31. Langbaum, *Mysteries,* 308.

psychic link for him between his boyhood and the present. A few pages earlier he feels himself divided between a "lower, deeper self" that suffers with Lydia and a mind that "remembered the sound of owls that used to fly around the farmstead when he was a boy" (*Rainbow,* 71). Now, after feeding the animals and undergoing the vital contact with Anna, Tom realizes what was not quite clear before even to the reader: that the cry of the woman in labor and the cry of the owls are *the same:* "The child slept, pushing her small fists from the shawl. He could tell the woman her child was asleep. But he must go to the other landing. He started. There was the sound of the owls—the moaning of the woman. What an uncanny sound! It was not human—at least to a man" (*Rainbow,* 77). The development and evolution of Tom's psyche through the encounter with Anna is indicated by his more penetrating "hearing": he can now hear the owl in Lydia's moan and Lydia in the owl's cry—what were unconnected sounds before now have the music of true metaphor. Likewise, he is himself more whole, finding, as he stands before his laboring wife, harmony among the boy he was, the husband he is, and the father he is becoming: "She looked at him as a woman in childbirth looks at the man who begot the child in her; an impersonal look in the extreme hour, female to male. Her eyes closed again. A great scalding peace went over him, burning his heart and his entrails, passing off into the infinite" (*Rainbow,* 77). Tom Brangwen, from whom Anna hid as from "the fact of the man" on the morning after her mother wed him, has, in the course of this chapter, become a father to both his infant son and his stepdaughter.

In *Fantasia* Lawrence makes his case for fathers by claiming that the original sperm cell becomes the infant's solar plexus and insisting that the father, though not necessarily intimately involved with the baby, is nonetheless its greater support and the equilibrator of the baby's relations with its mother. This sperm theory, I think, evinces Lawrence's wish to prove male superiority, a theme that provides an agenda for much of his work in the twenties. If the basis of paternal relation is, as Lawrence wishes to claim, in the literal male nucleus that "still lies sparkling and potent within the solar plexus . . . the tie of blood" (*FU,* 70), then it is hard to know what to make of Tom's success as a father to Anna, who is not his biological child. Nonetheless, Tom Brangwen more than fills the prescription Lawrence gave fathers in *Fantasia:* "The business of the father, in all this incipient child-development, is to stand outside as a final authority and make the necessary adjustments. . . . the father, from his distance, supports, protects, nourishes his child, and it is ultimately on the remote but powerful father-love that the infant rests, in a rest which is beyond mother-love" (*FU,* 87). Tom does indeed protect and nourish Anna, but not from a distance. From the moment he crosses the room to undress his stepdaughter—because she cannot stop crying and he cannot stand hearing her cry—the two are engaged in a relationship that Lawrence himself, still heedless of incest theories and sperm theories, does not hesitate to call, simply, father and daughter. By doing so he binds himself to few of the conventions about the range of emotions that may exist within such a relation. Thus it is that the "father spark" touches Anna Lensky the child, and prepares her to become a Brangwen, as in the title of *The Rainbow*'s following chapter, "The Girlhood of Anna Brangwen."

Anna's formal childhood, and the chapter entitled "The Childhood of Anna Lensky," ends with the first arching of the rainbow symbol in the novel. F. R. Leavis noticed many years ago that this arch/pillar image marks the full turn of Lawrence's attention from one generation to the next, "the point in the action at which we begin to know that Anna will be a major representative of our second cycle of life."[32] Anna will shortly be seen as a mother, the mother of *The Rainbow*'s eventual heroine Ursula, and of the sister heroines of Lawrence's next novel, *Women in Love.*

Before looking at the episodes that bring her to the happy position of freedom beneath the arch, one must consider that image:

> Anna's soul was put at peace between them. She looked from one to the other, and she saw them established to her safety, and she was free. She played between the pillar of fire and the pillar of cloud in confidence, having the assurance on her right hand and the assurance on her left. She was no longer called upon to uphold with her childish might the broken end of the arch. Her father and mother now met to the span of the heavens, and she, the child, was free to play in the space beneath, between. (*Rainbow,* 91)

This image of free, playful childhood under the protection of a father and mother who are evenly balanced in their relationship with each other marks the end of a two-year period in which, as we have seen, the family has been seeking such equilibrium. For Anna that equilibrium is achieved when she recaptures some of the childishness she lost when she was alone with her mother, and when she has some experiences of the outside world that shape her adult character.

32. Leavis, *D. H. Lawrence,* 125.

Anna is eager for that world now because she has overcome her jealousy of her stepfather; he, in turn, relies upon her for the companionship his wife does not give him. After the birth of young Tom, Lawrence tells us, "Tom never loved his own son as he loved his stepchild Anna" (*Rainbow,* 78). She, in turn, seeing her mother content with the infant, "Of her own choice . . . loved Brangwen most, or most obviously" (*Rainbow,* 79). Lawrence provides only a few episodes to illustrate the two years between the birth of Tom and the raising of the arch/rainbow. After the raising of the arch, a quick summary of Anna as a schoolgirl leads to her meeting of Will Brangwen. These few episodes involve Anna in movement and social circumstances beyond Marsh Farm.

Anna's passage to maturity is conspicuously marked by a sort of aggressive childishness. In her "little life together" with Tom, Anna actually regains her "spontaneous consciousness and freedom":

> He remembered for her all the little nursery rhymes and childish songs that lay forgotten at the bottom of his brain.
> At first she thought them rubbish. But he laughed and she laughed. They became to her a huge joke. Old King Cole she thought was Brangwen. Mother Hubbard was Tilly, her mother was the old woman who lived in a shoe. It was a huge, it was a frantic delight to the child, this nonsense, after her years with her mother, after the poignant folk-tales she had had from her mother, which always troubled and mystified her soul. (*Rainbow,* 79–80)

Tom instinctively combines the sexual energy that we can recognize in Anna ("frantic delight") with his own enjoyment of childish things to give the child an opportunity to regress into the early childhood silliness she missed. He is motivated as much by his wife's keeping him at a distance as by any recognition of Anna's need. The unusual loverlike intensity of the relationship probably endangers Tom more than it does Anna, threatening him with what Balbert, in his overdetermined reading of the scenes, calls a "destructive and permanent need for his daughter."[33]

Anna begs Tom to take her on what seem to be extraordinary outings into the world of men during their years of particular closeness. Lawrence shows her new self-confidence as a child when she goes to the pub with Tom:

> The landladies paid court to her, in the obsequious way landladies have.
> "Well, little lady, an' what's your name?"

33. Balbert, *Psychology of Rhythm,* 48.

"Anna Brangwen," came the immediate, haughty answer.

"Indeed it is! An' do you like driving in a trap with your father?"

"Yes," said Anna, shy, but bored by these inanities.

She had a touch-me-not way of blighting the inane inquiries of grown-up people.

"My word, she's a fawce little thing," the landlady would say to Brangwen.

"Ay," he answered, not encouraging comments on the child. Then there followed the present of a biscuit, or a cake, which Anna accepted as her dues. (*Rainbow,* 81)

Anna's boredom with the inanities adults produce in their attempts to converse with children is the correct Lawrentian response to all false relations. Afterward she asks her father, " 'What does she say, that I'm a fawce little thing?' " but does not understand his answer, that it means she's " 'a sharp-shins.' Anna hesitated. She did not understand. Then she laughed at some absurdity she found" (*Rainbow,* 81). Her ability to turn her attention from what she does not understand to finding her own amusement indicates that she is losing that "unskinned sensibility" that made her vulnerable when she first came to Cossethay. The landlady, Anna intuitively recognizes, uses empty words and has no sincere interest in her as an individual. Tom, though he brings her where she hears such inanities, nonetheless protects her and fosters her growth by his own refusal to patronize her.

For Anna this phase of close attachment to her father is not one of dependency and development of specifically female identity, but rather a period that promotes her independence and anticipates the particular combination of indomitability and femaleness that marks her early maturity. Hence, she further challenges the conventional behavior of little girls in novels by insisting that her father take her to the market in Nottingham. This six-year-old girl who chooses to accompany her father to cattle markets rather than stay home on the farm with her mother and baby brother becomes the adult Anna. Here I think we may see Anna in training for the role of "Anna Victrix"—sure of herself and somewhat oblivious of and superior to the world of male activity.

Again however, Lawrence is sensitive to the child's rapid alternations of mood. Even though Anna has begged Tom to take her to market with him, she is quite miserable waiting for him in the refreshment booth while he does his business. That strange and apparently threatening environment encourages Lawrence to move into her mind and emphasize her isolation. For the first time, she is separated from both her mother and Tom, out of whose perspectives Lawrence has created his prismatic view of her. The first sustained rendering of Anna's consciousness from her own point of view occurs in the following passage:

> Farmers, butchers, drovers, dirty uncouth men from whom she shrank instinctively stared down at her as she sat on her seat, then went to get their drink, talking in unabated tones. All was big and violent about her.
> "Whose child met that be?" they asked of the barman.
> "It belongs to Tom Brangwen."
> The child sat on in neglect, watching the door for her father. He never came; many, many men came, but not he, and she sat like a shadow. She knew one did not cry in such a place. And every man looked at her inquisitively, she shut herself away from them. A deep, gathering coldness of isolation took hold on her. He was never coming back. She sat on, frozen, unmoving. (*Rainbow*, 82)

These moments of isolation in the midst of a rough male world toughen Anna until she gradually holds her own against the teasing of the men:

> She was very angry because Marriott, a gentleman-farmer from Ambergate, called her the little pole-cat.
> "Why, you're a pole-cat," he said to her.
> "I'm not," she flashed.
> "You are. That's just how a pole-cat goes."
> She thought about it.
> "Well, you're—you're—" she began.
> "I'm what?"
> She looked him up and down.
> "You're a bow-leg man."
> Which he was. There was a roar of laughter. They loved her that she was indomitable.
> "Ah," said Marriott. "Only a pole-cat says that."
> "Well, I *am* a pole-cat," she flamed. (*Rainbow*, 84)

The degree to which the men accept the anomaly of her presence in their society is illustrated by the influence Anna has on the fate of Nat-Nut, a crippled cretin with a cleft palate who sells nuts in the public houses. With the naturalistic portrayal that marks most of his characterizations of children, Lawrence shows Anna's outspoken revulsion from this man, who has until now been the object of the men's unkind, but perhaps inconsequential, mockery:

> "Why does he do that when he walks?"
> " 'He canna 'elp 'isself, Duckie, it's the make o' th' fellow.'"
> She thought about it, then she laughed nervously. And then she bethought herself, her cheeks flushed, and she cried:

"He's a *horrid* man."

"Nay, he's non horrid; he canna help it if he wor struck that road."

But when poor Nat came wambling in again, she slid away. And she would not eat his nuts, if the men bought them for her. And when the farmers gambled at dominoes for them, she was angry.

"They are dirty-man's nuts," she cried.

So a revulsion started against Nat, who had not long after to go to the workhouse. (*Rainbow,* 84–85)

Lawrence suggests with the word "so" that Anna is the effective cause of Nat's banishment; as in many other instances in this novel, mere juxtaposition suggests cause and effect. Such a notion of causes is typical of children, and, as I suggested before, Lawrence's way of composing events retains something of the child's. Anna's intolerance for deformity is adopted by the men, as if her being a child sanctioned this scorn. Such intolerance is brought into the Brangwen family by Lydia and maintained by the women of the following generations. When her daughter Ursula is twelve, for instance, Anna honors Ursula's distaste for the "common school and the companionship of the village children," by sending Ursula to Grammar School in Nottingham, allowing her to escape from the "belittling circumstances of life, the little jealousies, the little differences, the little meannesses" (*Rainbow,* 245).

The superior attitude that Anna inherits from her mother and expresses in her objection to Nat is enhanced by her mother's connection with the Polish Baron Skrebensky. A visit to the Baron when Anna is about ten years of age is the subject of the other outing that illustrates Anna's initial movement beyond Marsh Farm. At this time Anna is, Lawrence tells us, "too much the centre of her own universe, too little aware of anything outside" (*Rainbow,* 92). This visit, where she accompanies her mother, widens her experience and provides a contrast to the rough atmosphere of the markets and public houses she experiences with her father. To Anna, it is a first encounter with anything different enough from home to seem objectively real:

The first *person* she met, who affected her as a real living person, whom she regarded as having definite existence, was Baron Skrebensky. . . . Anna was very much impressed by him. . . . Anna loved to watch him. . . . She felt a sense of freedom near him. . . . [He] represented to the child the real world, where kings and lords and princes moved and fulfilled their shining lives, whilst queens and ladies and princesses upheld the noble order. (*Rainbow,* 92–93)

Anna's response to the Baron echoes that of young Tom Brangwen to his one school friend and to the traveler at Matlock. But Anna is less dreamy than Tom. She feels that she has encountered a different sort of being, and Lawrence seconds that intuition, as he does not second Tom's: the Baron "went to the north of England expecting homage from the common people, for he was an aristocrat. He was roughly, even cruelly received. But he never understood it. He remained a fiery aristocrat. Only he had to learn to avoid his parishioners" (*Rainbow,* 93). The fiery blue eyes of the Baron that impress young Anna also confirm her identity with him: fieriness has been an epithet for Anna too—her hair is flamy, her temper fierce.

Anna makes the strangeness and superiority of this outsider a part of her own identity, while Tom longs for and yet is threatened by such fineness. For Anna the Baron becomes "a memory always alive." She is permanently marked by the idea he has enacted, that there is a noble world, to which she belongs, that is more real than Cossethay: "She kept an ideal: a free, proud lady absolved from the petty ties. . . . She would see such ladies in pictures: Alexandra, Princess of Wales, was one of her models. This lady was proud and royal, and stepped indifferently over all small, mean desires: so thought Anna, in her heart" (*Rainbow,* 95).

The desire to unite himself with exquisite, foreign beings whose experience extends beyond his own marked Tom Brangwen in his youth and drew him to Lydia Lensky. Now it kindles in him a desire to make a lady of his stepdaughter. It is odd, perhaps, but typical of Lawrence, that he sandwiches a bare statement of Tom's desire between two apparently unrelated episodes:

> So a revulsion started against Nat, who had not long after to go to the workhouse.
> *There grew in Brangwen's heart now a secret desire to make her a lady.* His brother Alfred, in Nottingham, had caused a great scandal by becoming the lover of an educated woman, a lady, the widow of a doctor. (emphasis added, *Rainbow,* 85)

By juxtaposing three apparently unrelated statements, Lawrence maps out Anna's development, a movement out of the ordinary life that tolerates Nat and toward the imagined nobler life represented by the Baron and by Alfred's mistress. These aspirations toward the noble foreshadow the appearance of Alfred's son, Will Brangwen, to court and marry Anna, and eventually the advent of Anton Skrebensky, the Baron's son, as Ursula Brangwen's first lover. In each case the young man is less than the imagined prince, but nonetheless carries with him an aura of nobility that increases his appeal to the Brangwen girl's mind and memory.

The earliest, most difficult years of Anna's childhood are eclipsed for many readers by the image of Anna as the happy offspring thriving beneath the "span of heavens" of her contented parents in the days before consciousness became a problem. Yet the many episodes that focus on Anna before she reaches the age of ten and goes off to the dame's school in Cossethay show that Lawrence brings his sense of the visionary nature of childhood *and* his realist's awareness of complex family relations to the portrait of Anna. The individuality with which he conceives this small girl will become even more evident in my next chapter, when I show how different from hers is the childhood of her daughter, Ursula.

Earlier I suggested that Lawrence's attitude toward children parallels Cézanne's attempt (as perceived by Lawrence) to let the apple in a still life "live of itself." Likewise, his portrait of Anna may be described by invoking his comment about another painter, Vincent Van Gogh. He says, "When Van Gogh paints sunflowers, he reveals, or achieves, the vivid relation between himself, as man, and the sunflower, as sunflower, at that quick moment of time."[34] Anna Lensky Brangwen is Lawrence's sunflower study. The relation between Lawrence and his creation is enormously flexible, full of air and light, with the result that the child stands revealed—a new individual in the world.

34. Lawrence, "Morality and the Novel," in *Study of Thomas Hardy,* 171.

The Spirit of Modern Childhood
5 Ursula Brangwen, Winifred Crich, Loerke

When Lawrence was beginning the draft of the novel called "The Sisters," which became *The Rainbow* and *Women in Love,* his intended subject for it was "woman becoming individual, self-responsible, taking her own initiative" (*Letters,* 2:165). Ursula Brangwen is, of course, the character who represents this independent modern woman. The story of her young womanhood occupies the second half of *The Rainbow,* and she is the Brangwen sister who marries the hero/Lawrence figure, Rupert Birkin, in *Women in Love.* She is also the first child of *The Rainbow*'s Anna Brangwen. In that novel Lawrence probes the sources of consciousness in her babyhood and then follows her development into a tenuously independent young woman.

The story of Ursula's childhood, related in the middle third of *The Rainbow,* differs markedly from that of her mother, Anna Lensky Brangwen, who appears as a little girl earlier in the novel. The role Lawrence has already prescribed for Ursula as the heroine of his double novel dictates the kind of childhood and youth she must have. In a letter to Edward Garnett, Lawrence explains that his plan to link Ursula (then called Ella) with Birkin requires her to have a love affair with someone else before she meets Rupert Birkin: "In the scheme of the novel I *must* have Ella get some experience before she meets her Mr. Birkin . . . tell me whether you think Ella would be possible, as she now stands, unless she had some experience of love and of men. I think, impossible" (*Letters,* 2:142). Lawrence assumes a linear view of character development here, even though he has the resulting woman in view before he creates the child. As a result of the exchange with Garnett, Skrebensky was brought in to replace a tepid Mr. Templeman as Ursula's first lover. Like the Skre-

121

bensky affair, Ursula's childhood is detailed in the novel to support Lawrence's idea of her as a woman. In composing the third state of his manuscript known as "The Wedding Ring," Lawrence added about two hundred pages devoted to Ella's childhood and girlhood.[1] Thus, the particular nature of Ursula's childhood derives not so much from Lawrence's conception of her parents' characters as from the demands of intense individuality and modernity that Lawrence had already determined would be part of her character in the later chapters of "The Sisters." Lawrence provides Ursula with an appropriate history, a myth of origins, for her role as the modern, independent woman in his study of "*the* problem of today, the establishment of a new relation, or the readjustment of the old one, between men and women" (*Letters,* 1:546).

As we already have seen, in handling childhood Lawrence yokes the realistic and the visionary. The yoking that results in *The Rainbow* is comparable to the combination of the *historical* and the *apocalyptic* that Frank Kermode finds in *Women in Love.*[2] By these terms Kermode means that the time-specific account of the two Brangwen sisters, their men, and their travels from Cossethay to the Alps embodies a revelation of the world in collapse that transcends particular historical time. I think that for the first half of *The Rainbow* what Kermode describes as the historical mode is more aptly termed the *domestic,* because the settings and events of this book are generally of the home and family. What Kermode calls apocalyptic I call the *generative* mode, meaning that Lawrence seeks to embody, within his account of ordinary events, a revelation of beginnings rather than endings, the first things, not the last. In the creation of Ursula's childhood, Lawrence's style stretches this visionary impulse further in a direction I would call *mythic.* As a result, the development of her consciousness is distinctly different from that of Anna's.

The scene in which Anna Brangwen tells her parents she is expecting her first child (Ursula) is a crucial example of this merging of the domestic and generative modes. The context is entirely ordinary: A disagreement with her husband, Will, has prevented Anna from giving the news of her pregnancy to him and she has turned to her parents instead. As they sit at the parents' kitchen table, her father reminds her that she may be as obstinate as her husband. When Will passes by on his way home from work, the family servant

1. Ross, *The Composition of "The Rainbow" and "Women in Love,"* 26.
2. Kermode, "D. H. Lawrence and the Apocalyptic Types," 121–51.

calls him in to join the group at the table and, reluctantly, he does so:

> They talked of trivial things. Through the open door the level rays of sunset poured in, shining on the floor. A grey hen appeared stepping swiftly in the doorway, pecking, and the light through her comb and her wattles made an oriflamme tossed here and there, as she went, her grey body was like a ghost.
>
> Anna, watching, threw scraps of bread, and she felt the child flame within her. She seemed to remember again forgotten, burning, far-off things. (*Rainbow*, 164–65)

Oriflamme, or *auriflamme,* originally referred to the orange or red-orange flag of the Abbey of St. Denis that was used as an inspirational banner by early French kings. Associated here with the comb and wattles of an ordinary chicken, the image transcends medieval quaintness and near-ludicrousness to magnify and beautify the fowl. Lawrence reveals a certain holiness in everyday life by sketching unmediated, mythlike connections between the evening light, the ghostly body of a hen with its comb like an aureole, and the movement of Ursula in Anna's womb. In the biblical event known as the Visitation, the child of Elisabeth leaps in her womb when her sister Mary visits her after the Annunciation. This sign of recognizing God is followed by Elisabeth's words to Mary, "Blessed art thou among women, and blessed is the fruit of thy womb."[3] The aura imposed on the scene with the flame imagery is actually felt by all those present, including the recalcitrant Will, and thus becomes a palpable force toward reconciliation of the family. As he listens to his wife and her mother speak of Anna's Polish birth father, whom Lydia describes as a "figure . . . alive and changing . . . like a running stream," Will finds that "instantly he was in love with [Anna] again" (*Rainbow*, 165).

As they walk home from this gathering, Anna tells Will she is pregnant; she feels glorified and aloof from her husband: "The blaze of light on her heart was too beautiful and dazzling, from the conception in her womb." Will, though, feels cut off and frightened: "She seemed fulfilled and separate and sufficient in her half of the world. . . . Why could he not always be one with her? It was he who had given her the child" (*Rainbow*, 166). This conflict between the parents—between Anna's beatified sense of her pregnant self and Will's insecurely patriarchal desire to merge with his wife and possess his child—eventually lodges in Ursula's consciousness, which

3. Luke, 1:41–44.

exhibits a unique combination of expansive psychic qualities (like Anna's) and analytical emotional qualities (like Will's). These qualities make her spirit profoundly modern.

It is helpful to approach the modernity of the child Ursula by considering Lawrence's analysis of another child he considered modern, Pearl of Nathaniel Hawthorne's *Scarlet Letter.* In the first version of his study of American literature, Lawrence declares, "We cannot help regarding the phenomenon of Pearl with wonder, and fear, and amazement, and respect. . . . Nowhere in literature is the spirit of much of modern childhood so profoundly, almost magically revealed. . . ." Pearl, he writes, "by the very openness of her perversity, was at least straightforward . . . she has a sort of reckless gallantry, the pride of her own deadly being."[4] More caustic in the revised *Studies in Classic American Literature,* Lawrence displays his fear of modern women (such as Pearl will become) and his joy in the destruction he feels they are perpetrating against men who deserve no better: "Poor, brave, tormented little soul, always in a state of recoil, she'll be a devil to men when she grows up. But the men deserve it. . . . Poor little phenomenon of a modern child, she'll grow up into the devil of a modern woman. The nemesis of weak-kneed modern men."[5]

What is it that disturbs and fascinates Lawrence about Pearl, and what does he find in her that is modern? In answering these questions, one may identify some of the differences between Ursula's childhood and her mother's. To analyze Pearl, Lawrence applies the psychology he later elaborated in *Psychoanalysis* and *Fantasia.* Pearl, Lawrence argues, presents an exaggerated, abstracted version of the alternating impulses that exist in every child. Normally the child finds equilibrium between two planes of being and two modes of relating with the world outside the self. Lawrence terms the lower plane the *sensual* and the upper plane the *spiritual.* The impulses regarding relations he calls *sympathetic* (seeking or accepting union with the environment) and *voluntary* (claiming independence or resisting the environment). The sympathetic impulses are enacted by the soft front of the body, the voluntary impulses by the stiffer back of the body. Even a simple action like breast-feeding

4. Lawrence, *Symbolic Meaning,* 137. Even though the Hawthorne essay was composed after *The Rainbow* (and first published in the *English Review* in May 1919), I believe the connection made by Lawrence's descriptions of Ursula as a modern woman and of Pearl as a modern child justifies reading the later analysis into the earlier fiction.

5. Lawrence, *Studies in Classic American Literature,* 105.

activates the two impulses: From the sympathetic center the child "draws all things unto itself, winningly, drawing love for the soul, and actively drawing in milk." From the voluntary center issues "the violent little pride and lustiness which kicks with glee, or crows with tiny exultance in its own being, or which claws the breast with a savage little rapacity, and an incipient masterfulness of which every mother is aware" (*FU,* 76).

In Pearl, Lawrence finds that the principle of equilibrium has been replaced by "the truly deadly principle of betrayal for betrayal's sake—the real demon principle, which just neutralises the sensual impulse with a spiritual gesture, and neutralises the spiritual impulse with a sensual gesture, creates a perfect frustration, neutralisation, and laughs with recurrent mockery."[6] Unable to balance her spiritual and sensual beings, Pearl is never in accord with herself. She acts purely from one plane of consciousness and then from the other, making sudden and cruel reversals. Furthermore, Pearl's actions emanate from sources that are entirely indecipherable to others. Thus she may, for no reason that anyone else can guess, suddenly turn on one: "Pearl, the devilish girl-child, who can be so tender and loving and *understanding,* and then, when she has understood, will give you a hit across the mouth."[7]

Lawrence offers a bleak schema of Pearl, and suggests that her neutralizing principle and unpredictability indicate modernity. In this formulation, Lawrence's language indicates a peculiarly fatal relation: "This is the one single motive of Pearl's being, this motive of neutralisation into nothingness."[8] Lawrence collapses two terms of existential choice into one when he outlines a *being* that is motivated toward *nonbeing* or *nothingness.* Curiously absent from Lawrence's sentence is the object of neutralization: one is uncertain whether Pearl's being neutralizes itself, its environment, or both. Indeed, the modernity that Lawrence ascribes to Pearl is not only a failure to achieve equilibrium in relation to the world, but a negation of any basis for being.

The character Pearl, as Lawrence notes in his essay on Hawthorne, is more a symbol than a personality. Hawthorne's art neglects the character's "personal plane" in favor of the soul's "passional abstraction."[9] Likewise, in *The Rainbow* Lawrence also

6. Lawrence, *Symbolic Meaning,* 136.
7. Lawrence, *Studies in Classic American Literature,* 103.
8. Lawrence, *Symbolic Meaning,* 136.
9. Ibid., 127.

wishes to imagine his characters in a zone beyond that of realistic personal qualities. Much of the first part of *The Rainbow,* the part in which Anna grows up, seems to take place on preconscious levels of being. The apparent incongruity of the objective portrayal of young Anna within this undefined context is, as I showed in Chapter 4, actually a technique by which Lawrence emphasizes the inaccessibility of the child's consciousness and enacts its development. At the same time he asserts the mingling of the physical and the spiritual by representing Anna's psychic growth in terms of external events. By contrast, one of Lawrence's problems in creating the story of Ursula is that her modernity requires that she awaken to mental consciousness at an early age. Lawrence assigned himself to write about the interchange between conscious and subconscious in a modern character without creating the kind of diabolical moral split that he criticizes in Pearl. Ursula is, like Pearl, a study in the interaction of the various impulses that make up the consciousness (in which Lawrence includes the unconscious or his privileged, paradoxical "blood consciousness"). It is a complicating factor of her modern character that much which *ought* to be unconscious according to Lawrence's model of being becomes conscious in Ursula— or at least in Lawrence's prose about Ursula. This prose attempts to render the undivided blood-consciousness by creating a discourse that partakes of both the sensual and the spiritual planes of being. Thus, despite her links with the previous generations, Ursula represents a new conception of the child, one in which the unconscious and its manifestations are crucial.[10] She is even more modern than Pearl. To represent her consciousness Lawrence combines a style that might be called *psychomachic,* after the medieval drama of the soul, with a modern stream of consciousness. Lawrence's analysis of Ursula's being continues the medieval tradition of an allegorical drama of the soul as it is invoked in Hawthorne's romance novel. Notwithstanding these historical affinities, the technique of interior

10. See Mark Kinkead-Weekes, "The Marriage of Opposites in *The Rainbow,*" for a fine new discussion of the relationship of archetypes and individuality, social history and timelessness in this novel. Of Ursula, Kinkead-Weekes wrote: "What we are made to realize about Ursula from the start is that she embodies all the opposites of her family, at peak intensity, and in greater awareness and self-consciousness. She is intensely visionary and intensely sceptical, spiritual and fleshly, arrogant and unfixed, emancipated and primitive, and it is her fate (because of her world) to be aware of herself in all these aspects." Kinkead-Weekes's essay appears in *D. H. Lawrence: Centenary Essays,* ed. Mara Kalnins, 21–39.

presentation Lawrence uses for Ursula allows him to encompass the psychological dimension of consciousness as it was introduced by such technically experimental writers as Virginia Woolf, May Sinclair, or James Joyce.

Using this combination of techniques from medieval soul drama and modern psychology, Lawrence traces Ursula's psychological growth, as he did Paul Morel's, from a very early age. He begins with her first movements in her mother's womb, endowing her story with a mythic resonance that is seldom found in modern psychological novels, except as it appears in *Ulysses,* with a certain irony. One recalls that Lawrence professed more respect for those "supreme old novels" the Bible and works by Homer and Shakespeare than for any written since the genre's rise in the eighteenth century.[11] The biblical or mythic texture that many critics have noted in *The Rainbow* is partially due to its focus on the spiritual possibilities of ordinary births, marriages, and deaths. Lawrence's desire to bring epic grandeur, spiritual depth, and visionary characters to the novel form gives a mythic as well as an analytic dimension to his introduction of the heroine as an infant. Myths often begin with the telling of the protagonist's unusual birth or infancy. Recall Achilles being dipped by the heel; the baby Hercules killing two adders; three-year-old Davy Crockett killing a bear; the concealment and subsequent discovery of Moses; the immaculately conceived Christ, born in a stable. Similarly the birth of David Copperfield takes on an ominous quality when Dickens elaborates upon David's caul. Such concentration on a peculiar event is typical of myth. In contrast, Lawrence investigates unusual implications of apparently normal happenings. He lavishes these events with attention and expansively explores their significance in the lives of other characters. There is nothing at all unusual about Ursula's conception or birth, and yet—as we saw above—the sunlight shining through the hen's comb seems to make the child "flame" within Anna.

While she is pregnant with Ursula, Anna Brangwen herself lives within a sort of mythical childhood, a paradise of her own imagining:

> Day after day came shining through the door of Paradise . . . The child in her shone till she herself was a beam of sunshine . . . How happy she was, how gorgeous it was to live: to have known herself, her husband, the passion of love and begetting; and to know that all this lived and waited and burned on around her, a terrible purifying fire, through

11. Lawrence, "Why the Novel Matters," in *Study of Thomas Hardy,* 196.

which she had passed for once to come to this peace of golden radiance, when she was with child, and innocent, and in love with her husband and with all the many angels hand in hand. She lifted her throat to the breeze that came across the fields, and she felt it handling her like sisters fondling her, she drank it in perfume of cowslips and of apple-blossoms. (*Rainbow*, 167)

These images of a paradise achieved by passing through and beyond sexual love show Anna's enjoyment of herself pregnant, at the center of things—a child again herself. This connection between childhood and paradise is made also by Freud, who finds the origin of paradise in childhood. "Paradise," he states, is "no more than a group phantasy of the childhood of the individual. That is why mankind were naked in Paradise and were without shame in one another's presence; till a moment arrived when shame and anxiety awoke, expulsion followed."[12] Freud is interested in locating the root of the popular delusion of a paradisal human past; he does not question, it seems, his belief in the happiness of the individual child before the awakening of shame. Lawrence reverses the terms of fantasy: while the mother, Anna, wishes to believe in the placid joys of childhood, the child, "restless as a young eel," wears her mother out with the "day-long wrestling with its young vigour" (*Rainbow*, 179).

Later Anna becomes discontented, and wonders—as her stepfather did before her—if there is something beyond. But she forgoes the desire for a journey beyond her domestic world with the thought that her children will be the travelers. Pregnant again, Anna "with satisfaction . . . relinquished the adventure to the unknown. She was bearing her children. . . . Through her another soul was coming, to stand upon her as upon the threshold, looking out, shading its eyes for the direction to take" (*Rainbow*, 182). Anna's relinquishment of spiritual adventure seems to exemplify the failure of a female child to live up to the promise of precocious independence. This pattern surfaces in novels from Samuel Richardson's *Pamela* to George Eliot's *Middlemarch* and Henry James's *Portrait of a Lady*. Certainly Anna Brangwen's glorification of motherhood may seem a compromise deceivingly couched in language that promotes the patriarchal social contract. Like Gertrude Morel, Anna gives up personal ambitions in exchange for the hope that her children can succeed. Yet there are significant differences. Gertrude's ambitions are

12. Freud, "The Interpretation of Dreams," in *Complete Psychological Works of Sigmund Freud*, 4:245.

specifically for her sons, and the nature of those ambitions is circumscribed by the narrow-mindedness of her own middle-class background. Anna does not seek personal fulfillment from her children; she is herself appeased by marriage and biological motherhood and does not seek to possess her children's souls. Anna achieves self-esteem and independence through motherhood, whereas Gertrude Morel remains a victim of class, marriage, and her own values. Hence, it may be argued that Anna, like Tom Brangwen, is a success because she is content and self-sufficient; she finds a version of the *beyond* without leaving home.

The configuration of father-to-daughter influence that I have noted between Tom and Anna Brangwen is repeated in Ursula's childhood. In portraying her as a creature of complex being from her early years, Lawrence focuses on her relations with her father. While his wife revels in her maternity, Will Brangwen awaits the advent of his first child's *mental* consciousness: "He loved with a hot heart the dark-haired little Ursula, and he waited for the child to come to consciousness. Now the mother monopolized the baby. But his heart waited in its darkness. His hour would come" (*Rainbow,* 194).[13] Will's eagerness for Ursula to reach mental consciousness is a symptom of weakness in both himself and his marriage. His desire to possess his daughter is unhealthy. This unhealthiness is not specifically sexual—quite the contrary. Will's needful "daytime" self suffers most in his relationship with Anna and dictates his need to possess his daughter: "So they [Will and Anna] remained as separate in the light, and in the thick darkness, married" (*Rainbow,* 201). When Anna reveals her disappointment that her child is not a boy, "a great blazing passion of resentment and protest sprang up in [Will's] heart. In that moment he claimed the child" (*Rainbow,* 178). For Anna, the baby remains an *it,* a "little animal" who brings her "extravagant bliss" by nursing at her breasts. Will is impatient to

13. Most of Lawrence's fictional children are blonde, so Ursula's dark hair makes her unusual. Besides her hair color and a note that as a baby she has "golden-brown, wondering vivid eyes" there is very little physical description of Ursula as a child. I owe this observation to my daughter, Katherine Ryan, then five years old, who questioned me about Anna's and Ursula's appearance because she wanted to make an illustration for my book. Daniel Dervin acutely notes that Ursula as an adult shares a sort of physical negativity with the male semi-autobiographical characters Rupert Birkin, Aaron Sisson, and Richard Somers. Dervin maintains: "For all her 'becoming individual, self-responsible, taking her own initiative,' [Ursula] is strangely bodiless and is made to enthuse excessively over the 'marvelous flanks'. . . of Birkin's body. He scarcely does the same for her" (*Strange Sapience,* 194).

detach the baby from his wife and therefore wishes to rouse Ursula to spiritual response and mental consciousness too early.

In his description of Will as a new father, Lawrence emphasizes an element of self-concern that violates the Lawrentian doctrine of impersonal parenthood. Will needs the child's recognition to verify his own existence: "As the newly opened, newly dawned eyes looked at him, he wanted them to perceive him, to recognize him. Then he was verified. The child knew him, a queer contortion of laughter came on its face for him. He caught it to his breast, clapping with a triumphant laugh" (*Rainbow,* 197). Will errs both in his wish for recognition and in his sense of personal triumph when it occurs, for the connections between parent and child should be "mindless, healthy, pristine." In that trio of adjectives Lawrence is asserting his view that the potential problems in parent-child relations originate not in the sexual realm, but in the mental. This anti-Freudian diagnosis is expounded by Lawrence when he describes Pearl's mercurial temperament. In the hectoring style of *Studies in Classic American Literature,* he declares to Hester that she deserves the jeering she receives from her daughter: "Pearl, the devilish girl-child, who can be so tender and loving and *understanding,* and then, when she has understood, will give you a hit across the mouth, and turn on you with a grin of sheer diabolic jeering. Serves you right, you shouldn't be *understood.* That is your vice. You shouldn't want to be loved, and you'd not get hit across the mouth."[14]

Hester Prynne expects her child to provide the human companionship that the community denies her. Will, similarly, expects his child to respond to his individuality, and thus recompense him for his sense of inadequacy. Like King Lear, such parents request what ought not to be given. Ursula (if she were old enough to speak) should reply as Cordelia does: "I cannot heave my heart into my mouth. I love your Majesty / according to my bond, no more nor less." For both Shakespeare and Lawrence, the obligation is neither strictly legal nor purely emotional. The bond of parent and child, according to Lawrence, is a "preconscious dynamic relation" guided not by spiritual love, but by wisdom. Speaking in the persona of the parent, Lawrence defines such wisdom as "a deep collectedness in the soul, a deep abiding by my own integral being, which makes me responsible, not for the child, but for my certain duties toward the child, and for maintaining the dynamic flow between the child and myself as genuine as possible: that is to say, not perverted by ideals

14. Lawrence, *Studies in Classic American Literature,* 103–4.

or by my *will*" (*FU,* 90). When Lear asks his children to satisfy his pride and embody an ideal of filial devotion by making public testimony of their love, he violates the privacy of their feeling. Furthermore, he asks for what cannot be done honestly or wisely. As Cordelia says, and as the speeches of Goneril and Regan prove, the primordial feeling between parent and child cannot be conveyed by words, which emanate from the mental, idealizing consciousness. Just as Lear's request violates honesty and wisdom, Will's violates the natural development of his child. In Lawrence's physiology, the child's mental functions begin *after* the four centers of dynamic (un)consciousness are established: when the "eyes begin to gather their sight, the mouth to speak, the ears to awake to their intelligent hearings." At this same time the "mind wakens to its incipient control. For at first the control is non-mental, even non-cerebral. The brain acts only as a sort of switchboard" (*FU,* 87).[15] Will hurries this incipient cerebration when he rushes in and claims Ursula: "She was not more than a year old when the second baby was born. Then he took Ursula for his own" (*Rainbow,* 197).

Will Brangwen's wish for acceptance by his tiny daughter requires from her a precocious mental capacity and makes too great a demand on her spiritual capacity while neglecting the sensual aspects of her dynamic consciousness. Will, as his name suggests, is more willful than sensual, an imbalance that has been distorted, rather than corrected, by his marriage. Love, Lawrence maintains, is only the spiritual (willful) form of the complex fourfold relation between parents and children. It is the parent's responsibility *not* to exaggerate its place in the dynamic flow. Because of his own disequilibrium, Will pulls Ursula's nature out of proportion by requiring a strong unconscious spiritual response from her. The father and daughter develop a "strange alliance": "They were aware of each other. He knew the child was always on his side. But in his consciousness he counted it for nothing. She was always for him. He took it for granted. Yet his life was based on her, even whilst she was a tiny child, on her support and her accord" (*Rainbow,* 204). What, then, are the effects on Ursula of her father's mental expectations and his unconscious spiritual demands? One recalls that when Anna

15. Are Lawrence's descriptions of child development at all accurate? Comparison with the results reported from recent research shows that the stages of development occur in much the order that Lawrence describes, though at earlier ages than he—or anyone else writing in his period—realized. Princeton Center for Childhood and Infancy, *The First Twelve Months of Life: Your Baby's Growth and Development.*

Lensky Brangwen was relieved of similar responsibilities for her mother she became more childlike, settling on the "swivel" of her own being. For Ursula, though, supporting her father is coupled with the burdens of being the eldest child, and is never relieved by the advent of anyone analogous to Tom Brangwen. Lawrence is explicit about the damage Ursula incurs:

> Her father was the dawn wherein her consciousness woke up. But for him, she might have gone on like the other children, Gudrun and Theresa and Catherine, one with the flowers and insects and playthings, having no existence apart from the concrete object of her attention. But her father came too near to her. The clasp of his hands and the power of his breast woke her up almost in pain from the transient unconsciousness of childhood.
>
> . . . her sleep-living heart was beaten into wakefulness by the striving of his bigger heart, by his clasping her to his body for love and for fulfilment, asking as a magnet must always ask. From her the response had struggled dimly, vaguely into being. (*Rainbow,* 205)

Her emphasized spiritual impulse becomes a marked trait of her adult character, represented, for example, in her frequent demand that Rupert Birkin *tell* her he loves her. In scenes such as the following, Ursula becomes the father, the Lear demanding verbal reassurance while Birkin (equally irritating in his way) speaks for the unspeakable, imagistically projected relation that Lawrence prefers to articulated feelings:

> "Ah, well," he said, "words make no matter, any way. The thing *is* between us, or it isn't."
>
> "You don't even love me," she cried.
>
> "I do," he said angrily. "But I want—" His mind saw again the lovely golden light of spring transfused through her eyes, as through some wonderful window. And he wanted her to be with him there, in this world of proud indifference. . . .
>
> "I always think I'm going to be loved—and then I am let down. You *don't* love me, you know." (*WL,* 250)

Ursula asks him so often to confirm this spiritual dimension of their relationship that Birkin calls the question her war-cry: " 'A Brangwen, A Brangwen,'—an old battle-cry.—Yours is 'Do you love me?—Yield knave, or die' " (*WL,* 251).

Despite her yearning to be loved and her insistence on the supremacy of love over the individual, Ursula is fearful that she will be consumed by a man, and she sometimes becomes aggressive in her resistance to such envelopment. As we know, Lawrence cast Ursula as the modern woman when he planned his double novel, so it is not surprising that she has those "cock-sure," grasping, and spiritually succubunt qualities that he felt were signs of modern cultural degeneration. In the bathetic episode in which Birkin comes to propose to Ursula and ends up doing so with her father in the room, Ursula—flustered, "driven out of her own radiant, single world" by the unexpected proposal—cries out to both men, "Why should I say anything? . . . You do this off your *own* bat, it has nothing to do with me. Why do you both want to bully me?" (*WL,* 261). The genesis of Ursula's intense, mixed desire for both all-consuming love and independent power must be seen in her sometimes imitative, sometimes resisting response to her young father's attempt to graft her onto himself. Her contrariety about whether she is the owner or the owned is succinctly illustrated by a single sentence from her consideration of Birkin's proposal: "Let him be *her man* utterly, and she in return would be his humble slave—whether he wanted it or not" (*WL,* 265). This struggle to achieve some equilibrium between the impulses of her consciousness, rather than simply to maintain childhood impulses, presages Ursula's modern womanhood. Yet Ursula does not "neutralize" her being, as Pearl does, by entertaining contradictory impulses. Rather, as she develops in the two novels, she is able to find the balance that allows her to marry Birkin without sacrificing her independent soul.

The structure of the unusual pressures on Ursula anticipates the basic, impersonal impulses of consciousness that Lawrence will formulate in his psychological essays and in his study of Hawthorne. The division of mental and sensual consciousness is enacted through specific episodes of Ursula's growing up, which stem from her unusual attachment to her father and distance from her mother. Ursula's early years are marked by experiences of terror, solitude, and yearning. All of these emotions are related to and expressed stylistically by her particularly divided, modern configuration of consciousness.

Terror is the motif of Will's response to his first baby, and it remains—in inverted form—a part of their relationship. From birth Ursula elicits an element of sheer terror from her father. This is partially due to his feeling that he is helpless to protect the vulnerable infant; but the more striking cause of this terror is that the infant arouses Will's deepest consciousness (the solar plexus and the lumbar ganglion, Lawrence's blood consciousness or dark gods): "From the first, the baby stirred in the young father a deep, strong emotion he dared scarcely acknowledge, it was so strong and came out of the dark of him. When he heard the child cry, a terror possessed him, because of the answering echo from the unfathomed distances in himself. Must he know in himself such distances, perilous and imminent?" (*Rainbow,* 196). Though Lawrence provides for terror in the psychic diagrams of *Fantasia,* he does not explore it as a parental emotion in any detail elsewhere in his fiction. This response is particular to Will and, more importantly, to the childhood of Ursula.

The terror that seizes Will is the answer of his own inarticulate self to the howl of his daughter's inarticulate being. It is significant that when Will first visits Marsh Farm he is described several times as "half-articulate." Lawrence's development of this theme in relation to Will's religious and artistic experience has been the most common subject for critical considerations of Will. His longing for articulation, having been met with scorn or failure, is repressed into more mechanical activities such as the repair of the church building. Unlike the longings of his wife or his father-in-law, however, Will's yearning for the unknown world is not satisfied by his marriage or his hobbies and remains a volatile and sometimes terrifying element in all his relationships.

Will's tendency to terror is connected with his impotent desire to possess his surroundings with his mind. He lacks the capacity John Keats describes as *negative capability,* "of being in uncertainties, Mysteries, doubts, without any irritable reaching after fact & reason."[16] Hannah Lee-Jahnke's psychoanalytic study of Lawrence offers the following conclusion regarding Will Brangwen's lack of autonomy: "Here the crushing influence of maternal love on the infant's ego is demonstrated again. Will does not possess the will power, the energy of resistance that protects the ego from absorption into non-existence by its surroundings or by another being. For him, the goal of life is to attain an ecstacy of passivity. His desire is to return to the uterus."[17] If Lee-Jahnke means that Will's relation to Anna results from his mother's influence, the little information that Lawrence provides about Will's mother does not contradict that conclusion. I quote this passage, however, for the insight of the phrase "an ecstacy of passivity," which can, I think, point us back not to the uterus, but to Lawrence's psychology. Will's ineffectuality results not from mother-fixated *passivity,* but rather from inability to bring his sensuous experience into adequate relation with his

16. *Letters of John Keats,* selected and edited by Robert Gittings, 43.
17. Hannah Lee-Jahnke, *David Herbert Lawrence et la psychoanalyse,* 225 (my translation).

spiritual and mental life. Hence his artistic and religious efforts, his marriage, and his relations with his children—Ursula in particular—are all deeply flawed. The *ecstasy* he might feel in these relations seldom comes to fruition because he cannot put his whole self into them. The renewal of his marriage by means of obscure, uninhibited sexual practices allows him to gain in masculine confidence, but full integration of his being still eludes him. As some like to point out with great optimism, Will eventually achieves satisfaction in establishing woodworking classes. Lawrence approves of even modest self-fulfillment, but its inadequacy is evident from Will's confusion during the proposal scene in *Women in Love*. Tom Brangwen, equally inarticulate, would not have made such a fool of himself. Inarticulate terror of the unknown is on the loose in Will Brangwen, looking for occasions to present itself. The birth of his first child provides such an occasion. When Will asks "Must he know in himself such distances, perilous and imminent?" the diction, by the modification of "distances" with "imminent," insists on making the difficult, and for Will frightening, connection between the deep consciousness and the immediate surroundings. Lawrence anchors the swirling adjectival movement of his exploration of Will's unconscious to this particular baby's cry. The dike of ordinary consciousness is broken; Will cannot separate the irritation of a baby's cry in the night from more treacherous depths of fear. On a conscious and literal level Will doubts his ability to protect the baby both from "the whole universe" and from himself. He struggles between the impulse to respond sympathetically to Ursula's crying and a "voice" that tells him to stifle it. His heart (literally, for Lawrence would attribute this feeling to the cardiac plexus) tells him, "This was his own flesh and blood crying! His soul rose against the voice suddenly breaking out from him, from the distances in him." Nonetheless, the echo of her cries from those distances within him tempts him to suffocate her with his hand: "Sometimes, in the night, the child cried and cried, when the night was heavy and sleep oppressed him. And half asleep, he stretched out his hand to put it over the baby's face, to stop the crying" (*Rainbow,* 196).

Will does not smother Ursula, but the reasons given for his restraint are less than coherent: First, Ursula is "his own [human] flesh and blood" drawing her father's indulgence; then, a paragraph later, it is the "*inhumanness* of the intolerable, continuous crying" (emphasis added) that arrests his hand. The arrested hand is followed by "Yet he echoed to it directly, his soul answered its madness. It filled him with terror, almost with frenzy" (*Rainbow,* 196).

Lawrence's ambivalence in this passage may be seen as representing discord in a parent's feeling for a child, a discord that reflects Lawrence's rejection of humanist definitions of the self. In attending to Will's ambivalence, Lawrence again challenges received ideas about how parents ought to feel and transforms the conventional subject and feeling into a portrait of the individual.[18]

Although I have emphasized the particularity of Will's response and argued that his hypersensitivity results from his lack of a sufficiently integrated being, his response to Ursula is nonetheless an illustration of the mythicized circuit of relations Lawrence later outlines in *Fantasia*. An infant's crying, he writes there, affects everyone. He sketches a picture of the infant at the breast who suddenly pulls away to scream; the mother, less disturbed than others because she is "*sure* of her possession of the child," wonders whether it is "wind" or "stomach-ache," but Lawrence tells us to listen more carefully, for what we hear is: "The first scream of the ego. The scream of asserted isolation. The scream of revolt . . . from union. . . . Nothing acts more directly on the great primal nerve-centres than the screaming of an infant, this blind screaming negation of connections. It is the friction of irritation itself. Everyone is implicated" (*PU*, 23). It is, Lawrence goes on to argue, the voluntary center (not the sympathetic, as our received ideas about baby care would suggest) that responds to such crying, and it responds—appropriately—by fighting back. Everyone is implicated, apparently, because everyone feels both the desire to break connections with the world and the threat of the infant's revolt from union. The mother should fight back, Lawrence insists: "Sometimes she fights to keep her refractory child, and sometimes she fights to kick him off, as a mare kicks off her too-babyish foal. . . . So long as the force meets its polarized response all is well. When a force flashes and has no response, there is devastation. How weary in the back is the nursing mother whose great centre of repudiation is suppressed or weak; how a child droops if only the sympathetic unison is estab-

---

18. For an example of a more conventional, but not necessarily maudlin or unconvincing use of the effects of a baby's cry in an earlier novel, we may refer to Eliot's *Adam Bede*. Hetty Sorrel, recalling the moments before she partially buried her day-old infant in the woods to get rid of him, says: "I longed to be safe at home. I don't know how I felt about the baby. I seemed to hate it—it was like a weight hanging round my neck; and yet its crying went through me, and I daredn't look at its little hands and face" (chap. 45, p. 329). Later, Hetty is drawn back to the now-empty site of the burial by an incessant hallucination of the baby's crying, and is arrested there for child-murder.

lished" (*PU,* 24). Interestingly, in *The Rainbow* Lawrence focuses more on the fathers' responses to the infants than on those of the mothers. Motherhood is primarily a physical struggle for Lydia. She stays in the background as she nurses her two sons, though Lawrence does say that bringing forth new life after what she has suffered requires her to withdraw into herself. Anna also glories in the physical struggle and seems unaffected by the philosophical terrors that beset her husband. As for these fathers, the scene in which Tom undresses Anna exhibits the clean and necessary repudiation. Will's response to Ursula is more complex, more self-involved and less clear.

When Will accepts the physical strangeness of the infant, he is able to translate his terror of the depths from which her cries issue into a more conscious relationship that does not threaten him so much. By describing the baby's strange beauty immediately after examining Will's terror, Lawrence retrieves Will's relationship with Ursula into the realm of the visual and the understandable: "He learned to know the little hands and feet, the strange, unseeing, golden-brown eyes, the mouth that opened only to cry, or to suck, or to show a queer, toothless laugh. He could almost understand even the dangling legs, which at first had created in him a feeling of aversion" (*Rainbow,* 196). That aversion, like his terror of the cries, comes from his fear of the unconscious—her tadpole legs do not look human. He is able to encompass their strangeness with a somewhat belittling, though surely affectionate, perception that they are, after all, human: "They could kick in their queer little way, and they had their own softness" (*Rainbow,* 196). This understanding, as I have noted, is infused by mental possessiveness. To Lawrence such understanding is inevitably false and sure to produce a backlash if pursued too earnestly. At the end of a year, when Gudrun is born, Will takes Ursula "for his own. She his first little girl. He had his heart set on her" (*Rainbow,* 197). He is setting himself up for an eventual rejection.

Lawrence's interest in the inhuman aspects of human infancy may be elucidated by an observation Carl Jung makes about the archetype of the child as a symbol for the self. Jung states:

> The symbols of the self arise in the depths of the body and they express its materiality every bit as much as the structure of the perceiving consciousness. . . . The deeper "layers" of the psyche lose their individual uniqueness as they retreat farther and farther into darkness. . . . as they approach the autonomous functional systems, they become increasingly collective until they are universalized and extinguished in the body's

materiality, ie., in chemical substances. The body's carbon is simply carbon. Hence, "at bottom" the psyche is simply the world.[19]

The archetypal child symbol, Jung suggests, represents the self in an undifferentiated form, just emerging from the pure materiality of the body. Lawrence's unusual attention to Ursula as a baby, particularly with respect to the terror of "imminent distances" she arouses in her father, is an approach to the dimension of being that exists beyond the bounds of consciousness and merges with the world itself. Will's terror of incomprehensible realms of being aligns with Lawrence's critique of the modern world and, particularly, with his critique of modern men. Lawrence identifies and castigates the death-oriented conditions that patriarchal, militarist society has created in the world; pure willfulness, such as Will represents, opposes peace by denying life. In a 1917 essay Lawrence asks, "What is will, divorced from the impulse of the unknown? . . . With what rigid, cruel insistence we clutch the control of our lives . . . with what madness of ghastly persistence we break ourselves under our own will!"[20] Just as Ursula acquires archetypal dimensions as a modern woman, her father represents the willfulness of the old fathers of European civilization whose attempt to shape the world in their own image has failed so horribly.

The terror that Ursula's crying has tapped in Will's unconscious returns in new forms when he is about twenty-eight years old and she is five or six. She begins to relapse into "her own separate world of herself," making her father "grind his teeth with bitterness, for he still wanted her" (*Rainbow*, 208). His impulse to fight back re-emerges. Perhaps it is to test her loyalty, in revenge for her new independence, that Will begins to try to frighten Ursula. Lawrence introduces the theme right after he tells us of the bitterness Will

---

19. C. G. Jung and C. Kerényi, *Essays on a Science of Mythology*, trans. R. F. C. Hull, 92. Jung's words have an uncanny similarity to Lawrence's 1914 description of what he was trying to achieve in his new novel: "You mustn't look in my novel for the old stable ego of the character. There is another ego, according to whose action the individual is unrecognizable, and passes through, as it were, allotropic states which it needs a deeper sense than any we've been used to exercise, to discover are states of the same single radically-unchanged element. (Like as diamond and coal are the same pure single element of carbon. The ordinary novel would trace the history of the diamond—but I say 'diamond, what! This is carbon.' And my diamond might be coal or soot, and my theme is carbon.)" (D. H. Lawrence, *The Letters of D. H. Lawrence*, ed. James Boulton et al., 2:183. See also chap. 3, n. 3.)

20. D. H. Lawrence, "The Reality of Peace," in *Reflections on the Death of a Porcupine and Other Essays*, ed. Michael Herbert, 27–29.

feels when Ursula separates herself from him: "He had a curious craving to frighten her, to see what she would do with him" (*Rainbow*, 208). He has taught her to swim, and the two of them jump off the canal bridge together in "a curious fight between their two wills" that gives them "a strange blow" and afterward makes the girl look at him "wonderingly, darkly, wondering from the shock, yet reserved and unfathomable" (*Rainbow*, 209).

This diving repeats the terror that Will derived from Ursula's infant cries. In taking the child under the water (an archetypal visitation to the underworld) he brings her to a "sort of unconsciousness," after which she will cling "safely" to him while he swims in the deep water of the canal. As we have seen him do before, Lawrence joins the historical and the apocalyptic in this apparently simple episode. The canal marks the boundary between Marsh Farm, Cossethay, and the industrialized world beyond. It seems that Ursula's immersion in the darkness of the water, like Achilles' in the Styx, better prepares her for the unconscious forces she must meet when she leaves her family and village, determined to become an independent young woman.

Nonetheless, her father's motives are scarcely protective or educational. Sometimes he "daringly, almost wickedly" repeats the dive until the two of them nearly drown: "He saved her, and sat on the bank, quivering. But his eyes were full of the blackness of death, it was as if death had cut between their two lives and separated them" (*Rainbow*, 209). Will's experiments with terror create a more intense rhythm in his daughter's relationship with him: apparent disillusionment and rejection alternating with continuing, but colder intimacy. After he has kept her in the carnival swing boats until she is violently ill and made her promise not to tell her mother (who hears of it from onlookers), Ursula "went over to her mother. Her soul was dead towards him. It made her sick. Still she forgot and continued to love him, but ever more coldly" (*Rainbow*, 210).

After the lengthy passages in which Will frightens Ursula, honing the emerging strangeness and violence of his behavior toward her, Lawrence steers his story toward a new phase in the marriage of Will and Anna. Implicitly, Ursula plays a role in the transition and is affected by the change in the marriage. Shortly after Ursula turns away from him, Will attempts to seduce a young woman in Nottingham whose "*childishness* whetted him keenly" (my emphasis, *Rainbow*, 211). He then returns home to Anna who, perceiving the change in her husband, "challenged him back with a sort of radiance, very bright and free, opposite to him" (*Rainbow*, 218). While the parents move into "a sensuality violent and extreme as death" the children become "mere offspring" to them (*Rainbow,* 219–20). A fifth child, a boy, is born during this two-year period, but he doesn't reverse the revolution in the parents' inward life that makes the children less important to both of them. The change makes Will more manly (by Lawrence's standards) and thus turns his attention to public life: "His intimate life was so violently active, that it set another man in him free" (*Rainbow,* 220). The handicraft classes he begins now as nearly a volunteer project lead eventually to a position as the school district's director of handwork instruction that he holds in *Women in Love.*

The children, one senses, are better off for the lessening of attention to themselves and the expansion of interests in the household. As does Anna when her parents become reconciled to each other, eight-year-old Ursula thrives within the protection of the renewed marriage because it relieves some of the pressure her father had previously placed on her. Nonetheless, Will remains to Ursula a "centre of magic and fascination" and, less sanguinely, he casts over her "the shadow of some dark, potent secret of which she would not, of whose existence she dared not become conscious, it cast such a spell over her, and so darkened her mind" (*Rainbow,* 222). This darkness, I would argue, is the early division in her being, provoked by her father. Will himself remains fondest of Ursula and believes that, "somehow, she seemed to be at the back of his new night-school adventure" (*Rainbow,* 221). Insofar as his loss of power over Ursula led to his attempted seduction of the childish young woman, then to the revitalization of his marriage, and then to the night classes, he is quite right.

Will Brangwen's fragmented being and use of his child to hold himself together have drawn the attention of many *Rainbow* critics. Little attention has been paid to those materials as evidence of Lawrence's boldness in creating the consciousness of the child.[21] Something of this achievement may be gauged from the way Ursula refers to the swingboat incident later in the novel. When she is on the ride with her father, she agrees to let him take her higher and higher, even though she feels "as if she would turn to vapour, lose hold of everything, and melt away." Afterward, "for the first time in her life

21. Richard Swigg, in *Lawrence, Hardy, and American Literature,* offers a discussion of Will's development that attends nicely to Ursula's role, and I am indebted to him in my own consideration of the same material from the child's perspective.

a disillusion came over her, something cold and isolating" (*Rainbow,* 209–10). The freedom Lawrence exercises in phrasing Ursula's feelings and in moving between conscious and unconscious levels of her being (as opposed to his reticence about Anna's) emphasizes that a great proportion of her original being is unconscious. Certain events are implanted there but consciously forgotten. For instance, ten years later when she recounts the swingboat incident to her first love, Anton Skrebensky, at the Derby fair, it comes out quite differently:

> "My father used to take me in the swingboats."
> "Did you like it?" he asked.
> "Oh, it was fine!" she said.
> "Would you like to go now?"
> "Love it," she said, though she was afraid. But the prospect of doing an unusual, exciting thing was too attractive for her. . . . he set the boat swinging. She was not afraid, she was thrilled. . . . So they rushed through the bright air, up at the sky as if flung from a catapult, then falling terribly back. She loved it. The motion seemed to fan their blood to fire, they laughed, feeling like flames. (*Rainbow,* 274)

Though Ursula has forgotten that "her soul was dead towards" her father after he made her ill on the carnival ride, neither the reader nor Ursula's soul has forgotten. Lawrence conveys the divided nature of the child's consciousness without asking us to believe that she remembers all the details of her own childhood. Transformed, turned from "cold disillusion" to "fire," the connection between love and terror that prevailed in her relationship with her father becomes part of her relationship with Skrebensky. Now she feels free to enjoy the sensuality of the ride and the contact with the man, while before she sensed some unnaturalness in what her father was doing to her. She rejoices "to see her father retreating to himself against the young man" (*Rainbow,* 280). When the terror that the swingboat association suggests does become an element in the relation of Ursula and Skrebensky, it is she who terrorizes him.

At a very early age Ursula develops the capacity to be alone. This solitude is her escape not only from her father's bouts of fierceness, but also from the atmosphere of "violent fruitfulness" created by her mother and the younger children. Ursula's allegiance moves from her mother to her father and finally to herself. When Gudrun is born, displacing Ursula as the nursling, the elder girl begins to yearn for her father: "Her heart followed him as if he had some tie with her, and some love which he could not deliver. Her heart followed him persistently, in its love" (*Rainbow,* 205). This yearning—with its heightened spiritual intensity—inevitably produces conflicts and disappointments because it makes Ursula try to grow up too quickly. When she tries to help Will set potatoes, she finds that she dreads "work because she could not do it as he did it." The occasion becomes "a picture, one of her earliest memories":

> He gave her a little basket of potatoes, and strode himself to the other end of the line. She saw him stooping, working towards her. She was excited, and unused. She put in one potato, then rearranged it, to make it sit nicely. Some of the sprits were broken, and she was afraid. The responsibility excited her like a string tying her up . . . she was overcome by her responsibility. She put potatoes quickly into the cold earth.
> He came near.
> "Not so close," he said, stooping over her potatoes, taking some out and rearranging others. She stood by with the painful terrified helplessness of childhood. He was so unseeing and confident, she wanted to do the thing and yet she could not. (*Rainbow,* 206)

The crucial element in this scene, it seems to me, is its conveyance of the "painful terrified helplessness" felt by children in relation to those they love with a modernity that results from the very ordinariness of the encounter. Nineteenth-century novelists who conjured up similar feelings often used extraordinary means to do so. Dickens enhances the fright of Oliver Twist, David Copperfield, or Pip by turning a villainous adult on the child. Who wouldn't be terrified by Sykes, Murdstone, or Magwitch? Charlotte Brontë's handling of psychic drama is less symbolic than Dickens's. She relies considerably upon atmospheric details such as the red room where Jane Eyre's Uncle Reed had died, or the tall black pillar of Mr. Brocklehurst whose "grim face at the top was like a carved mask, placed above the shaft by way of capital."[22] Whereas Dickens employs complex plots and metaphorical patterns and Brontë translates much of the child's internal feeling into extraordinary descriptions, Lawrence bares the child's psychic complexity in the most ordinary of circumstances.

   G. H. Bantock casually remarks in his chapter on Lawrence and education: Lawrence has the "vitality of a Dickens from the *inside.*"[23] This notion might be elaborated to show that the childhood terrors embodied by Dickensian villains are located, by Lawrence, within the adults the child loves; thus very ordinary domestic events

22. Brontë, *Jane Eyre,* chap. 4.
23. G. H. Bantock, *Freedom and Authority in Education: A Criticism of Modern Cultural and Educational Assumptions,* 137.

may induce fear in the child. While the reader sees Will Brangwen as an unsure young man routinely planting his vegetable garden, to his daughter he is enormously imposing: "His solitariness drew the child like a spell. . . . He had another world from hers. She stood helplessly, stranded on his world" (*Rainbow,* 206). After her father has rearranged her potatoes, Ursula abandons the task and plays in another part of the yard. When he comes to find her, saying "You didn't help me much," Lawrence tells us, "Already her heart was heavy because of her own disappointment. Her mouth was dumb and pathetic. But he did not notice, he went his way" (*Rainbow,* 207).

Like any child, Ursula shifts rapidly from one mood to another, but she also divides her consciousness into levels, retaining one feeling or response in secret while displaying another. It is this trait that makes Ursula, along with Paul of "The Rocking-Horse Winner," especially modern among Lawrence's child characters. And it is another link with Pearl. Although Ursula does not neutralize one plane of consciousness with another, her private sufferings, perversities, and contradictions are laid bare by the interior point of view. One may see Ursula's division of consciousness in the following incident, which occurs when she is four years old. Her father, shocked to see "zigzagging lines of deep little footprints across his work," has shouted at her for trampling his seedbeds:

> Her soul, her consciousness, seemed to die away. She became shut off and senseless, a little fixed creature whose soul had gone hard and unresponsive. The sense of her own unreality hardened her like a frost. She cared no longer. . . .
> Yet far away in her, the sobs were tearing her soul. And when he had gone, she would go and creep under the parlour sofa, and lie clinched in the silent, hidden misery of childhood.
> When she crawled out . . . she went rather stiffly to play. She willed to forget. She cut off her childish soul from memory, so that the pain, and the insult should not be real. (*Rainbow,* 207–8)

Lawrence's language, which implies a diagram of the soul, ascribes a remarkable degree of intentionality to the young girl's management of her own psyche and experience. She is, in short, described in terms usually reserved for his adult characters. At the same time, Lawrence avoids idealizing the child or giving the confrontation a moral interpretation through a maudlin sympathy with Ursula. In the episode as a whole the father's anger is just as plausible as the child's misery.

The realistic elements that survive in *The Rainbow* (despite Lawrence's declared lack of interest in them) make Ursula an uneasy combination of passional abstraction and the realistic representation of domestic and dramatic events from which Lawrence composed the childhood of Anna Brangwen. Paradoxically, as Lawrence approaches the modern subject and heroine, he begins to abandon the realistic mode in favor of the mythic, the directly visual description in favor of the metaphorical. This blending of domestic history into a kind of abstract psychic patterning that leans toward myth is a development toward what Kermode calls Lawrence's "revised version of realism" in *Women in Love*. Lawrence, Kermode declares,

> gave his age of crisis the minimum of historical particularity and the maximum of mythical, or typological, or symbolic, reference. The very character of his narrative involves a recoil from mere history and from [what Proust calls] 'the vagaries of a plausible concatenation.' He will have none of the plotting which in George Eliot [specifically in *Middlemarch*] soaks up so much authentic, thematic interest.[24]

If *Women in Love* is apocalyptic, then *The Rainbow* may be said to follow the movement from Paradise into life in the fallen world. Here the children struggle to find the way to live vitally within the conditions of history, and the chosen ones, the Olympians—like Ursula—prepare for their transcendence out of history and into myth. The problematic dualities of this condition are illustrated by Ursula's struggles as an adolescent trying to identify herself. Her youthful solipsism takes the form of imagining herself as a Polish princess under a spell in England or, later, as one of the fair daughters of men to whom the Sons of God would come: "She lived a dual life, one where the facts of daily life encompassed everything, being legion, and the other wherein the facts of daily life were superseded by the eternal truth. So utterly did she desire the Sons of God should come to the daughters of men; and she believed more in her desire and its fulfillment than in the obvious facts of life" (*Rainbow,* 257). Ursula feels a painful necessity and freedom to choose the dimension in which she will live. For a while she chooses her father's "mystical passion" over her mother's generous fecundity and earthiness: "Ursula was all for the ultimate. She was always in revolt against babies and muddled domesticity. To her, Jesus was another world, He was not of this world" (*Rainbow,* 256). Then later, still an adolescent, she becomes a realist, finding that the religion that had been for her "a glorious sort of play-world . . . became a tale, a

24. Kermode, "D. H. Lawrence and the Apocalyptic Types," 149.

myth, an illusion. . . . she held that that which one cannot experience in daily life is not true for oneself" (*Rainbow*, 263).

Either choice, Ursula will learn, is false, an imposition of mental limits upon the larger realm of conscious and unconscious being. She must do, finally, what The Man Who Died in *The Escaped Cock* does, and what *The Rainbow* does—she must understand that there is no need to choose between the mythic and the ordinary, and no need to accept a moral structure that limits her participation in either dimension. As Lawrence's own philosophical writings demonstrate, it is difficult to find a language to describe the soul, particularly if one is a twentieth-century novelist and not a writer of epic poems. Nonetheless, the way to make a true paradox is with metaphor. In his essay on the child archetype, Jung states:

> An archetypal content expresses itself, first and foremost, in metaphors. . . . If such a content should speak of the sun and identify it with . . . the power that makes for the life and health of man, it is neither one thing or the other, but the unknown third thing that finds more or less adequate expression in all these similes, yet—to the perpetual vexation of the intellect—remains unknown and not to be fitted into a formula.[25]

In Ursula Brangwen the paradoxical elements that call for unity are the modern and the mythic, for while Ursula represents the spirit of modern childhood, she also represents a new branch in the heroic tradition. Jung, in his discussion of the persistent archetype of the child who is both helpless and all-powerful, warns that we dare not "succumb to the illusion that an archetype can be finally explained and disposed of." "The best we can do," he continues—and I think that Lawrence does this in his creation of Ursula—"is *dream the myth onwards* and give it a modern dress."[26]

The modernity represented by Ursula becomes a subject in itself in Lawrence's next novel, *Women in Love*. In this novel the generational concerns that pervade *The Rainbow* are replaced by a narrower focus on the new generation, on the young women and men who are inheriting a corrupt England and grappling with its increasing social and sexual democracy. In its large, visionary form, *Women in Love* (written 1916–1917) contains Lawrence's response to World War I, which he regarded as the suicide of European civilization. *Dies Irae*—the final days, the days of wrath—was one title he considered for the book, and it expresses his view of the times.

25. Jung and Kerényi, *Essays on a Science of Mythology*, 76.
26. Ibid., 79.

Lawrence was treated as an exile in his own country; he and his German wife endured the war years in ill health, poverty, and literary ill repute. Not surprisingly, the child characters and the images of childhood in this novel are very different from those in *The Rainbow*.

The relationship of the two eldest Brangwen girls—now young woman—Ursula and Gudrun, provides one axis upon which this story turns. For both of them, parents, home, and family have become a puzzling, even horrifying, legacy which they are determined to deny. They really repudiate their parents; their closeness to each other seems to be their only connection with their childhoods. In the dialogue that opens the novel, the two sisters discuss whether or not they themselves wish to marry:

> "Of course there's children—" said Ursula, doubtfully.
> Gudrun's face hardened.
> "Do you *really* want children, Ursula?" she asked coldly.
> A dazzled, baffled look came on Ursula's face.
> "One feels it is still beyond one," she said.
> "*Do* you feel like that?" asked Gudrun. "I get no feeling whatever from the thought of bearing children."
> Gudrun looked at Ursula with a mask-like, expressionless face. Ursula knitted her brows.
> "Perhaps it isn't genuine," she faltered. "Perhaps one doesn't really want them, in one's soul—only superficially." (*WL,* 9)

As young women have done in many novels before this one, Gudrun and Ursula wonder what it would be like to marry and to have children. This discussion is to be taken seriously, because these women are in their midtwenties and self-supporting in their careers as artist and teacher: they could choose not to marry. The dialogue builds to an essential and radical question, one that will become prominent in later feminist thought: whether the desire for children is essential to female nature or a social construction. While such a question on the third page of a novel would seem to be like Chekhov's famous gun brought on to the stage, it is not answered in the plot of this novel. Only one of the sisters marries, and neither becomes pregnant. (But, recall that near the end of *The Rainbow,* the miscarriage, of her pregnancy by Anton Skrebensky, liberates Ursula.) This avoidance of a key question, I think, implies that it is not possible to think of having children in a world deformed by hatred. As Maria DiBattista suggests, this "Sisters" chapter "centers on the radical isolation of modern woman, isolated from marriage and its central affirmations," one of which is provision for future generations.[27] The marriage of Ursula and Rupert proposes to span the distance between the modern female self and traditional marriage but, coming to an impasse at the close of the novel, shows no prospect of children. The Pussum, a London model with whom Gerald Crich spends a weekend, is ten weeks pregnant, a fact she calls "beastly" and Gerald finds "impossible, she was so young and so far in spirit from any childbearing" (*WL,* 68). Weeks later when she appears again, the Pussum is thinner than before, so apparently her pregnancy has somehow been aborted (*WL,* 381). Here Lawrence sees pregnancy as both a physical and a spiritual condition for which the contemporary Englishwoman is unsuited. Ursula's spontaneous abortion of Skrebensky's and her child at the end of *The Rainbow* is not just a convenient closure for the novel; it is an indication of her spiritual condition and—ultimately—a symbol of rebirth for Ursula's own body and soul. Elsewhere in *Women in Love* the Pussum is called a "flower of the mud," an image that connects her with the "mud-child" Loerke. Such childlike grown-ups are aberrations (generally with aspects that imply sexual perversity) whom childishness and reproductive disability mark as human failures. In this they differ from the asexual childlike adults such as Mr. Dick in *David Copperfield,* whose childish virtues make him superior to many adults.

In *Women in Love* childbirth becomes an abstraction, an exotic image to be collected for its aesthetic qualities. In the apartment where Gerald stays with Pussum, Halliday, and the others, he contemplates a West African wood carving of a woman in labor. At first he does not recognize her position: "a woman sitting naked in a strange posture, and looking tortured, her abdomen stuck out." Gerald calls the statue obscene, but also finds it "rather wonderful, conveying the suggestion of the extreme of physical sensation, beyond the limits of mental consciousness" (*WL,* 74). Birkin defends

27. Maria DiBattista, "*Women in Love:* D. H. Lawrence's Judgment Book," in *D. H. Lawrence: A Centenary Consideration,* ed. Peter Balbert and Phillip L. Marcus, 72. Gudrun's and Ursula's taking of last stands before they need to do so is, DiBattista says in an argument based on Nietzsche's *Twilight of the Idols,* "a symptom of their fall into the fragmented world of modernity." The "primary female negativity" thus introduced to the novel's sexual dialectic "signals a collapse of the time needed for the self's unfolding into the compacted and airless space of irony (Gudrun) or anomie (Ursula). Both responses measure the distance separating female desire from the established familial system of filiation and alliance" (72).

the carving against Gerald's opposition, calling it "pure culture in sensation, culture in the physical consciousness"—the culture that England, according to Birkin and Lawrence, lacks (*WL,* 79). The women in this novel do not bear children—as Gertrude Morel, Lydia Brangwen, Anna Brangwen, Alvina Houghton, and Lady Chatterley do—because they lack such physical consciousness.

Even though bearing children is not possible for this war generation, childhood remains a subject in *Women in Love* through the memories and histories of Ursula, Gudrun, and Gerald (but not Rupert Birkin), through the two child characters Diana and Winifrid Crich, and through increasingly enigmatic images and symbols. Only occasionally do allusions to childhood retain the familiar, Romantic connotations of happiness, innocence, and spontaneity. For instance, Gudrun and Ursula row their boat away from the Crich family's public party to a secluded spot where they bathe and dance naked, and take their tea in private: "the two girls were quite complete in a perfect world of their own. And this was one of the perfect moments of freedom and delight, such as children alone know, when all seems a perfect and blissful adventure" (*WL,* 165). More often when childhood is invoked, the image is accompanied by longing for a condition that is irretrievably lost: Rupert Birkin, "tired of the life that belongs to death," tells Ursula that he wants "love that is like sleep, like being born again, vulnerable as a baby that just comes into the world" (*WL,* 186). Between men and women, the nostalgia for childhood is frequently exploitative; when Gerald Crich, grieving for his father, makes love to Gudrun the first time, he finds in her "the great bath of life . . . Mother and substance of all life she was. And he, child and man, received of her and was made whole. . . . Like a child at the breast, he cleaved intensely to her" (*WL,* 344–45). As it becomes evident to Gudrun that she cannot love Gerald, she watches her sister with Rupert: " 'How good and simple they look together,' Gudrun thought, jealously. She envied them some spontaneity, a childish sufficiency . . . They seemed such children to her" (*WL,* 403). For Ursula, too, marriage carries the motif of childhood, but she must reject her actual childhood to be reborn: "[Ursula] wanted to have come down from the slopes of heaven to this place, with Birkin, not to have toiled out of the murk of her childhood and her upbringing, slowly, all soiled. She felt that memory was a dirty trick played upon her" (*WL,* 409).

The dirty tricks of memory figure strongly in *Women in Love* as historical and biological determinants of character. Only those characters who can free themselves of their own histories survive.

Gerald Crich's early death seems ordained by his inauspicious beginnings. Christiana Crich, Gerald's mother, locked in a marriage of "utter interdestruction" that shatters her mind and her husband's vitality, submits to him "like a hawk in a cage" and bears many children. Gerald was "a proper demon, ay, at six month's old" according to his nurse, and he later accidentally kills his brother with an old gun. As a young man he returns home to modernize the family business, but he cannot escape the family trait: "We're all of us curiously bad at living. We can do things—but we can't get on with life at all" (*WL*, 218, 212, 205). On the other hand, the characters who are imaginatively equipped to survive in this apocalyptic world have separated themselves from the past. Rupert Birkin seems not to have any family connections at all, and in the course of the story breaks his psychic loyalty to the social and political worlds represented by his former mistress, Hermione Roddice, and his job as a school inspector. Ursula must struggle to disengage herself from her family, but Rupert believes that she has the spirit to succeed. He is looking at her father:

> Birkin could see only a strange, inexplicable, almost patternless collection of passions and desires and suppressions and traditions and mechanical ideas, all cast unfused and disunited into this slender, bright-faced man of nearly fifty, who was as unresolved now as he was at twenty, and as uncreated. How could he be the parent of Ursula, when he was not created himself? He was not a parent. A slip of living flesh had been transmitted through him, but the spirit had not come from him. The spirit had not come from any ancestor, it had come out of the unknown. A child is the child of the mystery, or it is uncreated. (*WL*, 255)

Birkin is not frightened of the unknown in Ursula as her father had been when she was an infant. In the sterner dialectic of *Women in Love,* the traditional image of a child as bringer of new life and hope is circumscribed by the deathly conditions of modern life. The child represents hope only if she can reject her inheritance. On the night Ursula walks away from her parents' house, completing her revolt against her father, she weeps "from fathomless depths of hopeless, hopeless grief, the terrible grief of a child, that knows no extenuation" (*WL,* 366). After severance from her natural childhood, Ursula is to be reborn into new being with Birkin.

Perhaps the most stunning contrast *Women in Love* offers to previous novels on childhood is in the drowning of Diana Crich, Gerald's sixteen-year-old sister, who falls from a steam launch into a reservoir during a party. As I noted before, the death of a young person is a spiritual event in the nineteenth-century novel. In most cases, the child—Helen Burns, Paul Dombey, Little Nell, the children of Sue Bridehead and Jude, James's Morgan Moreen ("The Pupil") and Dolcino ("The Author of Beltraffio")—is too good, actively good in Brontë and Dickens, passively innocent in James and Hardy, to survive in this world. Only one exception, the sniveling Linton Heathcliff, of *Wuthering Heights,* might be seen as a precursor to the unregrettable Diana. The young seldom die in Lawrence's work, so the death of Diana is a significant anomaly. Diana's accident compels Gerald to dive fruitlessly in the cold, dark water to grope for her and the young doctor who tried to save her. The kingdom this child leads the doctor to is not heaven but the underworld: "If you once die," he [Gerald] said, "then when it's over, it's finished. Why come to life again? There's room under that water there for thousands" (*WL,* 184).[28] Later, Rupert Birkin asks, "What does it matter if Diana Crich is alive or dead? . . . Better she were dead— she'll be much more real. She'll be positive in death. In life she was a fretting, negated thing" (*WL,* 185). Found the next morning in the rotten water of the nearly emptied reservoir, Diana has her arms "tight around the neck of the young man, choking him" (*WL,* 189). The child savior of the old century has become a parasite whose embrace kills her would-be savior, leaving few to mourn her. Even her sister Winifred's scream of "Di-Di-Di-Di," when Diana falls into the water, as Richard Swigg observes, invokes "destruction at the same moment as it calls [Gerald] to save."[29]

There is really only one living child in *Women in Love:* Winifred Crich. Oddly enough, she is not really a child either, for she is introduced as being thirteen or fourteen. Nonetheless, her behavior—she has a French nurse, speaks in baby talk to her pets, and is warned by Birkin not to fidget lest she fall out of the front seat of the car—makes her seem much younger. Apparently Lawrence needed a child in this role and forgot about the age he had assigned her. Winifred, like Ursula Brangwen, possesses a peculiar sort of modernity. Ursula, I argued, is troubled by the difficulties of being pulled too soon into mental consciousness—she strains under the pressure to create herself in modern terms. Winifred, on the other hand, may be approaching postmodernity. She is unconnected and unaffected, an individual whose self is made up of loose fragments of existence:

28. This doctor's lifesaving effort contrasts sharply with a similar episode in "The Horse-Dealer's Daughter" wherein both Dr. Jack Ferguson and Mabel Pervin discover love and new life when he saves her from drowning.

29. Swigg, *Lawrence, Hardy, and American Literature,* 168.

"quite single and by herself, deriving from nobody. It was as if she were cut off from all purpose or continuity, and existed simply moment by moment" (*WL,* 220). Leo Bersani notes that in Lawrence's "frictional repetition" of abstract character traits Winifred is "a strange hybrid of Loerke and Birkin."[30] Her singleness of being amounts to a preference for those who will cater to her spontaneity: "She was like a changeling indeed, as if her feelings did not matter to her, really" (*WL,* 219). This apparently unfeeling child is the object of her dying father's concern:

> The father, as by some strange final illusion, felt as if all his fate depended on his ensuring to Winifred her happiness. She who could never suffer, because she never formed vital connections, she who could lose the dearest things of her life and be just the same the next day, the whole memory dropped out, as if deliberately, she whose will was so strangely and easily free, anarchistic, almost nihilistic, who like a soulless bird flits on its own will, without attachment or responsibility beyond the moment, who in her every motion snapped the threads of serious relationship, with blithe, free hands, really nihilistic, because never troubled, she must be the object of her father's final passionate solicitude. (*WL,* 220)

When Gerald suggests that Gudrun be hired to give drawing lessons to Winifred, his father acts immediately, believing that the artist who shows her sculptures in London is a "tree of utterance" to which he can "graft" his favorite daughter before he dies. Gudrun, in her own detached way, takes a liking to Winifred, but she regards her connection with the Crich family as a prelude to an affair: "Gudrun knew that it was a critical thing for her to go to Shortlands. She knew it was equivalent to accepting Gerald Crich as a lover. . . . She also wanted to know what Winifred was really like" (*WL,* 234). Neither Winifred nor Gudrun is the sort of being who can be "grafted" to another.

In Winifred one finds the romantic, sentimental idea of the child fully overturned; she does wicked, grotesque, comical drawings of her pets and shows them around with an "almost inhuman chuckle" that delights the misanthropic Gudrun. Her obliviousness makes her a survivor in a dying family. Of all the children, she is the only one who is not repelled by her father: "They talked and prattled at random, he always as if he were well . . . Winifred, with a child's subtle instinct for avoiding the painful things, behaved as if nothing serious was the matter. Instinctively, she withheld her attention, and

30. Bersani, *A Future for Astyanax,* 176.

was happy. Yet in her remoter soul, she knew as well as the adults knew: perhaps better" (*WL,* 284). When her father finally dies, Winifred avoids the funeral gatherings, hating the conventional sentiments expressed there: she "hid in the studio, and cried her heart out, and wished Gudrun would come" (*WL,* 337). It is a strange conclusion, one that seems to vindicate the child's character as possessing—despite its changeling quality—more integrity than any adult's.[31] Lawrence comes close, in *Women in Love,* to revoking his admiration for childhood, but Winifred Crich's honest "nihilism" seems finally to place her in the company of young Anna and Ursula as a being Lawrence can admire.

Admire, but not reward, because the postwar moral landscape holds no rewards. Winifred is whisked off to London for a few days by her older sister Laura (the one whose wedding Ursula and Gudrun are watching as the novel opens) and never heard from again. Since Gudrun is not returning to England after the trip the two couples make to the Alps, it does not seem likely that Winifred will meet her "tree of utterance" again. Still, Winifred extends the spirit of modern childhood that Lawrence recognized in Pearl Prynne, and she shares Ursula and Gudrun's hostility to conventional English living, so—were I to predict—I would wager that Winifred, like these others, would find her way to the Continent where she could exchange the Crich family's death compulsion for one that is more ironic and aesthetically appealing.

In the closing episodes of *Women in Love,* the Dresden sculptor Loerke becomes the perverse bearer of the child motif that I have been tracing. The four main characters of *Women in Love* are, as Mark Schorer put it years ago, "compounded of a double drive" and are free in the plot to choose between life and death.[32] In the event, Ursula and Rupert leave the Alps to choose life, while Gudrun and Gerald stay in the mountains, engaged in a mortal contest of wills.

31. Swigg notes that figures such as Winifred "provide a subservient innocence for the benefit of adults, acting up to preserve them in their roles as proud or compassionate benefactors, like Billy Brangwen who plays a cherub, with 'a great solemnity of being good' to Birkin's angel." Winifred plays such a role for her father, who needs help to sustain his code of Christian paternalism, and for Gudrun and Gerald, for whom the interlude at Shortlands is a "last disguise of innocence" before they embark on the "hellish course" of their European journey. So read, this child becomes parodic of the romantic child whose innocence could not be sullied. Her baby talk to her pets, then, can be seen as an act put on for the benefit of adults who crave such pretenses (Swigg, *Lawrence, Hardy and American Literature,* 167–70).

32. Mark Schorer, "*Women in Love* and Death," 53.

Gudrun is now repelled by Gerald, who seems to her "like a child that is famished crying for the breast . . . he needed her to put him to sleep, to give him repose" (*WL,* 466). Gudrun rejects both the child-man she sees in Gerald and the role of nurturer in which he has tried to cast her. For her everything has become "intrinsically a piece of irony" (*WL,* 418). To replace Gerald she singles out Loerke, a "small, dark-skinned man with full eyes, an odd creature, like a child, and like a troll, quick, detached" (*WL,* 405). Loerke has a "mocking, penetrating understanding" that provides an exact reversal of the open, unjudging, pristine perceptions Lawrence attributes to natural children. Nonetheless, like a child, Loerke has a certain freedom because he owns no social and mental preconceptions. His freedom is made from "subconscious, sinister knowledge, devoid of illusions and hopes." To Gudrun he is a "mud-child . . . the very stuff of the underworld of life. There was no going beyond him" (*WL,* 427).

Indeed, this "mud-child," this man who is again a child because he has known every kind of degradation and given up every illusion of meaning in relationships or art, marks an end to Lawrence's exploration of the modern spirit of childhood. After this he must re-open the question of the meaning of childhood in a new way: through theory in *Psychoanalysis and the Unconscious* and *Fantasia of the Unconscious,* through visual images in two of his paintings, through allegorized social realism in "England, My England" and *Lady Chatterley's Lover,* through supernaturalism in "The Rocking-Horse Winner," and through mystical fable in *The Escaped Cock.*

6 "Yet you have children!"
Emergence of Theory and the Symbolic Child

In *The Plumed Serpent,* two characters debate whether having children is an act of human faith or one of mere animal reproduction. Kate Leslie, an Irishwoman, speaks with Don Ramón, a Mexican:

> "Sometimes," she said, "I think that is my *permanent* feeling toward people.—I like the world, the sky and the earth and the greater mystery beyond. But people—yes, they are all monkeys to me."
> He could see that, at the bottom of her soul, it was true. . . . "Pure monkeys! And the things they do, sheer monkeydom!" Then he added: "Yet you have children!"
> "Yes, Yes!" she said, struggling with herself. "My first husband's children."
> "And they?—*monos y no mas?*" [Monkeys and nothing more?]
> "No!" she said, frowning and looking angry with herself. "Only partly." (*PS,* 250)

Kate, the heroine of this 1926 novel, is at the end of her rope when she comes to Mexico, but she says she has felt since she was a girl that people are nothing but performing monkeys. Yet, she has children, and she admits, with anger, that these children are more than monkeys.

There are fewer children in Lawrence's later work. More important, those children who do appear are less realistic than Paul Morel, Anna Lensky, Ursula Brangwen, or even the daughters in his early novels and stories. This less realistic portrayal of children is part of a general movement toward a more symbolic—often pointedly allegorical—style in Lawrence's postwar writing. Lawrence's loss of interest in writing realistic fiction and his preference for "the greater mystery beyond" coincide with his own ill health, the failure of any of his utopian projects to attract followers, and the disillusionment with natural man that he experienced in the American West.

154

In other words, Kate Leslie's sentiments are very nearly Lawrence's own. But that does not settle the issue. The other speaker, Don Ramón, wants to find a way beyond Kate's European disillusionment. His is the voice of the regenerative Lawrence, the one whose hope rises like the phoenix from the ashes of despair.

These two attitudes, despair and hope, are both represented in Lawrence's work after *Women in Love.* For some years following World War I, Lawrence lost interest in the human scene, and his work reflects a loss of enthusiasm for the themes of generation and childhood. Lawrence's personal fear of being replaced by posterity (see Chapter 1) takes political form as fear of putting children into the world, a view that is shared by Lovat Somers and Jack Calcott in *Kangaroo* (1923) and repeated by Oliver Mellors in *Lady Chatterley's Lover* (1928). Lawrence's novels during this period attempt to teach mystical prescriptions for political leaders (*Kangaroo* and *Plumed Serpent*) in a dying culture. He finds the world inhospitable to children, whose parents are no longer able to teach them wisdom and responsibility. As early as 1916, in a letter to Catherine Carswell, Lawrence discusses a friend for whom he believes children are now a mistake, and goes on to contrast simple reproduction and true hope:

> There are plenty of children, and no hope. If women can bring forth hope, they are mothers indeed. . . . This is a winter. Children and childbearing do not make spring. It is not in children, the future lies. . . . It is the truth, the new-perceived hope, that makes spring. And let them bring forth that, who can: they are the creators of life. There are many enceinte widows, with a new crop of death in their wombs. What did the mothers of the dead soldiers bring forth, in child-bed?—death or life? And of death you gather death: when you sow death, in this act of love which is pure reduction, you reap death, in a child born with an impulse toward the darkness, the origins, the oblivion of all. (*Letters,* 2:635–36)

To realize the contrast between this attitude and Lawrence's earlier, more hopeful outlook, recall that *The Rainbow*'s Anna Lensky, born to refugees from the Polish insurrection of 1863, is just such a war baby. Yet Anna exhibits no impulse toward death and is a source of vitality for her mother, husband, and children.

In a poem written about 1917, "War-Baby," Lawrence again addresses the issues of faith and childbearing, but leaves room to believe that the biological ability to reproduce is accompanied, in the blood consciousness, by the faith required to do so:

> The child like mustard seed
> Rolls out of the husk of death

Into the woman's fertile, fathomless lap.
. . . .
As for our faith, it was there
When we did not know, did not care;
   It fell from our husk in a little hasty seed.

Say, is it all we need?
   Is it true that the little weed
     Will flourish its branches in heaven when we
      slumber beneath?

               (*CP*, 172)

The middle stanza makes the radical speculation that faith and meaning are literally *embodied* in the promulgation of the species. The profound question posed in the last stanza of the poem is answered variously in Lawrence's work during the last ten years of his life. As I shall later show, Lawrence expounds this idea in *Fantasia of the Unconscious* and expresses it vividly in *Lady Chatterley's Lover*. First, though, I want to look at two stories that present the question—and the answer—more austerely.

These two short stories illustrate the consequences for children who are born to parents or a world that cannot receive them. Like the children in many of the works of Charles Dickens and Henry James, these children become victims. In "England, My England" (1915, expanded and revised 1922), the failure is primarily that of the parents' marriage: a woman named Winifred and a man named Egbert marry and set up their home in a cottage on her father's estate. They are passionate and happy there, though Egbert has no fixed profession and earns little money: "He was always doing something, in his amateurish way. But he had no desire to give himself to the world, and still less had he any desire to fight his way in the world." [1] When they begin to have babies, expenses increase until "Egbert was living on his father-in-law." Winifred has "what the modern mother so often has in place of spontaneous love: a profound sense of duty towards her child. . . . Strange, that this sense of duty should go deeper than the love for her husband. But so it was. And so often is." [2] In many respects the story is a Lawrentian morality play, with lessons on appropriate behavior for each of the

---

1. D. H. Lawrence, "England, My England," *England, My England and Other Stories,* 10. Lawrence's substantial revision of the story in 1922 expanded the section devoted to the marriage and Joyce's injury from less than five to more than twenty-two pages. The 1915 version is reprinted as an appendix in the Cambridge edition.
 2. Ibid., 11.

sexes. Then what of the child in this short-circuited modern family? Her name is Joyce and, a Lawrence child, she has hair like thistledown. She becomes her parents' victim indirectly, by severely cutting her leg on a sickle that her father has (typically, one is led to think) neglected to put away. Her father's own casualness, exacerbated by his resentment of Winifred's tendency to play the "*Mater Dolorata*" in the sickroom, leads to poor medical care. Joyce becomes a cripple. The mother moves the child to London for therapy and Egbert is virtually cast out of the family, though the narrator adds that Joyce's "flamy, reckless spirit was her father's."[3] Egbert joins the army and is killed in Flanders. Although her grandfather spares no expense of money, effort, or will so "that Joyce should save her liberty of movement, should win back her wild, free grace," the reader knows that liberty and grace cannot be achieved by will. The focus of "England, My England" is mostly on Egbert, but in the end it is Joyce who must survive and carry, in her crippled leg, her "odd flippancy," and her debt to the "honourable effort on her behalf," the legacy of a flawed marriage and a corrupt English culture. The circuit of family love becomes a noose, tightened on the child's neck as well as on the adults'.

Again in "The Rocking-Horse Winner" (1925) the child is victimized by the failures of his parents, but from the beginning this later story is more stark and more stridently imbued with Lawrence's critique of the parents' values. The mother, Hester, and the very house want more and more money. The father, who barely appears in the story, has no luck for making it. The child—another Paul, like Paul Morel not only in name but as one of the few notable boy children in Lawrence's work—is spiritually close to his mother and wishes to help her by getting her some money. He does so by riding his rocking horse until he enters a visionary trance and learns the name of the winning horse in an upcoming race. His uncle places bets for him and deposits his winnings anonymously to Hester's bank account, but the money is never enough to satisfy his greedy mother. When she discovers him in a desperate trance, Paul collapses and dies, leaving his mother rich. The story neatly illustrates Lawrence's theory of the mother-induced oedipal complex. Both popular and elusive, "The Rocking-Horse Winner" has elicited many interpretations. As W. D. Snodgrass puts it, this story "seems the perfect story by the least meticulous of serious writers."[4] Its

3. Ibid., 26.
4. W. D. Snodgrass, "A Rocking-Horse: The Symbol, the Pattern, the Way to Live," in Mark Spilka, ed., *D. H. Lawrence: A Collection of Critical Essays,* 117. Snodgrass's article is a little gem, though its identification of Paul's secret as

formal perfection may owe something to Lawrence's lack of enthusiasm for his subject. He wrote the story to satisfy Cynthia Asquith,
who had rejected his first submission ("Glad Ghosts") to her book of
supernatural stories, and, as far as I know, he never recorded any
enthusiasm about it afterward. It is a set piece in what was to him a
closed form, the ghost story. All the same, Lawrence's little fable
about loveless houses, money, and sex pushes some of his theories
about family affection and children to brutally logical conclusions.
This family's problem is familiar from *Fantasia* and "England, My
England": Hester has a malady Lawrence diagnoses in *Fantasia* as
"neurasthenia of the heart," caused by living "terribly and exhaus-
tively from the upper centres." Thus, her need for things is an attempt to placate her impoverished heart:

> She had bonny children, yet she felt they had been thrust upon her, and
> she could not love them. . . . This troubled her, and in her manner she
> was all the more gentle and anxious for her children, as if she loved
> them very much. Only she herself knew that at the centre of her heart
> was a hard little place that could not feel love, no, not for anybody.
> Everybody else said of her: "She is such a good mother. She adores her
> children." Only she herself, and her children themselves, knew it was
> not so. They read it in each other's eyes.[5]

Hester's lap, unlike the one in "War-Baby," is neither fertile nor
fathomless. This mother's heart "turned actually into a stone."[6] The
tale illustrates Lawrence's remark in *Psychoanalysis of the Unconscious* that without the "nourishing creative flow between himself
and another" the individual's life becomes a "slow collapse into
corruption" (*PU,* 46). The allegorical mode of "The Rocking-Horse
Winner" forces Lawrence to a conclusion that is implicit in much of

---

masturbation seems insufficient to me. In "Two Modern Incest Heroes" Selma
Fraiberg argues that "The Rocking-Horse Winner" is a successful story because
it does not name the oedipal fantasy but, with the symbol of the rocking, keeps
the "erotic undercurrent silent" while "making it present; it conceals and yet it
is suggestive; a perfect symbol" (650). Michael Goldberg, in "Lawrence's 'The
Rocking-Horse Winner': A Dickensian Fable?" takes issue with Snodgrass and
answers affirmatively the question of his title; Lawrence's fable, he argues,
makes the same point about children and money that *Dombey and Son* makes.
Charlotte Goodman's article "Henry James, D. H. Lawrence, and the Victimized
Child" compares James's "The Pupil" with "The Rocking-Horse Winner" and
James's "The Author of Beltraffio" with "England, My England."

   5. D. H. Lawrence, "The Rocking-Horse Winner," in *The Complete Short
Stories,* 3:790.

   6. Lawrence, "Rocking-Horse Winner," in *Complete Short Stories,* 3:804.

his other work: without his parents' elemental, egoless love, the child *literally* dies.

That bleak image, the dead child and stone-hearted mother, is not Lawrence's final vision of the parent and child. Just as Don Ramón is able to discover a remnant of faith in the skeptical Kate Leslie, so Lawrence retrieves, during his years of disaffection with humankind, a vision of the child as a symbol of hope. He takes up the dilemma of the "War-Baby" poem again and finds that "our faith . . . was there / When we did not know, did not care." To get a sense of how this retrieval of faith comes about, one must turn to two crucial book-length essays written in the years between *Women in Love* and *Lady Chatterley's Lover.*

Psychoanalysis and the Unconscious and *Fantasia of the Unconscious,* published in 1921 and 1922 respectively, have often been reprinted as a pair. The first purports to be a reply to Freud's concept of the unconscious. The second, nearly four times the length of the first, extends the ideas sketched there in a somewhat more combative style. These essays have been called many things, including the dismissive "pollyanalytics" by a 1921 reviewer of *Psychoanalysis,*[7] but Lawrence's own description is clear: "a book— nay, a booklet—on the child consciousness" (*FU,* 190). Lawrence admits that he seems to digress when he discusses, say, evolution or astronomy, but, he counters, "Child-Consciousness it is. And we have to roll away the stone of a scientific cosmos from the tomb-mouth of that imprisoned consciousness" (*FU,* 190). That sentence, I believe, furnishes an agenda for these essays. Lawrence insists that they are derived from his fiction and poetry ("pure passionate experience"), but he also believed that the artist is governed by a metaphysic that is both cultural and personal. In these essays and many of his other nonfiction pieces, Lawrence articulates his rather unorthodox, polemical metaphysic.[8]

Lawrence's concept of the child is, as I have emphasized, neither Freudian nor Romantic. The fictional characterizations of Paul Morel and of each of the Brangwens all reveal a basic authorial assumption

7. According to David Ellis, "pollyanalytics" was coined by John V. A. Weaver in the *Brooklyn Daily Eagle* (May 28, 1921) (*D. H. Lawrence's Non-Fiction: Art, Thought and Genre,* p. 182, n. 23).

8. Testimony to Lawrence's acuity about mothers and sons comes from the unlikely source of T. S. Eliot, who reportedly once told a class at Harvard that "Lawrence had, in *Fantasia of the Unconscious,* written with more acumen about 'mother love' than any psychologist" (John Soldo, "The Tempering of T. S. Eliot, 1888–1915, qtd. from Peter Ackroyd, *T. S. Eliot: A Life,* 20.)

of vital, independent being in the infant and young child. There are even scenes in which a response from a fetal consciousness is integral to the development of plot and character. In these essays, Lawrence makes no consistent distinction between the terms *unconscious* and *consciousness.* To avoid confusing Lawrence's meaning with the Freudian terms, David Ellis proposes adopting another Lawrentian phrase, *the biological psyche,* for what Lawrence means.[9] This biological psyche is the "spontaneous life-motive in every organism" (*PU,* 13). In the individual human being it originates at the moment of union between egg and sperm and absolutely precedes any kind of mental activity. Often Lawrence describes this biological psyche (or "blood consciousness" or "true unconscious") as "pristine." The adjective is appropriate because it eludes both the moralistic overtones of the Romantics' "innocent" and the mechanical overtones of Freud's "unconscious" (a zone populated through the dynamics of defense reactions). Lawrence himself describes his true, pristine version of the unconscious as the "well-head, the fountain of real motivity" in contrast to the Freudian "cellar in which the mind keeps its own bastard spawn" (*PU,* 9). The Lawrencian biological psyche is premental, preverbal, and never, in the finely balanced person, fully dominated by mental consciousness. Lawrence's theory counters the Western dualistic conception of body and mind with a highly specified anatomy and physiology of the biological psyche. While many readers deny the system any factual validity and seek to understand it metaphorically, recent research shows that Lawrence grounded his scheme in nineteenth- and early twentieth-century thought about the involuntary nervous system.[10] Lawrence's theory of consciousness, like William Blake's cosmology and W. B. Yeats's *Vision,* cannot be understood unless the reader is willing to suspend disbelief. Texts of this kind demand to be read as they were written, as accurate descriptions of their authors' worlds. As scientists also know, the attitude of the observer influences the outcome of an experiment. Therefore I find it best to read Lawrence's essays both as serious statements, based on research and thought, which claim to be literal

9. David Ellis, "Lawrence and the Biological Psyche," 90.

10. John B. Vickery, in "D. H. Lawrence and the Fantasias of Consciousness," suggests that these writings are generically related to W. B. Yeats's *A Vision,* Robert Graves's *The White Goddess,* and W. H. Auden's *The Enchafèd Flood.* Christopher Heywood, in "'Blood Consciousness' and the Pioneers of the Reflex and Ganglionic Systems," presents a review to date of Lawrence's use of theoretical neurology.

representations of the growth of consciousness, *and* as literary texts that reveal Lawrence's imagination at work on subjects he also treats in his fiction.

In both *Psychoanalysis* and *Fantasia* Lawrence tracks the consciousness to its headwaters in the union of egg and sperm. The united egg and sperm "remains always primal and central, and is always the original fount and home of the first and supreme knowledge that *I am I.*" This original cell, lodged at the solar plexus, is the center of the "sympathetic" impulse of consciousness, of the sense that the individual encompasses all: "I am I, the vital centre of all things. I am I, the clue to the whole. All is one with me." The "voluntary" impulse of consciousness comes into existence with the first division of that primary cell, making its center in the lumbar ganglion: "Because I am set utterly apart and distinguished from all that is the rest of the universe, therefore *I am I*" (*FU,* 75). These analyses of the infant's connection with the world and his resistance to it undergird Lawrence's exploration of the revolutionary potential of the novel for revealing character.

By "child consciousness" Lawrence means four primary centers of the biological psyche that emerge during childhood. These exist at two planes of being within the body: the lower, sensual plane comprising the solar plexus and its opposite, the lumbar ganglion; the upper, spiritual plane comprising the cardiac plexus and its opposite, the thoracic ganglion. The dynamism that occurs between these four poles of unconscious being is the "first great field of individual, self-dependent consciousness" (*PU,* 34). The plexuses located on the front of the body reach toward union with the world, while the ganglia on the backside pull away. The child possesses two sympathetic (front) centers and two voluntary (back) centers. These four poles of the psyche (to which four more are added in puberty) constitute a necessary basis for development of healthy adult psychological being and marriage: "There cannot be a perfect transition [into puberty] unless all the activity is in full play in all the first four poles of the psyche. Childhood is a chrysalis from which each must extricate himself. And the struggling youth or maid cannot emerge unless by the energy of all powers" (*FU,* 150). A balanced individual consciousness saves the child a later struggle to establish integrity of the ego; thus the secure young adult is free to engage in the more important struggle for relationship with others and the world at large. Without balanced development in the four primary areas of child consciousness, the adult will be out-of-kilter—perhaps prematurely sexual or belatedly striving for equilibrium and strength in the solar and lumbar areas. In this context Lawrence's famous ideal of "blood consciousness" must be understood not as a rejection of mentality, but as a unifying term that takes its meaning from the bloodstream's role as link among brain, heart, lungs, lower organs, and extremities.

An old joke concludes that an idea may work in practice but not in theory. Such could be the case with Lawrence's theory of child consciousness and the biological psyche. Where does the practice occur? Not only in the fiction that preceded the theory (as I have illustrated throughout my previous chapters) but in the anecdotes and examples in *Psychoanalysis* and *Fantasia*. In one case Lawrence asks why the touch of fur evokes pleasure in one child and pain in another:

> How now? Is it a complex? Did the father have a beard?
> It is possible. But all-too-human. The physical result of rubbing fur is to set up a certain amount of frictional electricity . . . one of the sundering forces. It corresponds to the voluntary forces exerted at the lower spinal ganglia, the forces of anger and retraction into independence and power. An over-sympathetic child will scream with fear at the touch of fur; a refractory child will purr with pleasure. (*PU,* 30)

Although the children and the furred creature are undetailed, they provide a realistic basis for the impersonal explanation. The jab at Freud—"Did the father have a beard?"—criticizes analyses of mental states based on a theory of sexual motivations.[11] Implicitly, Lawrence also mocks his own analysis. I have suggested that one should suspend disbelief in order to read these essays thoroughly. Nonetheless, there are passages within the essays that circumvent the problem. Does one need to take literally Lawrence's theory of ganglionic centers in order to accept this story of the two different children and the fur? The precision of observation and the impulse toward narrative that attend the explanation reinforce Lawrence's claim that his theory evolved from his fiction. In fact, Lawrence does not abandon the techniques of fiction in these essays.[12] Here is a second example of sympathetic and voluntary reactions:

> In its wonderful unison with the mother [the child] is at the same time extricating itself into single, separate, independent existence. . . . At

11. See also the opening page of James Joyce's *A Portrait of the Artist as a Young Man,* Harmondsworth: Penguin Books, 1960, in which Stephen recalls "his father looked at him through a glass: he had a hairy face" (7).

12. For a provocative discussion of Lawrence's use of fictional techniques in his nonfiction, see M. Elizabeth Wallace, "The Circling Hawk: Philosophy of Knowledge in Polanyi and Lawrence," 109–10.

first the child cleaves back to the old source. . . . The sympathetic centre of unification, or at least unison, alone seems awake. The child wails with the strange desolation of severance, wails for the old connection. With joy and peace it returns to the breast, almost as to the womb.

But not quite. Even in sucking it discovers its new identity and *power*. . . . The child stiffens itself and holds back. What is it, wind? Stomach-ache? Not at all. Listen to some of the screams. . . . The first scream of the ego. The scream of asserted isolation. (*PU,* 22–23)

Fragmented vignettes such as this one about the nursing baby are woven through Lawrence's exposition of the biological psyche. With their "love and wrath, cleaving and repulsion, inglutination and excrementation" (*PU,* 24), these scenes give the work a persuasiveness that overwhelms the scheme itself.[13] This mixture of abstract discussion and realistic examples parallels the blending of the domestic and the visionary modes that I noted in *The Rainbow*.

Polemical vigor in these essays is directed against scientific or rationalist attitudes, which, Lawrence argues, distort the natural and essential development of human consciousness—most dramatically in children. In *Psychoanalysis,* Lawrence attacks Freud, who to him represents the nadir of rationalization because he applies reason to those sexual and physical realms of human experience that, Lawrence believes, offer the only hope of salvation from reason. The exact degree of Lawrence's acquaintance with Freud's work remains unknown, but certainly Lawrence's subjects are more diverse than those he attributes to the Viennese psychoanalyst. Superficially, an opposition exists: Freud, a physician, based his theories on case histories from clinical experience; Lawrence, an artist, drew his from his imagination. Nonetheless, Freud was deeply influenced by literary imagination, while Lawrence took an intellectual and prophetic interest in scientific thought. If Lawrence had really set out to refute Freud on specific points, he might have deserved serious attention. But he did not. His project is much broader, and—in my opinion—he makes a tactical error in using Freud as his straw man. *Psychoanalysis* and *Fantasia* have suffered, I believe, from the critics' attempts to defend them on Freud's home court. Difficul-

---

13. When I first read *Psychoanalysis* and *Fantasia,* I was a new mother and I was stunned by Lawrence's accuracy. Though I had read a dozen respected baby-care manuals, none of them explained, as Lawrence does, the pride a parent takes in her baby's excrementation (*PU* 30); or "how weary in the back is the nursing mother whose great centre of repudiation is suppressed" (*PU* 24); or why a newborn infant may emit screams of temper that stiffen its little back with "amazing power" (*PU* 23).

ties of terminology keep discussions from getting to substantive issues. Worse, they promote an exaggeration of the differences between the two thinkers. Philip Rieff claims that "the confrontation between Freud and Lawrence recapitulates the historic controversy—on what is the function of reason in the character of man— that divides Western culture still. Lawrence was the most profound spokesman in our century for the irrationalist minority position." More recently, Ellis proposes comparing Lawrence's essays with Freud's metapsychological texts such as *Beyond the Pleasure Principle* and thus salvages them from charges of scientific inaccuracy in order to focus on their wider address to the state of the human mind in his time.[14]

Both these critics carry on the enterprise on which Lawrence's own project foundered, the "debate" between Lawrence and Freud. Technically speaking, of course, there was no debate, because Freud did not respond to Lawrence's attack. London psychoanalysts had praised *Sons and Lovers* seven years before, but as I argue in Chapter 2, *Sons and Lovers* was Lawrence's only Freudian novel. Yet he was still tethered to Freud. Lawrence's debate with Freud is only apparently about infantile sexuality, and must be seen more accurately as a debate about the meaning of sexuality and its relation to the rest of life. Lawrence quibbles with Freud's definition of sex, not because of its limits, but because it is different *in kind*. Although Lawrence takes account of the erotic aspect of childhood in his fiction, he nonetheless remains at issue with Freud. Freud's scientific allegiance reduces sex to biological function, but his extension of his theories toward philosophical conclusions aggrandizes the realm influenced by this sexual function. Lawrence, on the other hand, associates sex with creativity of the soul. For him sex becomes a way of connecting with all of life—it can be transcendent. Since Rieff reopened the Lawrence-Freud debate in 1960, literary attitudes toward Freud have changed enormously. Literature reflects more skepticism of his findings and prescriptions but increased appreciation of his textual quality and influence. The diversity and complexity of thought now surrounding psychoanalytic theory, thanks largely to feminist and Lacanian critiques, make Lawrence's theory more easily countenanced.[15] This deconstruction of Freud

14. Philip Rieff, Introduction to *Psychoanalysis of the Unconscious* and *Fantasia of the Unconscious,* ix; Ellis, "Lawrence and the Biological Psyche," 93.
    15. For a Lacanian view of Lawrence, see Ed Jewinski's "The Phallus in

calls for a reconstruction of Lawrence. Increasingly, critics will be able to bring Lawrence's work into position as a subject, no longer an eternal *other* to Freud's.

The development I am charting between Lawrence's postwar disillusionment and his eventual return to the subject of childhood must take into account the period of the leadership novels, which express precious little interest in children. Paradoxically, as Judith Ruderman points out, the beginnings of Lawrence's interest in leadership, the theme that dominates Lawrence's male supremacist works from *Aaron's Rod* through *The Plumed Serpent,* may be found in *Fantasia.*[16] Here Lawrence argues, as he did not in *Psychoanalysis* the year before, that a man must have a goal in the world beyond that of an achieved relationship with a woman.[17] This goal, he states, must be established in a man's mid-thirties (Lawrence's own age) after he has become "deeply fulfilled through marriage, and at one with his own soul." Now he must "undertake the responsibility for the next step into the future . . . give himself perfectly to some . . . passionate purposive activity" while his wife, if she has "greatness of soul," will relinquish "her own self-assertion, and believe in the man who believes in himself and in his own soul's efforts" (*FU,* 157, 160).

Within this announcement of his doctrine of male mission, Lawrence asserts and explicates the paternal role in child development. Even now, in the late twentieth century, male participation in the care of infants is an embattled subject. Yet Lawrence, seventy years ago, attempted to establish a male role within this female domain. He notes two levels of participation. First, he emphasizes the role of the sperm—"the bright male germ" in the making of the individual child, which he connects with two other privileged subjects, the solar plexus and blood consciousness. This original germ "still lies

---

D. H. Lawrence and Jacques Lacan." Jewinski finds that Lawrence is the first English writer to reject the humanist notion of the self and compares this rejection with Lacan's concept of difference; for both men the phallus becomes the central signifier. My own sense is that Lacan and Lawrence mean different things by phallus, particularly in regard to language and symbolic order. Lawrence challenges humanism's assumptions about the human spirit by insisting upon its (prelinguistic) basis in the body; Lacan undermines humanism by insisting upon the constructed nature of language and the human subject.

16. Ruderman, *D. H. Lawrence and the Devouring Mother,* 31–36.

17. For comparisons of the two essays, see Evelyn Hinz, "The Beginning and the End: D. H. Lawrence's *Psychoanalysis* and *Fantasia*"; and David Ellis and Howard Mills, "Poetry and Science in the Psychology Books," in *D. H. Lawrence's Non-Fiction: Art, Thought and Genre,* chap. 3.

sparkling and potent within the solar plexus" (*FU*, 70). The physical connection of the child to its mother is more obvious because of the navel; however, he asks, "because the mother-child relation is more plausible and flagrant, is that any reason for supposing it deeper, more vital, more intrinsic? . . . the smaller, brilliant male-spark . . . may be even more vivid, even more intrinsic. So beware how you deny the father-quick of yourself. You may be denying the most intrinsic quick of all" (*FU*, 70). Second, Lawrence insists upon the importance of the father in raising the child because, in order to develop a proper psychic balance and independence, the child must grow "in the interplay of two great life-waves, the womanly and the male" (*FU*, 73). The role Lawrence recommends for fathers need not be stereotypically masculine; if a mother is "too generally hard or indifferent, then it rests with the father to provide the delicate sympathy and the refined discipline" (*FU*, 88). Whether the father is called upon to be sympathetic or stern, he must "stand outside as a final authority and make the necessary adjustments . . . to maintain some sort of equilibrium between the two modes of love in his infant" (*FU*, 87). A feminist reading of these sections of *Fantasia* perhaps depends on one's response to the essentialist issue in feminist theory: either Lawrence's masculinism has run rampant, trying to usurp a clearly female realm of influence; or Lawrence recognizes the importance of child nurture and wishes to elevate it by removing its historic segregation by gender. While the sagacity and unilateral authority Lawrence imputes to the father are plainly patriarchal, his overall attitude evinces continuing respect for the child, and a wary regard for the mother's biological being.

If Lawrence's pronouncements regarding women and their roles during the 1920s often seem damnable, many critics remain struck by the fact that his best fiction takes women seriously. This profound engagement parallels the earnestness with which he addresses the development of children, usually female, in his novels and the more abstract child in the theoretical books. His theories caution both fathers and mothers not to let an idealized notion of love replace a more essential respect between individuals: "never forget your own honour as an adult individual towards a small individual. It is a question of honour, not of love" (*FU*, 115). He abhors possessive parental love, which leads to fatal interference: "Instead of leaving the child with its own limited but deep and incomprehensible feelings, the parent . . . stimulates the child into a consciousness which does not belong to it, on the one plane, and robs it of its own spontaneous consciousness and freedom on the other plane" (*FU*, 151).

Children must be treated honestly and directly, not bullied, patronized, or idealized: "Children are more sagacious than we are. They twig soon enough if there is a flaw in our own intention and our own true spontaneity" (*FU*, 91). Parents cannot teach or demand love of a child; rather they must "always remember that it is a single little soul by itself; and that the responsibility for the wise, warm relationship is yours, the adult's" (*FU*, 115). The revision of character that Lawrence wants cannot occur unless the sources of consciousness are recognized in their earliest phases. Hence, the essays on child consciousness are a continuation of the project begun in the earlier novels. The attention to child characters in his novels is a part of Lawrence's surgery on the novel, his effort to "have the courage to tackle new propositions without using abstractions . . . to present us with new, really new feelings, a whole new line of emotion . . . to break a way through, like a hole in the wall . . . and [find] a new world outside."[18]

The two paintings by Lawrence reproduced in this book offer another way to regard his attitudes toward the family and the child in the last decade of his life. They present contrasting images of the circuit of family relations described in *Fantasia of the Unconscious,* one father-centered and the other mother-centered. The first painting, from 1926, Lawrence originally called *An Unholy Family.* Before it was exhibited, the painting was retitled *A Holy Family,* thus making the contrast with Christian painting less pointed and suggesting that any family might be holy. The painting parodies portraits of the holy family by medieval and Renaissance masters in which the Christ child and the Virgin are at the center and, usually, graced by the most brilliant nimbuses. In Lawrence's painting, the child is the focus of light from an unseen source, but he is not the center of the composition. The medial position is filled by the swarthy father, who gazes directly at the viewer; his wife, placed in front of him, looks in his direction but apparently beyond the picture space. Both adults have halos that crudely imitate the translucent late Gothic style. The father's is marked with radiating orange lines that emphasize the painted quality of the image. He wears a chest-exposing shirt of blue, the color traditionally worn by the Virgin Mary, while the woman is naked above the waist. The man's right hand holds and raises her left breast. (In Christian holy family paintings, the madonna sometimes offers one breast to the Christ child.) The boy, who looks to be at least eight years old, is

18. Lawrence, "The Future of the Novel," in *Study of Thomas Hardy,* 155.

seated behind his parents and watching them with a bemused expression, though the perspective would not allow him to see their faces.[19] He wears a red shirt much like his father's; another garment beneath his shirt covers his chest. The boy does not have a painted halo: rather, one is suggested by the shape of his hair, which is repeated and emphasized by the back of his chair. The setting is domestic, with a table, bowl, and several shelves of crockery suggesting a kitchen. One surprising detail unites the domestic elements and the religious allusions of the painting: A round window appears in the thick wall just above the boy's head. It is about the same size as the boy's head and at the same level as the man's head. The image it contains is not absolutely clear, but what it most suggests is a monk. This figure in a brown, cowled robe seems to be looking in the same direction the woman is—beyond the picture frame—toward an unidentified source of illumination. The iconography here, I would propose, is that the daily spiritual life represented by the monk is also lived by the ordinary family through its sensual contentment and what Lawrence regards as appropriate balance between man, woman, and child. The repetition of round forms—heads, breasts, crockery, window, halos—projects a scene of harmony despite the iconoclastic treatment of the subject.

The second painting, *Family on a Verandah* (1928), shows a family in an attitude Lawrence distrusts: the nude woman reclines at the center, while the man crouches at her feet and eyes her crotch, reverently or salaciously. Two children play in the foreground, on the verge of climbing up on the mother or perhaps searching for something beneath her. The woman's facial expression is enigmatic in reproductions—one might imagine her either exasperated or content. In any case, the mother's passive domination of the scene and the family represents Lawrence's often expressed, complex fears of female dominance.[20] The inwardly directed gazes of all the

19. The child's sex is not obvious to me, but Lawrence refers to him as "the *bambino.*" This was the first painting Lawrence made on some canvases Maria Huxley gave him. To the Huxleys he writes: "I call it the 'Unholy Family' because the *bambino*—with a *nimbus*—is just watching anxiously to see the young man give the semi-nude young woman *un gros baiser* [a big kiss]. *Molto moderno* [Very modern]!" This commentary is rather unreliable in that the child does not have a nimbus, though his parents do, and the man makes no movement to kiss the woman. What seems clear, though, is that Lawrence enjoys the prospect of surprising an audience with his unorthodox painting.

20. See Ruderman, *D. H. Lawrence and the Devouring Mother,* and Cornelia Nixon, *Lawrence's Leadership Politics and the Turn against Women.*

D. H. Lawrence, *Family on a Verandah*. 1928. Oil 19 × 14 inches.
(Whereabouts unknown. Photograph courtesy University of Illinois at
Chicago, the University Library, Department of Special Collections. Used
with permission of Laurence Pollinger Ltd. and the Estate of Mrs. Frieda
Lawrence Ravagli.)

family members betray a closed, possibly unhealthy circle of emotional energy. Yet the entire picture, especially when seen in color,
yields an alternate interpretation: its flesh tones are warm, the children and father seem very comfortable in their nudity, and the entire composition conveys the kind of mutuality and sensual tenderness Lawrence celebrated in *Lady Chatterley's Lover,* an effect
heightened by the inclusion of the children. Both paintings, with
their different representations of family politics, evince Lawrence's
continuing absorption in the question of how children form and are
formed by the nexus of women, men, and spirit.

In *Lady Chatterley's Lover* and *The Escaped Cock* (1929), Lawrence breaks a way through to new novelistic propositions again by
challenging social definitions of pornography and blasphemy. At
the same time, perhaps paradoxically, he returns to childbearing as
a symbol for renewed life. *Lady Chatterley's Lover,* though rooted
in a critique of class structure, rejects political themes and proposes
that tenderness in personal relations is the way to transcend history.
That novel and one of his very last works, *The Escaped Cock* (also

known as *The Man Who Died*), a retelling of Christ's resurrection, celebrate the flesh and return, tenuously, to a vision of the unborn as an embodiment of hope. Early in *Lady Chatterley's Lover,* Lawrence introduces the question of how Connie Chatterley is to provide an heir for her husband's estate, Wragby. Clifford Chatterly is an impotent cripple and, like several of his intellectual friends, thinks the "sex-business" is more trouble than it is worth. For instance, one woman visiting Wragby is reading a novel (probably Aldous Huxley's *Brave New World,* which Lawrence knew in manuscript) about the future "when babies would be bred in bottles, and women would be 'immunized.'" Clifford comments,"All the love-business . . . might just as well go. I suppose it would if we could breed babies in bottles" (*LCL,* 76). Connie, who regards such talk as mere palaver, is quite stunned when her husband suggests that she become pregnant. Clifford has little concern about who would father the child, because he assumes that "we ought to be able to arrange this sex thing, as we arrange going to the dentist" (*LCL,* 46). The idea of a baby pulls Connie out of the meaninglessness into which she is sinking and makes her receptive to the estate's gamekeeper, Oliver Mellors. Living in Wragby's arid, postwar ambience where "love, joy, happiness, home, mother, father, husband, all these great, dynamic words were half dead now," Connie finds herself drawn to the idea of a child: "But a child, a baby! That was still one of the sensations. She would venture very gingerly on that experiment. There was the man to consider, and it was curious, there wasn't a man in the world whose child you wanted" (*LCL,* 64, 66).

Thus, when Connie begins to love Mellors, she is already thinking of having a child. Her first orgasm with Mellors makes her feel pregnant: "In her womb and bowels she was flowing and alive now . . . and helpless in adoration of him as the most naïve woman. It feels like a child, she said to herself; it feels like a child in me" (*LCL,* 140). Within a few months, Connie makes a trip to Venice in order to create a cover story for the pregnancy she hopes will occur. While she is gone, accusations made by his first wife cause Mellors to lose his position as Wragby gamekeeper. Now certain that she is pregnant, Connie must decide whether she will return to Wragby, pretending she became pregnant in Italy, or go off with Mellors. The coming child kindles the tenderness of the novel's resolution:

> "And say you're glad about the child," she repeated. "Kiss it! Kiss my womb and say you're glad it's there."
> But it was more difficult for him.
> "I've a dread of puttin' children i' th' world," he said. "I've such a dread o' th' future for 'em."

> "But you've put it into me. Be tender to it, and that will be its future
> already. Kiss it!"
> He quivered because it was true. . . . He kissed her belly and her
> mound of Venus, to kiss close to the womb and the foetus within the
> womb. (*LCL,* 291–92)

Thus, the child is the force that urges the couple to break entirely
with their pasts and wait for their uncertain future together. The
"hopeful heart" with which Mellors concludes his letter, and the
novel, owes much to the expected baby, this spark that, in his words,
the "Lord blew a bit too soon on" (*LCL,* 298). Lawrence implies that
the Lord here is the flux of life itself moving into the future, rolling a
"hasty little seed" out of the husk of death that Wragby represents.

In Lawrence's most parabolic tale of all, *The Escaped Cock,* a
resurrected man (called simply "The Man Who Died") chooses to
try sensual life rather than ascension to heaven. He engenders a
child in the priestess of Isis, who calls him the god Osiris. The
language at the end of this story becomes so metaphorical that the
personal, even the given name, is expunged. Oddly enough, in a tale
that revises the Christian story of the God who becomes man, Lawrence creates a man and a woman who are gods. Then with another,
perhaps inevitable, enlargement of the view, those gods turn into
representations of natural elements:

> "Hast thou conceived?" he asked her.
> "Why?" she said.
> "Thou art like a tree whose green leaves follow the blossoms, full of
> sap. And there is a withdrawing about thee."
> "It is so," she said. "I am with young by thee. Is it good?"
> "Yea!" he said. "How should it not be good?" (*EC,* 59)

The priestess says she is "with young," as one would say of an
animal. The Man Who Died, sounding like a voice from Genesis,
says, "How should it not be good?" In this story Lawrence moves
almost entirely into the mythic and visionary mode that has all
along coexisted with the realistic in his fiction.

Throughout this study I have noted that Lawrence elevates ordinary events of childhood to visionary significance while he domes-
ticates Romantic and mythical images of the child. This re-vision of
the child in literature is part of his larger effort to reconceive the
relation between humankind and the universe in the novel itself.
The Escaped Cock brings the issue to a strange and seemingly inevitable conclusion. What appears *in theme* to be Lawrence's most
earthly story of all, the one in which he has the temerity to rewrite
the story of the Resurrection, making Christ take on the flesh rather

than shed it, emerges *in tone* as the most mythical of all. Indeed, what child *is* this? Who are we waiting for at the end of this story? It is the most mythical, the most ordinary child of all—the archetypal child who emerges from the natural processes of the body and moves into the unknown visionary space of the future, the one we conceive of ourselves.

Bibliography

Works by D. H. Lawrence

Aaron's Rod. Edited by Mara Kalnins. Cambridge: Cambridge University Press, 1988.

The Boy in the Bush. Coauthored by Mollie Skinner. New York: Penguin Books, 1963.

The Collected Letters of D. H. Lawrence. Edited by Harry T. Moore. 2 vols. New York: Viking, 1962.

The Complete Poems of D. H. Lawrence. Edited by Vivian de Sola Pinto and Warren Roberts. New York: Viking, 1971.

The Complete Short Stories. 3 vols. New York: Penguin, 1976.

D. H. Lawrence and Italy. Introduction by Anthony Burgess. New York: Viking, 1972.

England, My England and Other Stories. Edited by Bruce Steele. Cambridge: Cambridge University Press, 1990.

The Escaped Cock. Edited by Gerald M. Lacy. Santa Barbara: Black Sparrow, 1976.

Four Short Novels. New York: Viking, 1965.

Kangaroo. Harmondsworth: Penguin, 1950.

Lady Chatterley's Lover. Harmondsworth: Penguin, 1960.

The Letters of D. H. Lawrence. Edited by James T. Boulton et al. 5 vols. to date. Cambridge: Cambridge University Press, 1979, 1981, 1984, 1987, 1989.

The Letters of D. H. Lawrence. Edited by Aldous Huxley. London: Heinemann, 1932.

The Lost Girl. Edited by John Worthen. Cambridge: Cambridge University Press, 1981.

Love Among the Haystacks and Other Stories. Edited by John Worthen. Cambridge: Cambridge University Press, 1987.

Mr. Noon. Edited by Lindeth Vasey. Cambridge: Cambridge University Press, 1984.

173

The Paintings of D. H. Lawrence. Edited by Mervyn Levy. London: Cory, Adams and Mackay, 1964.

The Paintings of D. H. Lawrence. London: Mandrake, Privately printed for subscribers only, 1929.

Phoenix: The Posthumous Papers. Edited by Edward McDonald. New York: Viking, 1972.

Phoenix II: Uncollected Writings. Edited by Warren Roberts and Harry T. Moore. New York: Viking, 1970.

The Plumed Serpent (Quetzalcoatl). Edited by L. D. Clark. Cambridge: Cambridge University Press, 1987.

The Princess and Other Stories. Edited by Keith Sagar. Harmondsworth: Penguin, 1971.

Psychoanalysis and the Unconscious and *Fantasia of the Unconscious.* New York: Viking, 1960.

The Rainbow. Edited by Mark Kinkead-Weekes. Cambridge: Cambridge University Press, 1989.

Reflections on the Death of a Porcupine and Other Essays. Edited by Michael Herbert. Cambridge: Cambridge University Press, 1988.

St. Mawr and Other Stories. Edited by Brian Finney. Cambridge: Cambridge University Press, 1983.

Selected Letters. Edited by Richard Aldington. Introduction by Aldous Huxley. Harmondsworth: Penguin, 1950.

Sons and Lovers. Edited by Keith Sagar. New York: Penguin, 1981.

Studies in Classic American Literature. Harmondsworth: Penguin, 1971.

Study of Thomas Hardy and Other Essays. Cambridge: Cambridge University Press, 1985.

The Symbolic Meaning: The Uncollected Versions of Studies in Classic American Literature. Edited by Armin Arnold. New York: Viking, 1964.

Ten Paintings. Redding Ridge, Conn.: Black Swan, 1982.

The Trespasser. Edited by Elizabeth Mansfield. Cambridge: Cambridge University Press, 1981.

The Virgin and the Gipsy. New York: Vintage, 1984.

The White Peacock. New York: Penguin, 1950.

Women in Love. Edited by David Farmer, Lindeth Vasey, and John Worthen. Cambridge: Cambridge University Press, 1987.

Secondary Sources

Ackroyd, Peter. *T. S. Eliot: A Life.* New York: Simon and Schuster, 1984.

Adrian, Arthur A. *Dickens and the Parent-Child Relationship.* Athens: Ohio University Press, 1984.

Albright, Daniel. *Lawrence, Woolf, and Mann: Personality and Impersonality.* Chicago: University of Chicago Press, 1978.

Alden, Patricia. *Social Mobility in the English Bildungsroman.* Ann Arbor: UMI Research Press, 1986.

Ariès, Philippe. *Centuries of Childhood: A Social History of Family Life.* Translated by Robert Baldick. New York: Random House, Vintage Books, 1962.

Ariès, Phillippe, and Georges Duby, eds. *A History of Private Life.* Vol. 4, *From the Fires of Revolution to the Great War.* Edited by Michelle Perrot. Translated by Arthur Goldhammer. Cambridge: Harvard University Press, Belknap Press, 1990.

Austen, Jane. *Northanger Abbey* and *Persuasion.* Edited by Mary Lascelles. New York: Dutton, Everyman's Library, 1962.

Bachelard, Gaston. *The Poetics of Reverie: Childhood, Language, and the Cosmos.* Translated by Daniel Russell. Boston: Beacon, 1971.

Bakhtin, Mikhail Mikhailovich. *The Dialogic Imagination: Four Essays.* Edited by Michael Holquist. Translated by Caryl Emerson and Michael Holquist. Austin: University of Texas Press, 1981.

———. *Problems of Dostoevsky's Poetics.* Edited and translated by Caryl Emerson. Introduction by Wayne Booth. Minneapolis: University of Minnesota Press, 1984.

Balbert, Peter. *D. H. Lawrence and the Phallic Imagination: Essays on Sexual Identity and Feminist Misreading.* London: Macmillan, 1989.

———. *D. H. Lawrence and the Psychology of Rhythm: The Meaning of Form in "The Rainbow."* The Hague: Mouton, 1974.

Balbert, Peter, and Phillip L. Marcus, eds. *D. H. Lawrence: A Centenary Consideration.* Ithaca: Cornell University Press, 1985.

Bantock, G. H. *Freedom and Authority in Education: A Criticism of Modern Cultural and Educational Assumptions.* London: Faber & Faber, 1952.

Barbier, Françoise-Marie, and Simone Rozenberg. "Lawrence/Freud." In *Reflexions et directives pour l'étude de D. H. Lawrence: "Women in Love,"* edited by Anne-Marie Fraisse, 106–18. Paris: Minard, Carnet des Lettres Modernes, 1970.

Ben-Ephraim, Gavriel. *The Moon's Dominion: Narrative Dichotomy and Female Dominance in Lawrence's Earlier Novels.* Rutherford, N.J.: Fairleigh Dickinson University Press, 1981.

Bersani, Leo. *A Future for Astyanax: Character and Desire in Literature.* Boston: Little, Brown, 1976.

Blanchard, Lydia. "D. H. Lawrence and *l'écriture féminine.*" Presented at the International Conference on D. H. Lawrence, Montpellier, France, June 1990.

———. "Mothers and Daughters in D. H. Lawrence: *The Rainbow* and Selected Shorter Works." In *Lawrence and Women,* edited by Anne Smith, 75–100. London: Vision, 1978.

Bloom, Harold. "Freud, The Greatest Modern Writer." *The New York Times Book Review* (March 23, 1986): 1.

Bloom, Harold, ed. *Modern Critical Views: D. H. Lawrence.* New York: Chelsea House, 1986.

Bonds, Diana S. *Language and the Self in D. H. Lawrence.* Ann Arbor: UMI Research Press, 1987.

Boose, Lynda E., and Betty S. Flowers, eds. *Daughters and Fathers.* Baltimore: Johns Hopkins University Press, 1989.

Booth, Wayne. *The Company We Keep: An Ethics of Fiction.* Berkeley: University of California Press, 1988.

Brontë, Charlotte. *Jane Eyre.* London: J. M. Dent, 1950.

Brooks, Peter, ed. *The Child's Part. Yale French Studies* 43 (1969).

Brownmiller, Susan. *Against Our Will: Men, Women, and Rape.* New York: Bantam, 1976.

Buckley, Jerome Hamilton. *Season of Youth: The Bildungsroman from Dickens to Golding.* Cambridge: Harvard University Press, 1974.

Burgan, Mary. "Androgynous Fatherhood in *Ulysses* and *Women in Love.*" *Modern Language Quarterly* 44 (1983): 178–97.

Burns, Aidan. *Nature and Culture in D. H. Lawrence.* London: Macmillan, 1980.

Burrow, Trigant. *Preconscious Foundations of Human Experience.* Edited by William E. Galt. New York: Basic Books, 1964.

———. *A Search for Man's Sanity: The Selected Letters of Trigant Burrow.* Edited by William E. Galt. New York: Oxford University Press, 1958.

Carey, John. "D. H. Lawrence's Doctrine." In *D. H. Lawrence: Novelist, Poet, Prophet,* edited by Stephen Spender, 122–34. London: Weidenfeld and Nicholson, 1973.

Carter, Courtney. "Teaching D. H. Lawrence: Countering Kate Millet." Presented at the International Conference on D. H. Lawrence, Montpellier, France, June 1990.

Cavitch, David. *D. H. Lawrence and the New World.* New York: Oxford University Press, 1969.

Chambers, Jessie. *D. H. Lawrence: A Personal Record.* New York: Cambridge University Press, 1980.

Clarke, Bruce Cooper. " 'The Ragged Rose': D. H. Lawrence's Perils of the Soul." Ann Arbor: UMI Research Press, 1980.

Cobb, Edith. *The Ecology of Imagination in Childhood.* Introduction by Margaret Mead. New York: Columbia University Press, 1977.

Conrad, Joseph. "Amy Foster." In *The Portable Conrad,* edited by Morton Dauwen Zabel, revised by Frederick R. Karl, 155–91. New York: Viking, 1969.

Consolo, Dominick P., ed. *D. H. Lawrence: "The Rocking-Horse Winner."* Columbus, Ohio: Merrill, 1969.

Coveney, Peter. *The Image of Childhood: The Individual and Society: A Study of the Theme in English Literature.* Revised edition with introduction by F. R. Leavis. Baltimore: Penguin, 1967.

Cushman, Keith. "Domestic Life in the Suburbs: Lawrence, the Joneses, and 'The Old Adam.' " *D. H. Lawrence Review* 16 (1983): 221–34.

Dalsimer, Katherine. *Female Adolescence: Psychoanalytic Reflections on Literature.* New Haven: Yale University Press, 1987.

Defoe, Daniel. *Moll Flanders.* Edited by James Sutherland. Boston: Houghton Mifflin, Riverside, 1959.

Delany, Paul. *D. H. Lawrence's Nightmare: The Writer and His Circle in the Years of the Great War.* New York: Basic Books, 1978.

DeMause, Lloyd, ed. *The History of Childhood.* New York: Harper & Row, 1975.

Derrida, Jacques. "Freud and the Scene of Writing." In *Writing and Difference,* translated by Alan Bass, 198–231. Chicago: University of Chicago Press, 1978.

Dervin, Daniel. *A "Strange Sapience": The Creative Imagination of D. H. Lawrence.* Amherst: University of Massachusetts Press, 1984.

DiBattista, Maria. "*Women in Love:* D. H. Lawrence's Judgment Book." In *D. H. Lawrence: A Centenary Consideration,* edited by Peter Balbert and Phillip L. Marcus, 67–90. Ithaca: Cornell University Press, 1985.

Dickens, Charles. *Bleak House.* Boston: Houghton Mifflin, Riverside, 1956.

———. *David Copperfield.* Boston: Houghton Mifflin, Riverside, 1958.

———. *Dombey and Son.* New York: Signet, 1964.

———. *Great Expectations.* New York: Holt, Rinehart & Winston, 1948.

———. *Hard Times.* New York: Norton, 1966.

———. *Little Dorrit.* Baltimore: Penguin, 1967.

———. *The Old Curiosity Shop.* Baltimore: Penguin, 1972.

———. *Oliver Twist.* Baltimore: Penguin, 1972.

Dostoyevsky, Fyodor. *Netochka Nezvanova.* Translated by Ann Dunnigan. Englewood Cliffs, N.J.: Prentice-Hall, 1970.

Duncan, Carol. "Happy Mothers and Other New Ideas in Eighteenth-Century French Art." In *Feminism and Art History: Questioning the Litany,* edited by Norma Brode and Mary D. Garrard, 200–219. New York: Harper and Row, 1982.

Eagleton, Mary, and David Pierce. *Attitudes to Class and the English Novel, from Walter Scott to David Story.* London: Thames and Hudson, 1979.

Ebbatson, Roger. *Lawrence and the Nature Tradition: A Theme in English Fiction, 1859–1914.* Atlantic Heights, N.J.: Humanities, 1980.

Eliot, George. *Adam Bede.* In *The Best-Known Novels of George Eliot.* New York: Modern Library, n.d.

———. *The Mill on the Floss.* Edited by Gordon S. Haight. Oxford: Oxford University Press, 1980.

———. *Silas Marner.* In *The Best-Known Novels of George Eliot.* New York: Modern Library, n.d.

Ellis, David. "Lawrence and the Biological Psyche." In *D. H. Lawrence: Centenary Essays,* edited by Mara Kalnins, 89–109. Bristol: Bristol Classical Press, 1986.

Ellis, David, and Howard Mills. *D. H. Lawrence's Non-Fiction: Art, Thought and Genre.* Cambridge: Cambridge University Press, 1988.

Ellman, Mary. *Thinking about Women.* New York: Harcourt Brace Jovanovich, 1968.

Erikson, Erik H. *Childhood and Society.* New York: W. W. Norton, 1963.

Erlich, Gloria. *Family Themes in Hawthorne's Fiction: The Tenacious Web.* New Brunswick: Rutgers University Press, 1985.

Farr, Judith, ed. *Twentieth Century Interpretations of "Sons and Lovers."* Englewood Cliffs, N.J.: Prentice-Hall, 1970.

Felman, Shoshona, ed. *Literature and Psychoanalysis: The Question of Reading Otherwise.* Baltimore: Johns Hopkins University Press, 1982.

Fiedler, Leslie. "The Eye of Innocence: Some Notes on the Role of the Child in Literature." In *Collected Essays,* 1: 471–511. New York: Stein and Day, 1971.

———. "The Invention of the Child." *New Leader* 41 (1958): 22–24.

Flandrin, Jean-Louis. *Families in Former Times: Kinship, Household, and Sexuality.* Translated by Richard Southern. New York: Cambridge University Press, 1979.

Fleishman, Avrom. *Figures of Autobiography: The Language of Self-Writing in Victorian and Modern England.* Berkeley: University of California Press, 1983.

———. "He Do the Polis in Different Voices: Lawrence's Later Style." In *D. H. Lawrence: A Centenary Consideration,* edited by Peter Balbert and Phillip L. Marcus, 162–79. Ithaca: Cornell University Press, 1985.

Fogel, Daniel Mark. "The Sacred Poem to the Unknown in the Fiction of D. H. Lawrence." *D. H. Lawrence Review* 16 (1983): 45–57.

Ford, George H. *Double Measure: A Study of the Novels and Stories of D. H. Lawrence.* New York: Holt, Rinehart & Winston, 1965.

Fraiberg, Selma. "Two Modern Incest Heroes." *Partisan Review* 28 (1961): 646–61.

Freud, Sigmund. *The Standard Edition of the Complete Psychological*

Works. 24 vols. Edited by James Strachey. London: Hogarth Press, 1955–1962.

Furbank, P. N. "The Philosophy of D. H. Lawrence." In *The Spirit of D. H. Lawrence,* edited by Gamini Salgado and G. K. Das, foreword by Raymond Williams, 144–53. London: Macmillan, 1988.

Gay, Peter. *Education of the Senses.* Vol 1. *The Bourgeois Experience: Victoria to Freud.* New York: Oxford University Press, 1984.

Goethe, Johann Wolfgang von. *Autobiography [Dichtung und Wahrheit].* Translated by John Oxenford. Introduction by Karl J. Weintraub. 2 vols. Chicago: University of Chicago Press, 1974.

Goldberg, Michael. "Lawrence's 'The Rocking-Horse Winner': A Dickensian Fable?" *Modern Fiction Studies* 15 (1969): 525–36.

Goodman, Charlotte. "Henry James, D. H. Lawrence, and the Victimized Child." *Modern Language Studies* 10 (1979–1980): 43–51.

Gordon, David J. *D. H. Lawrence as a Literary Critic.* New Haven: Yale University Press, 1966.

———. *Literary Art and the Unconscious.* Baton Rouge: Louisiana State University Press, 1976.

Greenleaf, Barbara Kaye. *Childhood through the Ages: A History of Childhood.* New York: Barnes & Noble, 1978.

Grylls, David. *Guardians and Angels: Parents and Children in Nineteenth-Century Literature.* Boston: Faber & Faber, 1978.

Hamalian, Leo. *D. H. Lawrence in Italy.* New York: Taplinger Publishing Co., 1982.

Hamalian, Leo, ed. *D. H. Lawrence: A Collection of Criticism.* New York: McGraw-Hill, 1973.

Hardy, Thomas. *Jude the Obscure.* Boston: Houghton Mifflin, Riverside, 1965.

Harper, Howard M., Jr. "*Fantasia* and the Psychodynamics of *Women in Love.*" In *The Classic British Novel,* edited by Howard M. Harper, Jr., and Charles Edge, 202–19. Athens: University of Georgia Press, 1972.

Heilbrun, Carolyn. *Reinventing Womanhood.* New York: W. W. Norton, 1979.

———. *Toward a Recognition of Androgyny.* New York, Harper & Row, 1974.

Heywood, Christopher. " 'Blood Consciousness' and the Pioneers of the Reflex and Ganglionic Systems." In *D. H. Lawrence: New Studies,* edited by Christopher Heywood, 104–23. London: Macmillan, 1987.

Hinz, Evelyn. "The Beginning and the End: D. H. Lawrence's *Psychoanalysis* and *Fantasia.*" *Dalhousie Review* 52 (1972): 251–65.

Hoffman, Frederick J. *Freudianism and the Literary Mind.* Revised edition. New York: Grove Press, 1959.

Howe, Marguerite Beebe. *The Art of the Self in D. H. Lawrence.* Athens: Ohio University Press, 1977.

Jacobson, I. "The Child as Guilty Witness." *Literature and Psychology* 24 (1974): 12–23.

James, Henry. *The Art of the Novel.* New York: Scribner's, 1962.

———. *Autobiography.* Edited by Frederick W. Dupee. Princeton: Princeton University Press, 1983.

———. *The Awkward Age.* New York: Penguin, 1966.

———. "The Pupil." In *The Complete Tales of Henry James,* edited by Leon Edel, vol 7. Philadelphia: Lippincott, 1963.

———. *The Turn of the Screw.* New York: Norton, 1966.

———. *Watch and Ward.* New York: Grove, 1959.

———. *What Maisie Knew.* Garden City, N.Y.: Doubleday, 1954.

Jewinski, Ed. "The Phallus in D. H. Lawrence and Jacques Lacan." *D. H. Lawrence Review* 21 (1989): 7–24.

Jones, Ernest. *The Life and Works of Sigmund Freud.* Edited and abridged by Lionel Trilling and Steven Marcus. New York: Basic Books, 1961.

Jones, Granville H. *Henry James's Psychology of Experience: Innocence, Responsibility, and Renunciation in the Fiction of Henry James.* The Hague: Mouton, 1975.

Jung, C. G., and C. Kerényi. *Essays on a Science of Mythology.* Translated by R. F. C. Hull. Princeton: Princeton University Press, 1969.

Kalnins, Mara. *D. H. Lawrence: Centenary Essays.* Bristol: Bristol Classical Press, 1986.

Kazin, Alfred. "Sons, Lovers, and Mothers." In *D. H. Lawrence: A Collection of Criticism,* edited by Leo Hamalian, 22–32. New York: McGraw-Hill, 1973.

Keats, John. *Letters of John Keats.* Selected and edited by Robert Gittings. New York: Oxford, 1970.

Kermode, Frank. *D. H. Lawrence.* New York: Viking, 1973.

———. "D. H. Lawrence and the Apocalyptic Types." In *Continuities,* 122–51. New York: Random House, 1968.

Kessen, William, ed. *The Child.* New York: John Wiley, 1965.

Kiely, Robert. *Beyond Egotism: The Fiction of Joyce, Woolf, and Lawrence.* Cambridge: Harvard University Press, 1980.

Kohut, Heinz. *The Analysis of the Self.* New York: International Universities Press, 1971.

Kuhn, Reinhard. *Corruption in Paradise: The Child in Western Literature.* Hanover, N.H.: University Press of New England, 1982.

Lacan, Jacques. *Écrits: A Selection.* Translated by Alan Sheridan. New York: Norton, 1977.

Lally, Margaret. "*The Virgin and the Gipsy:* Rewriting the Pain." Presented at the International Conference on D. H. Lawrence, Montpellier, France, June 1990.

Langbaum, Robert. "Lawrence and Hardy." In *D. H. Lawrence and Tradition,* edited by Jeffrey Meyers, 69–90. Amherst: University of Massachusetts Press, 1985.

———. *The Mysteries of Identity: A Theme in Modern Literature.* New York: Oxford University Press, 1977.

Lawrence, Frieda. *Not I, but the Wind. . .* Carbondale: Southern Illinois University Press, 1974.

Leavis, F. R. *D. H. Lawrence: Novelist.* Harmondsworth: Penguin, 1964.

Lee-Jahnke, Hannah. *David Herbert Lawrence et la psychoanalyse.* Berne/New York: Peter Lang, 1983.

McCabe, T. H. "The Otherness of Lawrence's 'Odour of Chrysanthemums.'" *D. H. Lawrence Review* 19 (1987): 149–56.

MacLeod, Sheila. *Lawrence's Men and Women.* London: Heinemann, 1985.

Marcus, Leah Sinanoglou. *Childhood and Cultural Despair: A Theme in Seventeenth-Century Literature.* Pittsburgh: University of Pittsburgh Press, 1978.

Marcus, Stephen. "Some Representations of Childhood in Wordsworth's Poetry." In *Opening Texts: Psychoanalysis and the Child,* edited by Joseph H. Smith and William Kerrigan, 1–16. Baltimore: Johns Hopkins University Press, 1985.

Martz, Louis L. "Portrait of Miriam." In *Modern Critical Views: D. H. Lawrence,* edited by Harold Bloom, 73–91. New York: Chelsea House, 1986.

Mayers, Oswald Joseph. "The Child as Jungian Hero in D. H. Lawrence's *The Plumed Serpent." Journal of Evolutionary Psychology* 8 (1987): 306–17.

———. "D. H. Lawrence Compared: Essays on His Literary Affinities with Hawthorne, Anderson, and Hemingway." Ph.D. diss., University of Oregon, 1981.

Meredith, George. *The Ordeal of Richard Feverel.* Boston: Houghton Mifflin, Riverside, 1971.

Meyers, Jeffrey. *D. H. Lawrence: A Biography.* New York: Alfred A. Knopf, 1990.

Meyers, Jeffrey, ed. *D. H. Lawrence and Tradition.* Amherst: University of Massachusetts Press, 1985.

Miko, Stephen J. *Toward "Women in Love": The Emergence of a Lawrentian Aesthetic.* New Haven: Yale University Press, 1971.

Millett, Robert W. *The Vultures and the Phoenix: A Study of the Mandrake Press Edition of the Paintings of D. H. Lawrence.* Philadelphia: Art Alliance Press, 1983.

Minard, Eugene Robert. "Fanny Price: The Still Center of *Mansfield Park.*" Unpublished essay, 1975.

Moore, Harry T. *The Priest of Love: A Life of D. H. Lawrence.* New York: Penguin, 1981.

Moore, Harry T., and Robert B. Partlow, Jr., eds. *D. H. Lawrence: The Man Who Lived.* Carbondale and Edwardsville: Southern Illinois University Press, 1980.

Moynahan, Julian. "Lawrence and the Modern Crisis of Character and Conscience." In *The Challenge of D. H. Lawrence,* edited by Michael Squires and Keith Cushman, 28–41. Madison: University of Wisconsin Press, 1990.

Murfin, Ross C. *Swinburne, Hardy, and Lawrence and the Burden of Belief.* Chicago: University of Chicago Press, 1978.

Murray, Henry A., ed. *Myth and Mythmaking.* Boston: Beacon, 1960.

Nehls, Edward, ed. *D. H. Lawrence: A Composite Biography.* 3 vols. Madison: University of Wisconsin Press, 1958.

Nietzsche, Friedrich. *The Birth of Tragedy* and *The Genealogy of Morals.* Translated by Francis Golffing. Garden City, N.Y.: Doubleday, 1956.

Nin, Anais. *D. H. Lawrence: An Unprofessional Study.* Chicago: Swallow, 1964.

Nixon, Cornelia. *Lawrence's Leadership Politics and the Turn against Women.* Berkeley: University of California Press, 1986.

Picard, Harwood Brewster. "Remembering D. H. Lawrence." Presented at the D. H. Lawrence Centennial Conference, Boston, June 1985.

Plath, Sylvia. *The Collected Poems.* Edited by Ted Hughes. New York: Harper & Row, 1981.

The Princeton Center for Infancy and Childhood. *The First Twelve Months of Life: Your Baby's Growth and Development.* Edited by Frank Caplan. New York: Putnam, 1982.

Pritchett, V. S. *The Living Novel and Later Appreciations.* New York: Random House, 1964.

Raleigh, John Henry. "Victorian Morals and the Modern Novel." In *The Victorian Novel: Modern Essays in Criticism,* 462–85. New York: Oxford, 1971.

Rich, Adrienne. *Of Woman Born: Motherhood as Experience and Institution.* New York: Norton, 1978.

Rieff, Philip. Introduction to *Psychoanalysis and the Unconscious* and *Fantasia of the Unconscious,* by D. H. Lawrence. New York: Viking, 1960.

———. "A Modern Mythmaker." In *Myth and Mythmaking,* edited by Henry A. Murray, 240–75. Boston: Beacon, 1968.

———. "Two Honest Men." *The Listener* 62 (1960): 794–96.

Rilke, Rainer Maria. *Letters on Cézanne.* Edited by Clara Rilke. Translated by Joel Agee. New York: Fromm International, 1985.

Ross, Charles L. *The Composition of "The Rainbow" and "Women in Love": A History.* Charlottesville: University of Virginia Press, 1979.

Rousseau, Jean Jacques. *The Confessions of Jean Jacques Rousseau with Thirteen Etchings.* London: Hedouin, n.d.
————. *Émile or Education.* Translated by Barbara Foxley. New York: E. P. Dutton, n.d.
Ruddick, Sara. *Maternal Thinking: Toward a Politics of Peace.* Boston: Beacon, 1989.
Ruderman, Judith. *D. H. Lawrence and the Devouring Mother: The Search for a Patriarchal Ideal of Leadership.* Durham: Duke University Press, 1984.
————. "Orality and Animality in *The White Peacock.*" Presented at the D. H. Lawrence Centennial Conference, Boston, June 1985.
Sagar, Keith. *The Life of D. H. Lawrence.* New York: Pantheon, 1980.
Sagar, Keith, ed. *A D. H. Lawrence Handbook.* New York: Barnes & Noble, 1982.
Salgado, Gamini, and G. K. Das, eds. *The Spirit of D. H. Lawrence: Centenary Studies.* London: Macmillan, 1988.
Sanders, Scott. *D. H. Lawrence: The World of Five Major Novels.* New York: Viking, 1974.
Schiff, Richard. *Cézanne and the End of Impressionism: A Study of the Theory, Technique, and Critical Evaluation of Modern Art.* Chicago: University of Chicago Press, 1984.
Schneider, Daniel. *The Consciousness of D. H. Lawrence: An Intellectual Biography.* Lawrence: University Press of Kansas, 1986.
————. *D. H. Lawrence: The Artist as Psychologist.* Lawrence: University Press of Kansas, 1984.
Schorer, Mark. "*Women in Love* and Death." In *D. H. Lawrence: A Collection of Critical Essays,* edited by Mark Spilka, 50–60. Englewood Cliffs, N.J.: Prentice-Hall, 1963.
Schorer, Mark, ed. "*Sons and Lovers*" by D. H. Lawrence: A Facsimile of the Manuscript.* Berkeley: University of California Press, 1977.
Schorsch, Anita. *Images of Childhood: An Illustrated Social History.* Pittstown, N.J.: Main Street, 1985.
Schwartz, Murray M. "D. H. Lawrence and Psychoanalysis: An Introduction." *D. H. Lawrence Review* 10 (1977): 215–22.
Simpson, Hilary. *D. H. Lawrence and Feminism.* DeKalb: Northern Illinois University Press, 1982.
Sklenicka, Carol. "Lawrence's Vision of the Child: Reimagining Character and Consciousness." *D. H. Lawrence Review* 18 (Summer/Fall 1985–1986): 151–68.
Smith, Joseph H., and William Kerrigan, eds. *Opening Texts: Psychoanalysis and the Child.* Baltimore: Johns Hopkins University Press, 1985.
Smollett, Tobias. *Roderick Random.* New York: Dutton, Everyman's Library, 1927.

Sorel, Nancy Caldwell. *Ever Since Eve: Personal Reflections on Childbirth.* New York: Oxford University Press, 1984.

————. "A Look at 'Noble Suffering.'" *The New York Times Book Review,* January 26, 1986, 1.

Spacks, Patricia Meyer. *The Adolescent Idea: Myths of Youth and the Adult Imagination.* New York: Basic Books, 1981.

Spender, Stephen, ed. *D. H. Lawrence: Novelist, Poet, Prophet.* London: Wiedenfeld and Nicholson, 1973.

Spilka, Mark. "For Mark Schorer with Combative Love: The *Sons and Lovers* Manuscript." In *D. H. Lawrence: A Centenary Consideration,* edited by Peter Balbert and Phillip L. Marcus, 29–44. Ithaca: Cornell University Press, 1985.

————. "Lawrence and the Clitoris." In *The Challenge of D. H. Lawrence,* edited by Michael Squires and Keith Cushman, 176–86. Madison: University of Wisconsin Press, 1990.

————. *The Love Ethic of D. H. Lawrence.* Bloomington: Indiana University Press, 1955.

————. "On the Enrichment of Poor Monkeys by Myth and Dream; or How Dickens Rousseauisticized and Pre-Freudianized Victorian Views of Childhood." In *Sexuality and Victorian Literature,* edited by Don Richard Cox. *Tennessee Studies in Literature* 27 (1984) 161–79.

Spilka, Mark, ed. *D. H. Lawrence: A Collection of Critical Essays.* Englewood Cliffs, N.J.: Prentice-Hall, 1963.

Squires, Michael, and Keith Cushman, eds. *The Challenge of D. H. Lawrence.* Madison: University of Wisconsin Press, 1990.

————. *D. H. Lawrence's "Lady": A New Look at "Lady Chatterley's Lover."* Athens: University of Georgia Press, 1985.

Stone, Lawrence. *The Family, Sex and Marriage in England 1500–1800.* Abridged edition. New York: Harper Torchbooks, 1979.

Suransky, Valerie Polakov. *The Erosion of Childhood.* Chicago: University of Chicago Press, 1982.

Swigg, Richard. *Lawrence, Hardy, and American Literature.* London: Oxford University Press, 1972.

Tanner, Tony. *The Reign of Wonder: Naivety and Reality in American Literature.* Cambridge: Cambridge University Press, 1965.

Taylor, Dennis. "Lawrence and the Family Novel." Presented at the D. H. Lawrence Centennial Conference, Boston, June 1985.

Tedlock, E. W., Jr., ed. *Frieda Lawrence: The Memoirs and Correspondence.* London: Heinemann, 1961.

Temple, J. "The Definition of Innocence: A Consideration of the Short Stories of D. H. Lawrence." *Studia Germanica Gandensia* 20 (1979): 105–18.

Trilling, Lionel. "Freud and Literature." In *The Liberal Imagination,* 32–52. Garden City, N.Y.: Doubleday Anchor, 1953.
———. "Freud: Within and Beyond Culture." In *Beyond Culture: Essays on Literature and Learning,* 77–102. New York: Harvest/ HBJ, 1979.
Turner, John, F. "The Perversion of Play in D. H. Lawrence's 'The Rocking-Horse Winner.'" *D. H. Lawrence Review* 15 (1982): 249–70.
Ulmer, Gregory L. "Rousseau and D. H. Lawrence: 'Philosophes' of the 'Gelded' Age." *Canadian Review of Comparative Literature* 4 (1977): 68–80.
Van Ghent, Dorothy. *The English Novel: Form and Function.* New York: Harper Torchbooks, 1961.
Vickery, John. "D. H. Lawrence and the Fantasias of Consciousness." In *The Spirit of D. H. Lawrence: Centenary Studies,* edited by Gamini Salgado and G. K. Das, 163–80. London: Macmillan, 1988.
Wallace, M. Elizabeth. "The Circling Hawk: Philosophy of Knowledge in Polanyi and Lawrence." In *The Challenge of D. H. Lawrence,* edited by Michael Squires and Keith Cushman, 103–20. Madison: University of Wisconsin Press, 1990.
Wechsler, Judith, ed. *Cézanne in Perspective.* Englewood Cliffs, N.J.: Prentice-Hall, 1975.
Weiss, Daniel A. *Oedipus in Nottingham: D. H. Lawrence.* Seattle: University of Washington Press, 1962.
Williams, Judith. *Perception and Expression in the Novels of Charlotte Brontë.* Ann Arbor: UMI Research Press, 1988.
Williams, Raymond. *The English Novel from Dickens to Lawrence.* New York.: Oxford University Press, 1970.
Woolf, Virginia. "Mr. Bennett and Mrs. Brown." In *The Captain's Death Bed and Other Essays,* 94–119. New York: Harcourt Brace Jovanovich, 1950.
Wordsworth, William. *Poetical Works.* Edited by Thomas Hutchinson. Revised by Ernest de Selincourt. London: Oxford University Press, 1969.
———. *Selected Poems and Prefaces.* Edited by Jack Stillinger. Boston: Houghton Mifflin, Riverside, 1965.

Index

JOYCE CAMPUS LIBRARY

DATE DUE

DEMCO